THIS GREAT
BATTLEFIELD OF
SHILOH

THIS GREAT
BATTLEFIELD OF
SHILOH

HISTORY, MEMORY, AND
THE ESTABLISHMENT OF A
CIVIL WAR NATIONAL MILITARY PARK

TIMOTHY B. SMITH

The University of Tennessee Press / Knoxville

Library of Congress Cataloging-in-Publication Data

Smith, Timothy B., 1974–

This great battlefield of Shiloh : history, memory, and the establishment of a Civil War national military park / Timothy B. Smith.—1st ed.

p. cm.

Includes bibliographical references and index.

ISBN 1-57233-281-6 (cl.: alk. paper)

1. Shiloh National Military Park (Tenn.)—History.

2. Shiloh, Battle of, Tenn., 1862.

3. Memory—Social aspects—United States.

4. United States—History—Civil War, 1861–1865—Monuments.

5. United States—History—Civil War, 1861–1865—Influence.

I. Title.

E473.54 .S64 2004

973.7′31—dc22   2003014099

To D. W. Reed
The Father of Shiloh National Military Park

CONTENTS

ILLUSTRATIONS

FIGURES

MAPS

PREFACE

My fascination with Civil War battlefields began early in life. When I was growing up in central Mississippi, Shiloh and Vicksburg were frequent stops on Saturdays when our family had little else to do. Occasionally, we even branched out to smaller and lesser-known local battlefields, such as Brice's Crossroads and Corinth. Little did I know that years later, I would be working to administer one of those battlefields.

As the years went by and I began to have more than just a normal boy's fascination with war, guns, and soldiers, I began to look more closely at those same battlefields and many others. When I was ten, my dad took my brother and me on a two-week Civil War trip through Virginia, Maryland, and Pennsylvania. There, I visited the eastern battlefields such as Gettysburg, Antietam, and Manassas.

I continually read the history of these great battles and soon began to make a distinction in my mind between what I thought were "real" battlefields and those that were not so important. Oddly enough, I had decided that those battlefields preserved by the National Park Service were the real thing, and everything else really didn't matter. Now, of course, I realize much differently. Those battlefields administered by other organizations are imbued with a history of death, suffering, and honor just as Shiloh and Gettysburg are, and many played pivotal roles in the war. But in my mind, I had made the distinction between what was important to save and what, seemingly, was not so significant. After all, the really important battlefields had monuments and tablets and visitor centers.

This fascination with battlefields, monuments, and preservation affected my thinking. I can vividly remember staging battles on the dining room table with hundreds of little toy soldiers; I would venture to guess that almost every American boy does that. But I took it one step further. After the battle was over and the dead and wounded were disposed of, I would make small tablets and monuments and place them on my battlefield—at the precise locations where the heaviest actions had taken place. Preservation, monumentation, and memory were instilled in me from the beginning.

Fortunately, I have been blessed to become a member of the National Park Service family, whose duty it is to preserve and interpret not only Civil War battlefields but also many of America's other national treasures. And to be able to perform those duties at Shiloh National Military Park is an added blessing.

Shiloh has always been my favorite battlefield. I can remember visiting that hallowed ground as a boy and thinking my dream job would be to work there. I can also remember, as a seasonal employee of the park, telling my supervisor that I would "scrub the bathrooms with a toothbrush to get a permanent job at Shiloh." Fortunately, a toothbrush is not one of the tools I normally employ at work.

So, the matching of my background with my job has produced the following study of Shiloh's establishment. Since coming to Pittsburg Landing, my regard for the veterans and the resource has only deepened; my interest in administrative history and Civil War memory has only flourished; and my desire to tell the rest of Shiloh's story has only intensified. I am proud and humbled to live and work on *This Great Battlefield of Shiloh.*

In every book I've read, the author finds some new and catchy way to say, "Thanks to the people who have helped me, and any dumb mistakes are not their fault." I always thought that was a formality the author had to put in the front of the book. But now that I have written this book, I understand. And since possibly every new way of saying thanks and retaining all responsibility has been used, I will simply say, "Thanks to the people who have helped me, and any dumb mistakes are not their fault."

The list of people I need to thank is long. First and foremost are my parents. They not only raised me to honor the sacrifice of our veterans, past and present, but they took me to the hallowed ground on which some of our fiercest battles were fought. The patriotism they instilled in me led in large degree to this work. My dad, a minister, never missed an opportunity from the pulpit to honor America and her veterans on special holidays such as Veterans' Day and Memorial Day weekends: "Render unto Caesar the things that are Caesar's, and to God the things that are God's." Of course, their time, money, love, and advice has had more of an effect on whatever I am today than that of anyone else. For your unwavering support and love, I thank you, Mom and Dad.

Dr. John F. Marszalek, my major professor in the doctoral program at Mississippi State University, deserves special mention. He pushed, calmed, listened, advised, scolded, encouraged, and, most importantly, befriended me. He went through this work numerous times, and I can truly say that this would not be possible without him. Thanks, John, for everything.

Other members of the Mississippi State University History Department deserve special mention also. Dr. Ren Crowell made many helpful suggestions that helped me centralize my thinking on the entire subject of historical memory.

Professors Richard Damms, Robert Jenkins, and Don Mabry also read the manuscript and offered valuable suggestions. Mike Ballard was really the one who began my whole Shiloh experience. He sent a lowly graduate student to Shiloh to work in their archives, and the result thus far has been a job and this history. Peggy Bonner in the History Department at Mississippi State helped in more ways than she knows.

Many National Park Service people deserve special thanks. Terry Winschel at Vicksburg, Jim Ogden at Chickamauga, Ted Alexander at Antietam, and Scott Hartwig at Gettysburg all proved very helpful in discussing their own park histories with me, allowing me to place what happened at Shiloh in at least some context. A National Park Service authority on cultural and natural resources, Dr. Richard Sellars discussed the topic with me and also read the manuscript.

My colleagues at Shiloh National Military Park have probably heard more about the park's history than they ever wanted to know. Superintendent Woody Harrell deserves special mention. He not only gave me a job but really began the entire process by allowing me to write the park's administrative history. Joe Davis, Jim Minor, and Brook Garner have all discussed the park with me, put me in contact with people they met who mentioned that they had some connection to the park, and supported me through the whole process. Ashley Ball referred me to material that she thought might be helpful. A fine historian and my neighbor on the park, Tom Parson has spent many hours discussing monuments and history and tramping the battlefield with me. My former boss Janet Ambrose, now of Yellowstone National Park, encouraged me to publish this history. Brian McCutchen, formerly at Shiloh but now in the regional office in Omaha, also spent many hours discussing the park's history with me.

Special thanks goes to my boss, Stacy Allen. He read the entire manuscript and offered many valuable suggestions to make it better. His knowledge of Shiloh, both past and present, is unequaled, and his keen common sense allows him to see things that many miss. I am proud to call Stacy my colleague, neighbor, and friend.

Working with the University of Tennessee Press has been a pleasure. Jennifer Siler and Stan Ivester have made the entire process enjoyable. The press's readers, Earl Hess and John Hubbell, added helpful comments that only made the final product better, as did my copyeditor, Gene Adair.

Many others have offered valuable help during research for this book. DeLong Rice of Pickwick, Tennessee, made his collection of his grandfather's papers available to me. One of the most poignant moments was when he showed me Superintendent DeLong Rice's old name plate that sat on his desk back in the 1910s and 1920s. And it was made of the same cast iron with which the tablets at Shiloh were cast. What an amazing artifact! Thomas Van Ness pointed me toward papers of his ancestor, Robert F. Looney. Dan Hayes shared photos of his family—natives of the park area. The staffs at the National Archives, Library of Congress, Memphis Shelby County Public Library, and the Filson Historical Society all helped with the collection of material.

And finally, an enormous word of thanks must go to the veterans of Shiloh, both those who fought here on April 6 and 7, 1862, and those who returned forty years later to build a park. To men such as Cornelius Cadle, Atwell Thompson, and especially D. W. Reed, thank you for preserving the heritage of Shiloh so that we, one hundred years later, can enjoy, ponder, honor, and remember.

Timothy B. Smith
Pittsburg Landing, Tennessee

INTRODUCTION

April 6 and 7, 1903, were important days. Hundreds of veterans and thousands of visitors joined together for the momentous event. Famous senators and generals gave speeches, as did Indiana's governor. Even the United States Assistant Secretary of War was present. All these people came for the dedication of twenty-one Indiana monuments on a Civil War battlefield. The place of this gathering was not Gettysburg or Washington, however; it was the middle of rural west Tennessee. Congress had preserved the battlefield of Shiloh, and veterans not only from Indiana but also from many other states flocked to the site to erect monuments, then and later.

Why did so many people gather in such a remote area to dedicate elaborate monuments and memorials? The obvious answer is that one of the bloodiest battles in the Civil War had been fought on that land and that a park had been established to commemorate the event. That answer, however, provides only a partial explanation, and it also fosters other questions, such as why a park was established in the first place. These are not simple questions, and the complete answers are complex.

On one level, the preservation activities at Shiloh were the result of a nationwide phenomenon taking place in the 1890s and early 1900s. Patriotism, nationalism, and sectional reconciliation were feelings that were sweeping the nation at that time. The United States was debuting on the world stage as a great power and assuming a more active role in international affairs than it had ever undertaken before. Such an entrance onto the world stage, not just on a military level but also on economic and social levels, fostered a feeling of patriotism and pride. The war fought with Spain in 1898 only added to this nationalism.

As part of this nationalistic feeling, the United States was also charting a course of reconciliation between sections. Just three short decades earlier, the nation had split along sectional lines over the issues of race and slavery. The disputes had produced a civil war, which had lasted four long years and literally crippled an entire generation. Afterwards, two more decades of Reconstruction took place, ending only in the 1890s. In that decade, American white leaders finally compromised on racial issues and effectively placed black Americans in roles subordinate to whites. This decision allowed a reconciliation of North and South on the grounds of white supremacy; decades of Jim Crowism followed.[1]

In order to complete this reconciliation, both sections ignored the issues of race and slavery that had caused them to kill one another in the 1860s. Rather, they focused on other aspects of the war, such as the valor, courage, and bravery of the soldiers. On that issue, both sides could agree.

These nostalgic feelings of patriotism, nationalism, and reconciliation led to a nationwide memorialization of American military history in general and Civil War soldiers in particular. Throughout the North and South, in almost every town, veterans and their descendents erected statues of generals and placed memorials to common soldiers. The nation established cemeteries for the fallen and built national military parks to preserve the scenes of bravery and heroism.

Although this phenomenon was not a coordinated national effort, the entire nation became involved in a variety of ways. As in all war memorializations, three groups combined to support this effort. The veterans desired commemoration, the American public supported the idea, and the government provided funds. The requisite groups in the nation thus supported this memorialization and, by extension, reconciliation. This grassroots effort, of course, fit into the developing grassroots movements of the era. One has to look no further than the major movements of the time, such as Populism and Progressivism, to understand how frequently common Americans bonded together to accomplish their goals.[2]

The establishment of Shiloh National Military Park, therefore, was part of a larger national phenomenon. Shiloh and its sister parks—Chickamauga and Chattanooga, Antietam, Gettysburg, and Vicksburg—were all established in the 1890s and fit nicely into the memorialization movement. By studying the establishment and administration of these parks, the modern scholar can learn much about the mindsets both of veterans and of their non-veteran contemporaries regarding the Civil War.

The builders of Shiloh, as well as the other parks, were conscious of the context in which they worked. While almost never stating their cause bluntly in their mundane, day-to-day correspondence, they did show it in the more lofty labors of dedications and ceremonies. Speeches literally seeped with references to patriotism, nationalism, and honor. In the congressional deliberations and debates over establishment of the park, congressmen stated their reasons for building such parks. "It is the pride of succeeding generations to be able to point to these memorable fields as places where the destiny of our country was practically worked out in its awful civil war," the House Committee on Military Affairs reported. The park commission likewise frequently placed their efforts in the context in which they worked. One member of the commission spoke at the dedication of Illinois monuments: "This park is one of four national military parks created by the government to place in evidence for all time the gallant service of American soldiers." At the dedication of Ohio monuments, the same speaker reminded his hearers: "Five National Military Parks . . . evidence the feeling of the American people, Union and Confederate, as to the good results of the battle between the forces opposed." Another commission member spoke at the Illinois dedication, thankful for the "Power which, amid the clash of arms, preserved the liberties we prize and has restored the good feeling without which those liberties might little avail us—we come to testify to the patriotic sacrifices of these men who did not live to participate in the reconciliation at which we rejoice." The first two quotations about Americans honoring American soldiers, not just United States soldiers, came from a former Union soldier, while the latter quotation, speaking of rejoicing at reconciliation, came from a former Confederate. Patriotism, reconciliation, and honor were very much in the minds of the park builders.[3]

In fact, the dedication speeches, prayers, and poems vividly show the reconciliation, patriotism, and honor felt by Americans of the 1890s. Almost every dedication and gathering contained speeches full of phrases such as "citizens of a united country," "brothers of a reunited country—brothers in every respect," "unity of national sentiment," "a common glory," "patriotism and magnanimity of a common country," and "peace, forgiveness, love and reunion." Perhaps Judge Jacob Fawcett said it best when dedicating the Wisconsin monument at Shiloh: "As we of the North assemble here today for the purpose of dedicating this monument to the memory of Wisconsin soldiers who perished here, our hearts rejoice to feel that in coming to this place we are not coming into an enemy's country, and that our dead do not lie in an enemy's soil, but that we have assembled here among the people of the South and are mingling with them as members of a reunited family. That we are among those who honor our dead as we honor theirs. That we of the North join with the people of the South in saying that the heroes of this great battle wore both the blue and the gray."[4]

Thus, Shiloh National Military Park was a monument to veterans by veterans, supported by the government and the American people. It was also a personal labor of love for those who built and maintained the park. Many men and women made their contribution to Shiloh National Military Park. A study of the leaders of the establishment and the building of the reservation shows just how passionate and devoted these figures were and, by extension, just how important this national phenomenon was to America and its citizens. It also offers an earlier parallel to the present memorialization of the World War II generation.

Congressmen and senators who led in the effort to write, debate, and pass Shiloh's enabling legislation and then continually appropriated funds to run the park were primarily veterans of the Civil War. To them, Shiloh and her sister parks were not recreational areas for general use by the American public but rather were hallowed tracts (as Abraham Lincoln stated so eloquently in his Gettysburg Address) where friends and comrades died in causes that were bigger than all of them put together. These battlefields were important mile-markers in America's history, they believed, and should be preserved so that future generations would be able to chart the progress of the republic with tangible traces of the past.

On a more human level, the park commission and its officers were also passionate about the service they had rendered in the Civil War and the commemoration of that service. Many aged veterans literally gave the remainder of their lives in the effort to establish, build, and maintain Shiloh National Military Park for all veterans. The battlefield was to them a tangible link to America's most critical period—a period in which they had taken an active part. They realized the urgency of their work; soon, with the passing of veterans, the battlefields would be the only remaining link to that past, and the better this generation preserved and interpreted their fields of honor, the better the coming generations could understand what the veterans had done. Such an urgency to memorialize is being felt in the early twenty-first century with the passing of the World War II generation.

The best way to study the founding, building, and maintenance of Shiloh National Military Park as part of this memorialization movement is to look at the men and women who actually dedicated their lives to the work. In the case of Shiloh, three men stand out. Shiloh veteran Cornelius Cadle, the park commission chairman, was the dominant figure in building the park as well as in maintaining liaison with the War Department and Congress. Although neither a veteran nor an American citizen, the park's chief engineer, Atwell Thompson, likewise passionately poured his life into the park. Most importantly, Shiloh veteran David W. Reed, commission historian, had more to do with the interpretation of the battle of Shiloh and, for that matter with how the Shiloh battlefield appears even today, than any other man associated with the effort.

From different backgrounds, each man combined his specific talents with the others to produce the best park they possibly could. Cadle, the executive, ran the commission in the firm hope of producing an accurate rendering of what had happened in the battle. Thompson, the Irish immigrant engineer, produced the best engineering work he could to fulfill the American dream of professional success. Reed, the historian, insisted on highly accurate troop locations, an effort which was important not only to historians but also to the veterans and to succeeding generations who might hope to locate ancestors' positions. All brought their specific talents to Pittsburg Landing and worked together to produce something of which the veterans in particular and the nation as a whole could be proud. These three men wanted to memorialize the battlefield and the men who fought there, but they also wanted to be good stewards of the resources handed them. They wanted to be proud of their work.

Cadle, Thompson, and Reed, although well known in veterans' circles during the time, were not nationally known figures, but they did typify a generation of passionate individuals who worked for fame, fortune, and the satisfaction of doing a job well. The so-called "robber barons" of the late nineteenth century were just such individuals. Whether they were the famous Rockefellers, Goulds, and Carnegies, or the not-so-famous Cadles, Thompsons, and Reeds, all strove to be the best in their respective fields. In the case of Shiloh, Cadle, Thompson, and Reed produced a part of the memory of the Civil War that ultimately helped reconcile the sections.

Civil War memory has become a popular subject among historians. Because of the disjointed nature of the movement and its broad scope, however, study of this phenomenon has been of a topical nature. For example, one of the most recent and best studies of this topic is David Blight's *Race and Reunion: The Civil War in American Memory*. Blight investigates the role of race in producing a national memory of the war. Edward T. Linenthal, in *Sacred Ground: Americans and Their Battlefields*, takes a different perspective and looks at the American preoccupation with its fields of conflict. In *Ghosts of the Confederacy: Defeat, The Lost Cause, and the Emergence of the New South*, Gaines Foster explores a totally different angle, that of the Southern perspective of the war and how that section interpreted the conflict and its results. In *Remembering War the American Way*, G. Kurt Piehler takes a more general view, researching and analyzing the overall process of remembering America's wars.[5]

Each of these perspectives produces an important understanding of the way the United States viewed the Civil War, but gaps still exist. A study of Shiloh National Military Park can fill some of those holes, although by no means all. For example, Blight delves into race and its relationship to Civil War memory, but that study has very little to offer in terms of Shiloh, simply because racial issues had little direct effect on the work at Pittsburg Landing. Piehler focuses on national remembrance but does not deal with specific battle sites at all. Foster's view is important but likewise offers little in terms of Shiloh's role in remembrance. There was actually very little Lost Cause influence in the creation of the battlefield park. The best published work to deal with battlefields and memory is Linenthal's book, but he also takes a very limited view of Civil War battlefields, researching and analyzing only Gettysburg. In fact, the indexes of these four books, as well as countless others, do not even contain a reference to Shiloh.

Because of the need for additional approaches of investigation into Civil War memory, a study of Shiloh National Military Park can partially answer questions left unanswered by other studies and demonstrate the role of military parks in creating America's memory of the Civil War. Such a study can answer questions about these battlefields, including why Congress appropriated money for parks in isolated areas, why veterans pushed for these sites, how these veterans viewed their battlefields, and how these veterans perceived the memory of the war itself.

The following, then, is an attempt to answer such questions about Civil War battlefields by examining one park in detail. Just as the entire preservation and commemoration movement has been neglected, so also has the study of Shiloh. Only one published administrative history exists, printed in 1954. Written by Charlie Shedd, the park historian at the time, the short history is informative but in no way deals with commemoration, preservation, reconciliation, or memory. In sum, it provides facts but makes no attempt to place them in the context of American history. The only academic work to examine the history of the battlefields themselves is Herman Hattaway and A. J. Meek's *Gettysburg to Vicksburg: The Five Original Civil War Battlefield Parks.* However, this book is an illustrated history with very little detailed or analytical text. Even biographers of the major figures in Shiloh's establishment do not deal with the issue. Neither Stephen Engle's biography of Don Carlos Buell nor Richard L. Kiper's work on John A. McClernand treats the Shiloh establishment in any detail.[6]

This book is an examination of a veterans' movement to preserve a battlefield and how that movement fits into the larger context of American history. It seeks to show how and why the veterans of Shiloh lobbied for, established, and built Shiloh National Military Park in the closing years of the nineteenth and early twentieth centuries. As such, the book focuses on a certain time period, from the end of the battle in 1862 to the park's incorporation within the National Park Service in 1933. This period stands as the critical phase when veterans not only built the park but also produced the interpretation that is still presented at the park today. Likewise, this is the time period when America went through a reconciliation process, of which Shiloh was a major part.

Confined by such parameters, then, there is very little battle history itself. Many monographs have appeared by well-known historians, such as James Lee McDonough, Wiley Sword, Larry Daniel, and Stacy Allen, that trace tactical movements literally by the minute. There is little need to rehash the readily available battle history in a study that focuses on the veterans' movement to preserve the battlefield.[7]

Similarly, this is not a full administrative history of the park. During the time period after 1933, the park's history is so different from what came before that to discuss it in this book would be to lose the book's primary focus: to examine the veterans' memory of the Civil War through the history of a national military park.

The result, it is hoped, will provide a thorough understanding for the general reader and academic alike of what happened at Shiloh long after the armies marched away to fight on other fields. Those veterans were making statements about their war, speaking in their own time to generations in the future. It is important to learn why veterans did what they did so that when we visit their battlefields many years later, we may still hear what they had to say to us.

CHAPTER 1

Isolation

The area surrounding the crossing of latitude 35°09'02" north and longitude 88°19'23" east is perhaps one of the most tranquil places on earth. Encompassing Shiloh National Cemetery and the visitor facilities of Shiloh National Military Park, this riverside location is, for the most part, quiet and undisturbed. Urbanization, industrialization, and the hectic rush of the modern world seem far away. Each year, thousands of history enthusiasts, interested tourists, and families pace the tranquil brick walkways of the cemetery or quietly read the iron tablets and stone monuments that grace the land. The heavily wooded park provides a beautiful outdoor environment for these visitors, while the magnificent Tennessee River, bordering the eastern edge of the park, flows reverently past the almost four thousand honored dead buried atop the steep river bluffs. Adding to the tranquility, numerous animal species inhabit the area, allowing visitors the rare sight of a red fox, white-tailed deer, or gray squirrel.

One of the major factors contributing to the peaceful and serene atmosphere of the government reservation in Hardin County, Tennessee, is its isolation. White settlers first inhabited the region in the early nineteenth century, and for years thereafter, the population density remained rural at best. During the Civil War, Hardin County held no major strategic attributes beyond the Tennessee River. The sole reason the Union army arrived there in the spring of 1862 was to utilize roads that led from Pittsburg Landing, one of many small river landings, to Corinth, Mississippi, some twenty-two miles to the southwest. Corinth, by comparison, did have strategic value: it was the crossing point of two of the Confederacy's major railroads, the Memphis and Charleston and the Mobile and Ohio. The Union army that encamped at Pittsburg Landing and the later reinforcements who joined it constituted by far the largest city in the county, before or after that time. Continuing the nineteenth-century tradition, Hardin County is still mainly rural, with nothing but small hamlets dotting the countryside.

While this isolation has hampered modern development, no better scenario could have been planned for preservation of a battlefield. Urbanization has literally engulfed many Civil War battlefields since most battles took place over the possession of roads, railroads, and transportation corridors near towns, but such development has not affected Shiloh. Likewise, isolation has meant that land development in terms of roads, railroads, and industry has not drastically altered the field of battle. Thus, while isolation and a stagnant economy have created economic and social problems in the area, they have ironically bene-fited Shiloh, allowing the development and interpretation of the battlefield in a near-pristine condition.

This pattern of isolation existed even in prehistoric times. Very little is known about the civilizations that inhabited the region before Europeans explored the area; the majority of available information has come from Native American mounds found atop the steep bluffs overlooking the Tennessee River. Encom-passed within the boundaries of Shiloh National Military Park, these mounds have been the site of a number of excavations, ranging from amateur digs by the park founders in 1899 to exploration done by Smithsonian archaeologists in the 1930s. The park, even today, often hosts assorted archaeological groups working at the mounds.[1]

The first excavation of these mounds took place in 1899, led by government officials then in the process of building the park. Done "with more zeal than skill," this exploration consisted solely of a trench dug through the burial mound. These amateur efforts proved worthwhile, however. Within the excavation, workers found human remains as well as a priceless effigy pipe carved from red stone in the shape of a kneeling man. Because of the pipe's worth, the Smithsonian Insti-tution later attempted to acquire it, but the park commissioners would not give it up. One park employee responded tersely that "we would not care to part with it." Instead, he offered several human bones taken from the mound, which the Smithsonian accepted.[2]

This quick and unscientific dig exemplifies the pattern of disrespect white men have shown the mounds at Shiloh. After the battle in April 1862, members of the 28th Illinois buried their dead in one of the mounds. As late as 1915, men were still desecrating the site. DeLong Rice, a park employee, had a summer cottage built atop the largest one, along the bluffs of the river.[3]

This early native population ultimately declined, however, apparently giving birth to the later Choctaw and Chickasaw tribes of Mississippi. In their stead came a civilization of white men of European descent. Continual westward expansion eventually affected the region, although west Tennessee was one of the last loca-tions settled by whites. Tennessee became a state in 1796, but only the eastern and middle portions saw settlement by 1820; the interior of west Tennessee was still isolated and barren from the white perspective. By 1820, however, the United States government wanted to make additional territory available to settlers and brokered a treaty with the remaining natives for some ten thousand square miles of west Tennessee. The first area settled in west Tennessee was on either side of the river, just north of the Mississippi Territory. In 1819, the area became Hardin County, named for an early surveyor, Colonel Joseph Hardin.[4]

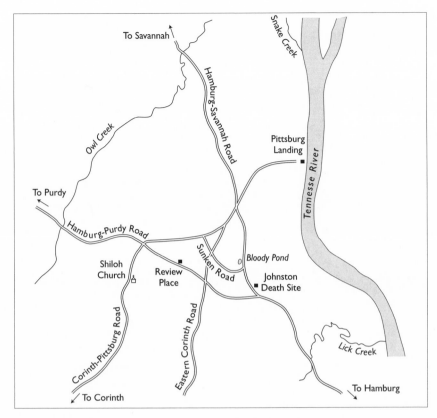

Map 1. The Shiloh National Military Park area. Map by the author.

Most early settlement in Hardin County occurred east of the river. Less activity took place in the western section of the county, with the few settlers concentrating along the river. As early as 1832, however, Tennessee granted John Chambers the area surrounding what would later become Pittsburg Landing. Apparently, Chambers did not develop his grant because, in 1843, Thomas B. Stubbs took a grant from the State of Tennessee for the same two hundred acres. Soon, a small hamlet containing a store and a few residences emerged on Stubbs's land, near the sloping landing dwarfed below high bluffs. Among the early settlers to reach the Shiloh plateau west of the river were three brothers, Pittser, Thomas, and Riley Tucker. By August 1848, the brothers had staked off fourteen hundred acres near the landing, from which they operated a ferry to the east bank. As early as 1835, the residents worshiped at a small Methodist church in the area, but this congregation split over the slavery issue around 1846. The southernmost church soon acquired the name Shiloh—one meaning of which is "place of peace." The title seemed fitting at the time because of the quiet, rural setting. Most important

Fig. 1. The commission dug this trench through the burial mound at Shiloh National Military Park. D. W. Reed, historian and secretary, stands at the far right of the back row. Commission Chairman Cornelius Cadle also stands on the back row, third from the left. Commissioner J. H. Ashcraft is seated on the left. Courtesy of Shiloh National Military Park.

to the development of the area and later history, Pitts Tucker operated a liquor store and tavern at the landing, which began to draw steamers plying the Tennessee River. The landing eventually became known as Pittsburg Landing, a corruption of the store operator's first name.[5]

Over the years, Hardin County developed slowly. By 1848, the population had reached eight thousand people. Savannah, on the east bank of the river, emerged as the principal town. Other hamlets grew, almost all of them along the river, the central transportation artery in the county. Landings became especial havens for activity, including Crump's, Pittsburg, and Hamburg Landings near the southern end of the county.[6]

Quickly, Pittsburg Landing became an important location. Several hundred yards long and sufficiently deep, the landing offered a gradual slope to a point where high water would not inhibit docking. The Tennessee River, before the Tennessee Valley Authority's work, was notorious for extremely rapid rises and falls, causing many landings to cease operation in high water. Thus, an all-weather landing such as Pittsburg had an important advantage. The best roads of the time led north to Crump's Landing, west to Purdy, south to Hamburg Landing, and, most importantly, southwest to Corinth, Mississippi.

By 1860, more than three-dozen families inhabited the plateau, bringing business and activity to Pittsburg Landing. In the years before railroads arrived in the area in the late 1850s, growing river traffic offered communication with the out-side world, particularly by attracting merchants who traveled by wagon to and from Corinth. Individual farmers owned and worked small plots of land on the high ground near the landing. These farmers had a wearisome job, however, for the soil around Pittsburg Landing was poor at best. One local historian con-cluded that "a more unprofitable spot of land, perhaps, could not have been selected . . . for a battleground, . . . with less loss to the county." Nevertheless, fam-ilies with names that would one day become famous because of the battle—Fraley, Duncan, Rea—made the best of their rural lives on the banks of the Tennessee.[7]

Despite its isolation, Hardin County still fell victim to the sectional controversy brewing in the nation during the 1850s. Savannah's leaders split over this contro-versy, which was based firmly on the issue of slavery. Very few slaves lived in the more populous eastern two-thirds of Hardin County because most large-scale farmers worked the semi-fertile and isolated land west of the river. As a result, Unionist sentiment prevailed within the county. Led by the eastern citizens, Hardin County voted against secession. The effort to avoid conflict was futile, however, as war clouds grew even larger on the horizon.[8]

Throughout 1861 and into early 1862, the first year of the war, the scene of con-flict lay far to the north of Hardin County. The inhabitants did, however, struggle with one another. The section east of the river, especially in and around Savannah, openly sided with the Union, while Confederate sympathizers in the western third of the county courted the Confederacy by organizing Southern mil-itary units. Secessionists within the area attempted to whip up public support, and efforts to woo young men to join the Confederate army took place, using young women, eloquent speeches, and Southern nationalism. Banquets and socials swelled feelings of Southern honor, and many young men joined the Confed-erate ranks. Conversely, large-scale Union enlistment did not take place until after United States forces occupied the region later in 1862.[9]

By March 1862, the war had finally reached Hardin County, particularly the area around Pittsburg Landing. The long Confederate defensive line in northern Tennessee and southern Kentucky commanded by General Albert Sidney Johnston fell to a variety of Union thrusts. The Cumberland Gap region fell in January 1862—the result of the small but important Battle of Mill Springs. By far the most important actions occurred along the Tennessee and Cumber-land rivers in northwestern Tennessee. A Union army commanded by little-known Brigadier General Ulysses S. Grant scored impressive victories at Forts Henry and Donelson in February 1862. With his successes, Grant neutralized three Confederate defensive locations, captured an entire enemy army, and effectively broke through the Confederate defensive perimeter in the Western Theater. The most important effect of these victories, however, was the opening of the twin rivers deep into the Confederate heartland. The Federals followed up

Grant's victories by capturing Nashville on the Cumberland River and undertaking a large-scale movement southward on the Tennessee. All across the line of the west, the Federals had Southern commander Johnston on the retreat. Accordingly, Confederates withdrew from locations as far apart as Columbus and Bowling Green, Kentucky.

Johnston moved to regroup his scattered units in north Alabama and Mississippi. Believing that the next Union expedition would be sent to break the railroads that crossed at Corinth, Mississippi, he concentrated his command there, calling in troops from all points of the compass; units arrived in Corinth from Tennessee and New Orleans and as far away as South Carolina, Florida, and Texas.

After nearly a month of planning, the Federals continued their southward push along the Tennessee River. Despite conflict with his department commander, Major General Henry W. Halleck, Grant continued his thrust deep into the Confederacy. Union forces now appeared in Hardin County. Grant and Major General C. F. Smith, both commanding the expedition at various times, made their headquarters at the Savannah home of Unionist William H. Cherry.

Meanwhile, Union gunboats plied the river as far south as Alabama and on March 1 encountered a small Confederate outpost and a battery of cannon at Pittsburg Landing. The gunboats shelled the area and landed accompanying infantry. The small skirmish resulted in the capture of one Confederate gun and several wounded soldiers. The Union patrol soon returned to the gunboats, however, when it confronted a Confederate picket line consisting of elements of the 18th Louisiana Infantry.[10]

In an effort to break the Memphis and Charleston Railroad in mid-March, Brigadier General William T. Sherman led another raid from Savannah toward Eastport, Mississippi. With his 5th Division crammed aboard transports, Sherman steamed past Pittsburg Landing on his way south. The raid ended unsuccessfully because of rain and high water, and Sherman could only return northward. With his commander's approval, he decided to disembark his division at Pittsburg Landing, the only landing in the vicinity still above high water. Sherman's and Brigadier General Stephen A. Hurlbut's divisions tramped up the steep bluffs around Pittsburg Landing and camped in the woods and fields surrounding Shiloh Church.

Sherman notified Grant that he had located a perfect site to encamp the army. The high plateau overlooking Pittsburg Landing contained many benefits, he believed. It lay between two large creeks, which offered protection to the army's flanks. Pittsburg Landing itself, which could facilitate large transports and supply ships even in high water, offered general communications. Good water was available because of the presence of several natural springs. Fields were abundant for the training and drilling of the relatively green army. Most importantly, several ridge roads ran from the landing to Corinth, the ultimate goal of the expedition.

Sherman summed up his thoughts in a letter to Grant: "The ground itself admits of easy defense by a small command, and yet affords admirable camping ground for a hundred thousand men." Grant agreed. By late March, five Union divisions lay encamped on the plateau above Pittsburg Landing. Drill and the leisure of camp life became the norm for the Federal army in the spring days of late March and early April 1862.[11]

Confederate commander Johnston knew that Grant's army only awaited the arrival of the Union Army of the Ohio, with Major General Don Carlos Buell commanding, before it moved forward to attack Corinth. Johnston decided to strike Grant before Buell arrived, thereby evening the odds. The Confederate Army of the Mississippi marched from various points on April 3, 1862, intending to assemble for the attack just south of Shiloh Church. Heavy rain, bad roads, and miscommunications delayed the Confederate march, however.

By the evening of April 5, Johnston and his second-in-command, General P. G. T. Beauregard, had deployed nearly forty-four thousand men in line of battle, four corps deep, within a mile of the Union camps. The unsuspecting Federal commanders, despite some contacts and even minor skirmishing, had no idea that the enemy army lay so near. Under orders not to bring on an engagement but to await the arrival of Buell, front-line division commanders William T. Sherman and Benjamin M. Prentiss chose not to act on reports of nearby Confederates. Fortunately for the Federals, one alert brigade commander ordered a morning patrol that uncovered the enemy a mere mile in front of the camps. The ensuing skirmish grew into a pitched battle that delayed the Confederate advance. With two to three precious hours wasted, Johnston lost the element of surprise, and the main assaults on the southernmost Union camps, where Johnston intended the battle to begin, did not occur until eight that morning.

Once the main Confederate assault began, however, it rolled up Union brigade after brigade. Attempting to flank the left of the Federal army and drive a wedge of Confederate troops between it and Pittsburg Landing, Johnston fell victim to faulty reconnaissance. Misunderstanding the deployment of the Federal army, Johnston concentrated the majority of his forces on what was actually the Union right flank. Instead of separating the Federals from the landing, this tactic created an opposite effect and drove Grant back onto his base, the landing, rather than away from it. Throughout the day, severe fighting erupted in and around now-famous places such as Shiloh Church, the Peach Orchard, Bloody Pond, and the Hornet's Nest.

Johnston's troops felt victorious at the end of the day. His brigades had driven the enemy back some two miles, and the bulk of the Federal army lay huddled along a final line of defense near the landing. Johnston, however, never realized his accomplishments. At half past two that afternoon, he died from a wound suffered while directing an attack. Dying from a loss of blood, Johnston became the highest-ranking American military officer (a full general) ever killed in battle, a distinction he still holds. Beauregard, the second-in-command, took control of the Confederate army.

By the time the Confederates had overrun the various Union positions in actions that included the capture of some twenty-two hundred Northern troops near the Hornet's Nest, nightfall was upon them. Accordingly, Beauregard never really tested Grant's final line. Confident of success, the Confederates spent a fitful night awaiting ultimate victory the next morning.

That was not to be, however. During the night, Grant received reinforcements from a number of directions. One of his own divisions, Lew Wallace's, arrived from Crump's Landing near dusk on April 6. Despite his unfortunate delay in reaching the field, Wallace added men to Grant's right flank. The majority of the fresh soldiers came from Buell's army, however. The first units arrived in Savannah on April 5, and divisions of Buell's army slowly made their way to the battlefield. One division marched overland and ferried the river during the evening and night while others came on transports from Savannah. By daylight on April 7, Grant had almost twenty-five thousand fresh troops in line alongside his battered yet still defiant soldiers.

Johnston's fears had come to fruition. He had wanted to defeat Grant before a combination of Union armies could take place, but he had failed. The two-day delay before the battle and even the two-hour delay on the morning of April 6 helped Grant to hold out until reinforcements arrived from Buell.

Beauregard now had no chance to continue the offensive and perhaps destroy the enemy armies. Fighting raged on April 7 as Union forces retook the ground lost the day before. The Union troops forced the Confederates to retreat, and they left the field in the early afternoon. The great Confederate offensive had failed.

In the days after the battle, both sides regrouped and tended to the wounded. Time would not allow a long cessation of hostilities, however. Soon, still another Union army, Major General John Pope's Army of the Mississippi, arrived in the vicinity of Pittsburg Landing. Department commander Henry W. Halleck himself came to lead the advance on Corinth.[12]

After a very slow march, Halleck reached Corinth and began to lay siege to the railroad city. Beauregard realized his position was untenable and retreated to Tupelo on May 29. An almost bloodless conclusion ended the campaign against Corinth. As it turned out, the battle for possession of the vital railroad junction at Corinth, the objective of the campaign, had actually raged at Shiloh.

The scene of operations now moved eastward and southward as dual Union thrusts against Chattanooga and Vicksburg developed. Although supplies still moved through the Pittsburg Landing area and minor skirmishing took place, the war was generally over for Hardin County. Inhabitants of the Pittsburg Landing area returned to their homes, more often than not to find them destroyed as a result of the battle. Frightened animals returned to their familiar surroundings. The ground that literally shook in April once again reverted to its pre-battle peace.

By the fall of 1862, the battlefield of Shiloh lay relatively quiet, and it would remain so for the rest of the war. The nation witnessed more terrible conflict and afterwards many years of arduous Reconstruction. There was no focus on preserving or remembering what had happened at Shiloh or, for that matter, on any other battlefield. Only single monuments or signs appeared on the less isolated fields of battle such as Gettysburg. All the while, Shiloh reverted back to its customary isolation, witnessing only the passing of a few inquisitive visitors or aging veterans and their interested offspring.

For more than thirty years after the battle, Americans gave very little thought to preserving their Civil War battlefields. Farmers with names made famous by the battle at Pittsburg Landing returned to their fields. Loggers cut and hauled wood from the area, careful to watch for bullets or cannonballs that would dull or bend their saw blades. Commercial steamboats once again plied the waters of the Tennessee River, stopping occasionally at a once-again-peaceful Pittsburg Landing.

The work of preservation at the battlefield of Shiloh, therefore, was practically nonexistent, and during those years of neglect, numerous changes took place. By the 1890s, the appearance of the battlefield had changed drastically from its condition in April 1862. Several new roads cut across the plateau. Wood and field lines had changed. War Department agent George B. Davis, inspecting the area for possible future preservation, noted that the battlefield had "changed much in detail, but little in its general aspect." One veteran, returning in 1894, was saddened by what he saw and lamented, "You will find the field has grown up to a thick underbrush of black gum and oak." He admitted "a feeling of disappointment, and with it a tinge of regret," that the field was not even recognizable, considering the sacrifice made there in 1862.[13]

The only real lasting physical remembrances of the battle, the burial places of both Union and Confederate soldiers, had also deteriorated badly by the 1890s. In 1878, one newspaper described the destruction that the weather and rooting hogs had on bodies barely covered by a thin layer of earth. "There are many bones scattered over the hills and hollows and lying in the woods exposed," related the reporter. B. G. Brazelton, a local historian writing in the 1880s, lamented the fact that buried Confederates were "without a tombstone to mark their last resting place." By the 1890s, some Confederate burial trenches were no longer even distinguishable. Similarly, smaller-scale burial sites were also in decay.[14]

Despite the lack of definitive action, anyone who wandered the field could see that there had been a battle on those grounds years before. The landscape itself told a disturbing tale: trees shot to pieces, the debris of battle everywhere.

Bayonets and muskets were a common sight, as were wagon parts and harnesses. Occasionally a visitor would find a ramrod or a cannonball embedded in a tree. Local farmers, who proudly led tours for visitors, occasionally found more gruesome remnants of the battle while working their fields. Plows would frequently unearth the skeletons of soldiers buried hastily on the battlefield. Jesse Curtis, a local farmer, found the remains of three Union soldiers near the Peach Orchard in 1880. One veteran remarked as late as 1893 that "they are ploughing up their bones all over the field." In 1934, M. A. Milligan uncovered nine Union soldiers on his land just two hundred yards southwest of the national park boundary. Even as late as 1977, relic hunters found two Confederate soldiers buried on private property near the park.[15]

The most telling indication to visitors that something momentous had taken place around Pittsburg Landing, however, was the National Cemetery, comprising some ten and one-half acres atop the steep bluffs overlooking the Tennessee River. The cemetery was one of the most beautiful in the nation. Large oaks shaded a majority of the site and were the home to squirrels and a variety of birds. Atop a massive flagpole fluttered the American flag.

The cemetery at Shiloh was the result of the nineteenth-century American national movement to memorialize the dead, most notably from its wars. Americans were not only creating park-like civilian cemeteries all around the nation but were also honoring their war dead with elaborate graveyards. Before the Civil War, individual soldiers were rarely honored; a central monument normally celebrated the dead as a group. This all changed in 1862 when Congress authorized the establishment of national cemeteries—the first fruits of a national Civil War memorialization process. In 1866, further congressional action authorized the establishment of cemeteries on Southern battlefields, and Quartermaster General Montgomery Meigs quickly issued General Orders 33, approving the location and reburial of Union soldiers on many battlefields, including Shiloh. Quartermaster Department inspector E. B. Whitman viewed the field, as well as many burial grounds along the Tennessee River, and recommended that a site on the bluff overlooking Pittsburg Landing was the appropriate place to honor the dead. The Quartermaster General approved the location, and Major General George H. Thomas, commanding the Department of the Tennessee, gave the order to begin work. As a result, the government established Pittsburg Landing National Cemetery in 1866 (changed to "Shiloh National Cemetery at Pittsburg Landing" on July 30, 1888), in order to provide decent and honorable burial for the thousands of United States soldiers killed at Shiloh and in surrounding areas. Significantly, the Confederates were left in mass graves on the battlefield.[16]

The legislature of the State of Tennessee ceded possession of the land to the federal government in an act of March 9, 1867, but there was immediate trouble regarding clear title to the land. The heirs of Thomas B. Stubbs, represented by

Stubbs's daughter Mary A. Harmon, would not accept the government price for the land. It was not until January 6, 1869, in *United States* v. *Mary A. Harmon,* that the United States District Court of the District of West Tennessee awarded the government title to the cemetery lands for the sum of five hundred dollars.[17]

Burial of soldiers began long before the government received clear title to the land. As early as March 1866, work parties under Quartermaster Department inspector E. B. Whitman spread themselves into a makeshift skirmish line and walked every inch of the field, in all some twelve square miles. Workers marked each grave by compass direction and distance from a prominent nearby object. Many bodies lay in regimental burial grounds, which burial details had usually placed near one of the regiment's battle positions or campsite. More difficult work came in locating individual burial plots scattered across the battlefield. Later in the month, Whitman returned to the field, this time with work parties to rebury those bodies he had discovered exposed to the weather and scavenging animals.[18]

By the fall of 1866, with the arrival of "the cool weather of autumn," workers began exhuming bodies from the battlefield. Many of these proved to be unknown, some because of the annual fires (begun by locals to clear out underbrush) that had destroyed the headboards. After carefully examining the bodies for clues to identity, workers placed them in strong boxes, which they then reinterred in the new cemetery. At Pittsburg Landing, laborers also buried deceased soldiers from engagements all along the Tennessee River, some arriving from as far north as Fort Henry, Tennessee, and as far south as Muscle Shoals, Alabama. In all, laborers gathered bodies from 178 locations at Shiloh and 565 different localities in the Tennessee Valley.[19]

Despite governmental regulations calling for conformity in all national cemeteries, planners of the Pittsburg Landing National Cemetery created what one laborer called "the handsomest cemetery in the South." Brevet Lieutenant Colonel A. W. Wills laid off sections of the cemetery into divisions, traversed by contoured avenues originally covered with shell and gravel but replaced with a brick walkway in the twentieth century. Workers reburied what soldiers they could in regimental plots, facilitated by the existence of wartime regimental burial sites on the battlefield. Some twenty-nine regimental plots encircled a central site, on which stood a "rostrum," a gazebo-type speaker's platform.[20]

By 1869, workers had interred 3,584 Civil War soldiers in the cemetery, 2,359 of them unknown. These soldiers represented 203 different regiments from thirteen separate states. Later, however, soldiers from other wars and government personnel were also buried in the cemetery. The burial ground also included cemetery employees and their families. Even two Confederate soldiers, having died as prisoners, were placed among the Union dead. By 2001, the cemetery held 3,861 graves, of which 2,370 were unknown.[21]

From the beginning, the cemetery contained a wide array of soldiers. At a point overlooking the Tennessee River, workers buried six color-bearers of the 16th Wisconsin in a semicircle. Laborers also erected a similar memorial, a circular group assembled around an upright cannon shaft honoring minor officers killed in battle. The grave of one drummer, John D. Holmes of the 15th Iowa, also helped to bring solemnity to the area. Another grave, supposedly of another drummer boy, was placed in a prominent position near the entrance to the cemetery. Cemetery builder A. W. Wills authorized the unusual placement of this grave in 1867 to secure the attention of visitors. Wills, however, seems to have stretched the truth somewhat. The soldier in the grave was not officially a drummer but, rather, "a member of a certain band." Even a local Daughters of the American Revolution chapter buried one Revolutionary War soldier at Shiloh.[22]

The government marked these soldiers' graves in several ways. As the bodies were interred, simple wooden "headboards," painted white with black letters, displayed a grave number. A congressional act of March 3, 1873, stipulated that permanent markers should replace the wooden headboards. Consequently, the temporary markers at Shiloh were replaced in 1876 and 1877 with marble headstones of varying shapes and sizes. Many of these were upright stones that

Fig. 2. A group of veterans at the Shiloh National Cemetery. D. W. Reed stands just left of the upright cannon. Courtesy of Shiloh National Military Park.

told the soldier's personal information and grave number, while others were simple square stones standing some eight inches in height and displaying only the grave number.[23]

Care of the cemetery fell to a local superintendent, assisted by a group of laborers. This governing organization remained in effect even after the establishment of a national park commission for Shiloh in the winter of 1894. Cemetery administration remained separate from that of the national park until 1933, when both the park and cemetery were transferred from the War Department to the National Park Service of the Department of the Interior. Even then, however, R. H. Bailey, cemetery superintendent, remained in direct charge of the cemetery until it was consolidated with the park under Blair Ross, the park superintendent, on July 31, 1943.[24]

Originally, the cemetery superintendent and builders lived in tents. In 1866, workers converted an existing wood building into a cemetery lodge, a simple structure that stood just west of the main entrance to the cemetery. With appropriated funds, laborers replaced this lodge in 1876 with a new facility, moving the older lodge several hundred feet northward and transforming it into a tool storage area. The new structure, located on the site of the former lodge, was a one-and-a-half-story brick building set atop a limestone foundation. The building contained six rooms, not counting the three rooms in the cellar.[25]

A wooden toolhouse and another storage building provided room for goods, and a wooden stable, later replaced by a more substantial brick one, housed the livestock used by the superintendent and his workers. Wells provided ample water for residents and visitors. A rostrum, erected in 1892, and a flagpole sat atop the river bluff, while a set of iron steps and a 154-foot-long brick walkway, erected in June 1891, allowed easy access to and from Pittsburg Landing. The War Department placed ornamental iron gates at the cemetery entrance in 1911.[26]

Perhaps the most distinctive feature of the cemetery was the "massive limestone wall" that encircled the area. Built in the fall of 1867 of stone brought by steamboat from a quarry eleven miles upriver, the wall measured 4 feet high, 2 feet thick, and 2,818 feet in length. A hedge of osage orange, totaling 3,172 linear feet, was planted in 1871 and for many years encircled the entire cemetery, while a simple wire fence separated the lodge and storage buildings (situated in the western portion of the tract—"outside the cemetery proper") from the gravesites.[27]

Several monuments immediately went up in the cemetery. Three upright cannon-shaft monuments have adorned the cemetery from the beginning. These were later joined by three cannon formed into a pyramid, denoting Grant's headquarters. Two guns overlooking the river have symbolically long kept watch over the cemetery. One, a solid brass, twenty-four-pound boat howitzer salvaged from a sunken riverboat near Diamond Island, weighed 1,305 pounds. A cannonball remains housed in the tube. An eight-inch siege howitzer also decorated the cemetery. Both long sat atop wooden frames, despite efforts by superintendents to acquire naval carriages. With no such carriages available, workers built platforms of stone and concrete to support the guns.[28]

The only major stone memorial that has ever existed within the cemetery was the 9th Illinois monument. Placed to honor the unknown dead and wounded of that regiment, which suffered 366 total casualties out of 578 present for duty, it was dedicated in early June 1896 with impressive cere-monies. Estimates placed the crowd at 5,000 people, including 15 or 16 veterans of the regiment itself. A band serenaded the crowd, the widow of one of the 9th Illinois's captains unveiled the monument, and a Confederate veteran laid a wreath. A major speaker at the event was the former commander of the Union Army of the Ohio, Major General Don Carlos Buell.[29]

From its origins, the cemetery needed continual upkeep. Periodically, foliage had to be removed to allow grass to grow. Likewise, trees stained the headstones, and they required cleaning. The wall proved a constant problem, requiring in 1891 a 450-foot reinforcement on the southern boundary. Filling sunken graves and sodding grass helped maintain a beautiful setting.[30]

Placed as it was on the bluffs overlooking the Tennessee River, the cemetery developed a serious problem with erosion. As early as 1871, washouts became a major concern. By 1903, erosion had caused so much damage that part of the eastern limestone wall enclosing the cemetery had disappeared into the water. Efforts to contain this destruction went forward, but even in 2004, the stream bank regularly experienced loss of land because of the Tennessee River's encroachment.[31]

Other acts of nature also adversely affected the cemetery. Periodically, inclement weather caused severe damage. Superintendent Leonard S. Doolittle reported a June 21, 1884, "hurricane" which did extensive damage to the ceme-tery's trees. On June 3, 1904, "the severest wind storm which has ever visited this section" downed even more.[32]

As the only governmental facility at Pittsburg Landing until the 1890s, the cemetery necessarily hosted returning veterans for special events and obser-vances, such as the dedication of the 9th Illinois monument and the yearly reunions on the anniversary of the battle, April 6 and 7. Most festivities, incor-porating both Northern and Southern veterans, took place at the rostrum in the center of the cemetery. Of course, the cemetery staff adorned the land for these observances, as well as on other special occasions such as Memorial Day. Every year on May 30, United States flags from the local Adamsville Grand Army of the Republic chapter marked each grave, and the main flag was lowered to half-mast. Other events necessitated the lowering of the flag to half-staff, among them the deaths of former presidents.[33]

Fig. 3. An assembly of veterans at the battlefield on Memorial Day 1895. Courtesy of Shiloh National Military Park.

Thus, for thirty years after 1862, only the cemetery stood as a reminder of the ultimate sacrifice made in the woods and fields around Pittsburg Landing. By the decade of the 1890s, while some efforts at safekeeping occurred near the landing itself, the conservationist's hand had barely touched the vast majority of the battlefield. Shiloh was in desperate need of preservation. Fortunately, a mood of nationalism, memorialization, and preservation was sweeping the nation in the 1890s. Even the isolated terrain around Shiloh Church and Pittsburg Landing would soon benefit from this spirit.

CHAPTER 2

"An Act to Establish . . ."

Since its foundation, the United States has witnessed sectional controversy, with the states and regions arguing over racial, political, and economic issues that have literally torn the nation apart. Although such sectionalism had existed throughout U.S. history, the problem became especially apparent in the 1840s with the territorial expansion inspired by the movement of Manifest Destiny. The 1850s led to outright killing over the slavery issue in places like Kansas and Missouri. Finally, the Southern states attempted to leave the Union in the 1860s, prompting the Civil War. The years following this conflict were also tinged with violence and controversy. Although the Civil War ended debates over secession and slavery, twelve years of Reconstruction failed to settle the bigger questions of liberty and freedom for the emancipated slaves. By the end of the 1880s, the nation still suffered from this sectional controversy.[1]

The 1890s, however, saw an upsurge in nationalism. Sparked by centennial celebrations of Revolutionary-era events, which included erection of monuments on several battlefields, this feeling of patriotism forced the sections to deal with their past and bond together as one nation of united states. In this decade, most aged veterans lost the animosity and hatred born in the Civil War and fueled by Reconstruction. Sectional politics became less heated as Republicans catered to white Southerners, hoping for their political support. Economic issues grew even more important, with industrialization and the desire to utilize the raw-material-rich South taking precedence over racial issues. The emergence of Jim Crow segregation seemed to satisfy whites of all sections. In this context, the nation began to pay tribute to the old veterans of the Civil War, both blue and gray. War rhetoric no longer elicited cries of blame. Now the nation sought to honor both sides as brave and heroic men who gave their lives for ideals each viewed as essential. As a result, the sections came closer together, forming firmer bonds over economics, politics, and even racial issues. The Spanish-American War, fought in 1898, also fueled this developing wave of nationalism.[2]

Tangible results emerged from this feeling of nationalism and tribute to Civil War veterans. All across the nation, patriotic societies emerged. Congress established a national holiday for both sides, Memorial Day, in 1889. More spectacularly, monuments went up all across the United States. On almost every county court-house lawn in both North and South, a statue of a common soldier commemo-rated local men who sacrificed for their respective causes. In the two Civil War capitals, veterans erected monuments to honor their commanders. In Richmond, statues of Jefferson Davis, Robert E. Lee, and "Stonewall" Jackson lined Monu-ment Avenue. In Washington, D.C., statues of Ulysses S. Grant, William T. Sherman, and other Federal leaders adorned Pennsylvania Avenue and other sites. Most telling, the magnificent memorial to Abraham Lincoln, with its inscrip-tion quoting the famous passage that begins "With malice toward none," symbol-ized the reunion of the sections.[3]

One of the most important results of this wave of nationalism was an effort to preserve and honor the actual scenes of Civil War conflict. Either during or immediately after the war, Congress had established national cemeteries on many battlefields. In 1890, Congress established the first national military park to commemorate the battle of Chickamauga and related scenes of combat around Chattanooga. In the same year, Congress established a park at the bat-tlefield of Antietam, near Sharpsburg, Maryland. Gettysburg received a park in 1895, as did Vicksburg in 1899. This wave of nationalism and preservation would also affect the isolated and seemingly forgotten field of battle located around Pittsburg Landing.[4]

Other factors also contributed to the congressional action that ultimately pre-served Shiloh. Veterans returning to the battlefield over the years grew appalled to hear stories of farmers plowing up soldiers' remains in the fields surrounding Pittsburg Landing. Road improvements also unearthed bodies. Aged veterans, growing more and more sentimental by the year, shuddered to think that their friends and comrades of the 1860s still lay buried in undiscovered common bat-tlefield graves. Realizing that all the graves could never be found, these veterans agreed that the next-best option was to preserve the entire battlefield, thus pro-tecting the lost graves.[5]

Army pride also played a role in this grassroots movement to establish a national park. Since Congress had already founded battlefield parks for the Army of the Potomac at Antietam and for the Army of the Cumberland at Chicka-mauga and Chattanooga, the veterans of the Army of the Tennessee desired a park to commemorate their actions in the late war. Fortunately for them, many veterans of the Army of the Tennessee held prominent political positions. Mere privates and sergeants in 1862, these men were now senators, representatives, and governors. One example was David B. Henderson, a lieutenant at Shiloh but des-tined to become Speaker of the House of Representatives.[6]

The first definite idea of establishing a national military park at Shiloh sur-faced in 1893. In April of that year, several Union veterans returned to the bat-tlefield to view the scene of their earlier conflict. Hearing the stories of farmers and workers unearthing skeletons, these veterans were determined to insure that such horrors would cease. Returning downriver on the steamer *W. P. Nesbit*, these aging soldiers mulled over the idea of establishing a national park like those already set aside at Chickamauga and Antietam. By the end of the trip, the veterans had formed an organization with temporary officers and called themselves the Shiloh Battlefield Association. Although the child of Union veterans, this organization actively sought the cooperation of former Confederates, who gladly lent their support.[7]

The association held a more formal meeting later that year at Indianapolis, Indiana. First, the veterans elected a permanent group of officers and appointed committees to work on various aspects of the project. Second, they decided on three major initiatives: to ask the United States government to purchase the field; to preserve the graves, both Northern and Southern, that still lay on the battlefield; and to mark the field with appropriate markers and monuments. Third, they appointed a special committee to gather the support of the major veterans' organizations, such as the Grand Army of the Republic and the Society of the Army of the Tennessee, and to lobby Congress. Finally, the association called for annual reunions on April 6 and 7 to be held at Pittsburg Landing.[8]

By 1894, the association had gathered the support of many prominent men. At the Indianapolis meeting, the veterans elected Major General John A. McClernand, who had commanded a division in the Army of the Tennessee at Shiloh, as its first permanent president. They further named a private of the 41st Illinois Infantry, E. T. Lee, as secretary, and Dr. J. W. Coleman, who had served as a surgeon in the 41st Illinois, as treasurer. Honorary vice presidents consisted of a vast array of famous officers who had served at Shiloh, including Army of the Tennessee division commanders Benjamin Prentiss and Lew Wallace, and Army of the Ohio commander Don Carlos Buell. Prominent Confederates named to the list ranged from Generals Basil Duke and Joseph Wheeler to former Tennessee governor and staff officer Isham G. Harris, now a Democrat in the United States Senate. In all, the association assembled an impressive array of veterans to push for the establishment of a national military park at Shiloh.[9]

With the association formalized, its leaders began working to convince the federal government to preserve the park. This effort, of course, required support from a variety of other well-established organizations. Since the mass of veterans themselves would have to lend their influence to the idea, the association sent delegations to the Grand Army of the Republic and the Society of the Army of the Tennessee. Both readily lent their assistance. They also called on Southern leaders, such as Senator Harris and former Confederate General Joseph Wheeler, now a member of the House of Representatives, to aid the work. Many of these former Confederates supported the idea, especially since the battlefield still contained the remains of some two thousand Confederate dead.[10]

Most of all, the Shiloh Battlefield Association needed the support of the United States Congress. Its "Congressional Committee" lobbied that body for the park and impressed many congressmen, gaining a "promise of assistance" from them. In the House, David B. Henderson of Iowa and Joseph Wheeler of Alabama, both Shiloh veterans, lent their support, while Senator John Sherman of Ohio, brother of General William T. Sherman, and Senator Harris of Tennessee led the effort in the Senate.[11]

The preservation activities of the Shiloh Battlefield Association seemed perfectly timed. The emerging sense of nationalism had put the American people in a mood to preserve the physical artifacts of the nation's heritage. Many organizations and even states had joined the growing body of conservationists calling for the federal government to maintain permanently some of the nation's most cherished historical sites.

The federal government, however, had been slow to join the popular movement to protect America's historic treasures. Differing views concerning the role of the government on this issue led to a stalemate regarding preservation legislation. Some argued that the federal government did not have the authority for such action. Others insisted that it was not the government's duty to preserve each and every battlefield, which would entail massive expense. Many pieces of legislation attempting to preserve battlefields had already met defeat as this policy conflict continued, but most battlegrounds, such as Wilson Creek, Stones River, and Appomattox, would eventually receive some preservation support from the federal government.[12]

As a result, veterans' groups and organizations were the driving force in the effort for historical preservation prior to the 1890s. The federal government had assumed sole responsibility for national cemetery construction during and after the Civil War, but it limited its role basically to establishing and maintaining these burial grounds. Yet, the establishment of cemeteries not only marked a change regarding memorialization of the individual soldier but also marked the first major organized effort by the federal government to erect memorials outside the capital.[13]

The Civil War helped to transform the national government into a massive bureaucracy. As its authority and responsibility continually evolved, Congress became slowly but increasingly involved in commemoration and veteran remembrance. First, congressmen established the national cemetery system. Then, by the 1880s, Congress recognized the importance of remembering veterans with pension bills and memorial holiday legislation. By the opening of the decade of the 1890s, the United States government was ready to take the ultimate step, that of buying and developing the battlefields of the Civil War. One of these would be the isolated but not forgotten battlefield of Shiloh.[14]

Within this context of nationalism and a supportive government, the Shiloh Battlefield Association acted by advertising its goal and requesting donations. Each member of the twelve-thousand-man association, almost all from the enlisted ranks, paid small dues. Members hosted reunions at the battlefield and encouraged battle survivors to write their senators and representatives to support the bill in Congress. In the spring of 1895, the group took concrete action by purchasing options on thirty-four plots of land at Shiloh—some twenty-six hundred acres—for a dollar a plot, intending, of course, to hand over the options to the government once Congress made the appropriation. Secretary E. T. Lee filed the options in the Hardin County Courthouse on March 26, 1895. In all, the land would cost $32,830.50. The veterans hoped this move would force the hand of Congress, for the options ran out in one year, on March 4, 1896.[15]

Through its efforts, the Shiloh Battlefield Association had called attention to the need for a national military park at Pittsburg Landing. The association, however, could only do so much. Their main goal remained the task of persuading Congress to fund the venture. Control of the process of establishing a park thus shifted to a more powerful group representing America as a whole—the United States Congress. With power to fund such an operation and authority to take land needed for a park, the federal government was the body that had to act to preserve the Shiloh battlefield. In an era when Congress was the dominant branch, the president would follow Congress's lead.

Some congressional ties with the Shiloh Battlefield Association did exist. As mentioned earlier, the association, at its 1893 organizational meeting held in Indianapolis, Indiana, had appointed a committee of congressmen known to favor the idea of a park. These congressmen met in early 1894 and gave David B. Henderson the job of actually writing a bill to establish the park.[16]

Representative Henderson, an Iowa Republican, seemed to be a good choice to write the bill. Born in Scotland in 1840, he had immigrated to the United States in 1846. After initially settling in Illinois, he moved to Iowa in 1849, where he received an education. Like many other young men, Henderson was swept into the Civil War. He joined Company C, 12th Iowa Infantry, which fought at Shiloh. Henderson had suffered a flesh wound in the neck at Fort Donelson in February 1862 and had only returned to the army on April 6, the first day of the battle. By the time he arrived on the field, he could not locate his unit and thus was spared capture in the Hornet's Nest. As the senior officer (first lieutenant) remaining in the regiment, he took command of remnants of the unit the next day and fought in the second day's battle. Later that year, he was hit in the leg at Corinth, necessitating amputation and discharge from the service. After recovering from the wound, Henderson reenlisted in the army and became colonel of the 46th Iowa. After the war, he worked as a lawyer and entered Congress in 1883. By the 1890s,

Henderson had become a powerful member of the House, serving as Judiciary Committee chairman and later as Speaker of the House. Both Henderson's service in the war and his ranking authority in Congress made him an obvious choice to advance the idea of a park at Shiloh. Personal interests also played a role: Henderson's brother Thomas, killed at Shiloh, lay buried in the National Cemetery at Pittsburg Landing.[17]

Even the prominent Henderson would need help, however. Although several battlefields had been preserved, no formalized process was in place within the government to oversee them. As a result, the different battlefields had their own sponsors, producing a disjointed but semi-coherent effort that would eventually serve as the forefather of a national park system. Despite his status in Congress, Henderson openly asked for assistance from those who understood more about the subject of legislation for national military parks than he did. Particularly, Henderson called on General Henry Boynton, an author and journalist who had been instrumental in establishing the park at Chickamauga.[18]

Fig. 4. Wounded at Fort Donelson, Lieutenant David B. Henderson missed the first day of Shiloh but arrived in time to lead the remnant of the 12th Iowa on the second day. After the war, Henderson became a powerful member of Congress, ultimately serving as Speaker of the House. He drafted the bill to establish Shiloh National Military Park. Courtesy of Shiloh National Military Park.

Henderson and Boynton, and doubtlessly others, soon produced a bill to establish a Shiloh National Military Park. A relatively short bill containing only eight sections, the legislation proposed a military park along the same lines as other such sites.[19]

Section 1 listed reasons for the action, namely preservation of the battle site in order to honor "the armies of the Southwest," which had no parks of their own. The section also explained the legal process of acquiring land: the government would buy the tracts in private ownership and the State of Tennessee would cede title to roads and public lands. The first section included a specific geographical boundary for the park, comprising some three thousand acres.[20]

Section 2 placed jurisdiction over the park within the executive branch, specifically under the War Department. The secretary of war was to maintain final authority over the park, and that authority included the right to acquire land by condemnation if necessary. The bill cited two laws giving the secretary of war the necessary authority, including the act of August 1, 1888, authorizing condemnation and the February 27, 1867, act protecting and establishing national cemeteries. The legislation left to the secretary of war's discretion which legal authority to use.[21]

The third section of the proposed legislation bypassed a potential problem with property owners at Shiloh. Several dozen families lived within the boundaries established in Section 1. Although the bill authorized condemnation procedures, Henderson saw no need to uproot the families and thus allowed for tenancy on the field. This section allowed the secretary of war to enter into agreements with locals to remain in their dwellings and to work their fields for subsistence and livelihood. Administrative authority over the tenants remained firmly in the government's hands, however; the legislation contained such clauses as "upon such terms as he [secretary of war] may prescribe" and "under such regulations as the Secretary may prescribe." The tenants were further required to preserve the historical features of the park, including maintaining wood and field lines and caring for the various monuments and markers that would eventually cover the battlefield.[22]

Section 4 of the Shiloh bill contained specific provisions regarding the actual establishment and governance of the park. While the secretary of war would retain ultimate authority, a three-man commission would carry on the actual day-to-day governmental affairs at Shiloh. The bill stipulated that each commissioner should be a veteran of the Civil War and a veteran of the armies that fought at Shiloh. To give equal representation to the three armies, one commissioner would be named from each army. Thus, the secretary of war was to appoint one veteran of the Union Army of the Tennessee, one of the Union Army of the Ohio, and one of the Confederate Army of the Mississippi. Such an arrangement would maintain the ratio of two Union commissioners and one Confederate, as established at Chickamauga. The section further stipulated that the commission would maintain an office in the War Department and that the commissioners would be paid for their work. Finally, the section authorized the secretary of war to employ "some person recognized as well informed concerning the history of the several armies engaged at Shiloh" to act as historian and secretary.[23]

The fifth section of the act to establish a park at Shiloh allowed for the transformation of a rural, isolated section of land into a national park. The bill authorized the commission to utilize existing roads and, if necessary, to even create new thoroughfares to allow access to the site. Further, the section stipulated that lines of battle be determined and marked with tablets or other monuments. This section also granted authority to the secretary of war to employ laborers and to gather supplies that might be needed. Finally, the act gave the secretary of war authority to make and enforce further rules governing the park.[24]

Section 6 authorized each state that had sent troops to the field of Shiloh to locate and mark with monuments the positions of their volunteer units on the field. The bill provided more authority for the secretary of war, requiring him to approve each monument or marker design and all inscriptions in collaboration with the park commission, which would provide written reports of the proposed action.[25]

The seventh section provided for protection of park resources. Crimes such as tampering with monuments or markers, destroying fences or buildings, cutting or damaging trees, removing battle relics, hunting within the park boundaries, or destroying earthworks brought fines of between five and fifty dollars, half of which would go to the park and half to the informer.[26]

The final part, Section 8, provided an appropriation of $150,000 "to begin to carry out the purpose of this act." Disbursements, of course, fell to the discretion of the secretary of war, who was required to report the status of the park to Congress each year.[27]

While the bill's authors seriously considered the legislation, it was nevertheless hurriedly contrived, disjointed, and poorly organized. Authorization for workers in the park appeared throughout the eight sections, as did a variety of regulations. Logically, these provisions should have been organized under one section. Second, the bill failed to place the reasoning for the battlefield park in its historical context. The sole reason mentioned in the bill was to establish a park to honor the armies of the "Southwest." Many of the factors established by the Shiloh Battlefield Association, such as preservation of graves, were overlooked. Third, several contradictions appeared in the bill. Although the secretary of war was authorized to set regulations, the bill mandated its own set of rules, which were by no means complete. The bill also seemed to work at cross purposes regarding preservation of the field. Several clauses spoke of maintaining historical accuracy, while other portions allowed for alterations of the field, most notably the opening of new roads. Fourth, Henderson seemed more interested in maintaining the authority of the secretary of war and the War Department than in allowing the commissioners on the field to make informed decisions.

Because the authors of the bill apparently wanted to centralize power in Washington, D.C., the bill stipulated that the commission would keep an office in "the War Department building." Fifth, the bill also contained many small grammatical and historical errors, most notably misspellings of names, such as "D. C. Buell" as "D. G. Buel," which even a casual familiarity with Civil War history would have eliminated. Finally, the amount of land in the area outlined by the bill was much greater than the stated three thousand acres; the total land within the prescribed boundary included nearly six thousand acres. This error either demonstrated a cursory knowledge of the field and limited background work or a possible effort to mislead congressmen into thinking less money would be needed. Still, the bill suited the purposes of establishing the park. On March 30, 1894, Henderson introduced the bill in the House of Representatives during the second session of the Fifty-third Congress. The bill was assigned a number, H.R. 6499, placed on the calendar, and referred to the Committee on Military Affairs.[28]

The committee took up the bill in June and ultimately returned unanimous approval. On June 22, 1894, Representative Joseph H. Outhwaite (Democrat) of Ohio, chairman of the Committee on Military Affairs, submitted his report to the entire House. The committee recommended that the "unsightly tract of land" be made a national military park along the lines of Chickamauga, Antietam, and Gettysburg. The committee also added its own historical interpretation. It demanded that the field be preserved for the reasons stated in the bill, as well as other factors, including the desire to mark the field before the veterans passed from the scene: it would be a "monument to them" before they "left this world." The committee also called on Congress to establish other national military parks on other prominent fields.[29]

Perhaps thinking the bill would face opposition because of the differences concerning battlefield preservation and its costs, Outhwaite placed the legislation in its most favorable light, a typical action by someone pushing a pet project. He talked about the roads leading to the field, making it "easily accessible." He continued that the only work required to preserve the field in battle condition was to remove underbrush and timber. Concerning costs, the chairman argued that the price tag would be very little once the initial appropriation set up the park. He also added that the land could be purchased for twelve dollars an acre, which was a small amount. Finally, Outhwaite argued that the historical knowledge gained from establishment of the park would "put at rest once and for all time to come the uncertainties and misrepresentations surrounding the battle."[30]

While trying to place the bill in its most acceptable form, Outhwaite no doubt let reality slip from his grasp. His arguments were inaccurate about the cost, amount of work needed, accessibility, and historical advantage to be gained. Nevertheless, the committee unanimously passed the bill with little change. Only seven minor amendments were made, mostly to correct spelling or grammatical errors.[31]

Once the bill was reported out of committee, Henderson advanced the legislation through the House. In doing so, he showed more ability as a politician than he had shown as author of the bill. He anticipated trouble ahead in the second session of the Fifty-third Congress because 1894 was an election year. Because the bill had come out of committee in June 1894, Henderson had only two or three months to get it passed before Congress adjourned. "Appropriations are unpopular before Congressional elections," Henderson admitted. He championed the bill as best he could in late summer, yet remained cautious because of Congress's desire to cut spending. Finally, Henderson worked out a deal by which he would delay the bill until the third session of the Fifty-third Congress, which began after the elections, when it would be passed. He made this deal by securing the verbal support of several key congressmen, including the Appropriations Committee chairman, Joseph D. Sayers (Democrat) of Texas, who promised he would give "generous cooperation" to H.R. 6499 in the coming session. Henderson, confident of victory, delayed his bill for several months but continued to call on citizens to encourage their congressmen to support the legislation.[32]

Fortunately for the Shiloh bill, Henderson was reelected. He arrived in Washington and immediately began preparations to get H.R. 6499 to the floor. He brought the legislation forward on December 4, 1894, the day after Congress assembled. The House resolved itself into the Committee of the Whole and set a limit of one hour for debate. Although not a veteran, Outhwaite acted as floor manager of the bill and, after calling the legislation to the House's attention, yielded to Henderson.[33]

The Iowa representative spoke briefly on "this great battlefield of Shiloh," basically reminding his colleagues of several points. He first stated that both the powerful Grand Army of the Republic and the Society of the Army of the Tennessee supported the bill. He then reminded the House that options were already being taken for tracts of land at Shiloh and that time limitations made quick passage of the bill a necessity. (Henderson took credit for these purchase options, never mentioning the Shiloh Battlefield Association.) Finally, Henderson promised that the land could be attained for approximately ten dollars an acre, a figure that Charles Grosvenor (Republican) of Ohio, author of the earlier legislation establishing Chickamauga and Chattanooga National Military Park, agreed was "a wonderfully low one." Grosvenor reminded the House that the government had paid twenty-eight dollars an acre for land at Chickamauga. Soon afterwards, because of the one-hour limit on debate, Henderson ended his speech and allowed questioning on the bill.[34]

Representative Alexander M. Dockery (Democrat) of Missouri took the floor and asked if Henderson would be content with half the requested appropriation—seventy-five thousand dollars. Henderson responded that he would, of course, like to have the full amount but that he would consent to a lower appropriation.

Grosvenor once again spoke up, stating that experience taught him that the park would not need so much money at the beginning, because of "controversies about titles and matters of that sort" that would delay the work. After conversing quickly with Outhwaite, the Military Affairs chairman, Henderson agreed to a lower appropriation.[35]

Following this exchange, the House began questioning the background investigation work done on the matter, and Henderson seemed unable to provide good answers. Nicholas Cox (Democrat) of Tennessee asked if the government had made an examination of the land and its price, and Henderson had to admit it had not. Nelson Dingley (Republican) of Maine inquired about an estimated figure of total appropriations, which Henderson could not give. When Dingley pressed for figures on costs of land improvements, monuments, and tablets, Henderson had to admit ignorance. He could only respond that "there will be the usual monuments and other things of the kind that these battlefield parks usually contain."[36]

Henderson's response opened the way for Dingley to press the matter concerning all military parks. Speaking of Gettysburg, Chickamauga, Antietam, and now Shiloh, he asked if the Committee on Military Affairs had "formulated any plan with reference to them." Henderson again had to admit that there was no formal plan but added somewhat foolishly that he was "meet[ing] the wishes of the Western armies." Such a statement only highlighted the lack of coordination, but Henderson knew that the veterans' desires and support were his strongest ally.[37]

Others chimed in with questions Henderson could not answer. Grosvenor asked about the language requiring commissioners to be members of the armies but not requiring that they had actually fought at Shiloh. Henderson responded that there would be no trouble finding veterans of the battle to serve as commissioners. Thomas R. Stockdale (Democrat) of Mississippi offered a successful amendment that "no discrimination shall be made against any State." Finally, Outhwaite took over, trying unsuccessfully on several occasions to cut off debate to save his rattled colleague, Henderson. Outhwaite moved that the appropriation be cut to seventy-five thousand dollars, which the House accepted. The Committee of the Whole also agreed to the Military Affairs Committee amendments and passed the bill. The chairman asked that the Committee of the Whole report favorably to the House. The entire House agreed to the amendments and bill, and Outhwaite asked that a motion to reconsider be laid on the table. With that action, the House passed the bill.[38]

The bill then moved to the Senate on December 6. That body placed it on its calendar and referred it to the Committee on Military Affairs. Chairman William Bate (Democrat) of Tennessee, a Shiloh veteran himself, held a hearing and reported the bill, without amendment, out of committee on December 13. Very little debate occurred in committee, although some opposition emerged regarding concerns about the need to create additional military parks.[39]

Senate debate came shortly thereafter. On December 18, Isham G. Harris (Democrat) of Tennessee, yet another Shiloh veteran, took the floor and gave notice that he or Senator Bate would call up H.R. 6499 the next morning, having been unable to do so that day during the morning hour. He ended with a plea that "I hope to get the consent of the Senate to pass it."[40]

The next morning, December 19, Bate called the bill to the floor. He asked for unanimous consent that the legislation be considered, but former lawyer and Indian fighter Joseph N. Dolph (Republican) of Oregon immediately objected, presumably over the same issue of creating too many military parks. A surprised Bate asked that the bill, because of its importance, be acted on at once. He also added that the House members had acted on it and "are very anxious that it should be passed at an early date." Dolph yielded "out of personal regard for the Senator from Tennessee," and consideration continued. The Senate resolved itself into the Committee of the Whole, and Bate presented the bill without amendment, asked for the final reading, and secured the body's approval. Soon thereafter, Confederate veteran Francis M. Cockrell (Democrat) of Missouri gained the floor and curiously offered his opposition to the idea of establishing any military parks. He did not want to register opposition to the Shiloh bill but informed the Senate that he had not supported the act in committee. "I think it is an entering wedge to an immense mass of business which will entail upon the country an annual expenditure of thousands and hundreds of thousands of dollars. This is only the entering wedge for making every battlefield a national park."[41]

Despite such minor opposition, the bill passed both houses of Congress and needed only the signature of the chief executive. Without comment, President Grover Cleveland signed the bill into law on December 27, 1894, and notified Congress of the action on January 4, 1895. Shiloh National Military Park was a reality.[42]

Other legislative actions affected Shiloh National Military Park in the years following its establishment. In accordance with the enabling bill, the Tennessee State Legislature ceded rights to the property on April 29, 1895. Congress acted again in 1896 with a bill that promoted use of the military parks for training and study by the United States Army and state National Guard units.[43]

The original bill, as well as the legislation that followed, always met minor opposition, such as the restrained hostility of Congressman Dingley over a formal policy toward military parks and of Senator Cockrell over the need for additional parks costing the government thousands of dollars a year. More vocal opposition came from eastern newspapers, which argued that too many parks would diminish the importance of the big eastern fields of Gettysburg and Antietam. Supporters of the Shiloh bill responded, however, and Henderson wrote that the assailants quickly "hauled down their battle flag."[44]

The most significant opposition, ironically, came from within the War Department itself. Some opponents there argued that too many large military parks would only bury the department in paperwork and drain valuable funds. The leader of this group was Major George B. Davis, chairman of the commission publishing the 128-volume *Official Records*, a compilation of after-action reports and correspondence from the Civil War. Davis argued, even for several years after Shiloh's establishment, that the park did not need the entire three thousand acres, that such a park would drain money from the government, that this bill would lead to other unnecessary parks, and that Shiloh was inaccessible to visitors anyway. In place of a full-sized park, Davis promoted the idea of a twenty-five-acre memorial near Pittsburg Landing. Realizing this argument was going nowhere, he argued for a two-hundred-acre fenced memorial and strips of land on the battlefield. This process, buying only roadways and lines of battle, would later gain support and become known as the "Antietam Plan," named for the park-building process on that battlefield. Ultimately, Davis did not persuade Congress to oppose the establishment of military parks and, to his credit, worked hard to implement Congress's order to build the park at Shiloh.[45]

Soon, however, control of Shiloh National Military Park passed from Congress to another group of men—the authorized park commission. Secretary of War Daniel S. Lamont exercised his authority to appoint the commission of veterans. In the hands of these veterans who had actually fought at Shiloh, the developing park would for many years be protected from outside opposition and from younger generations who did not always see the importance of preserving fields of battle such as Shiloh.

Although operational control passed to the commission, Washington still possessed ultimate authority over the future of Shiloh. In fact, the enabling legislation fractured control over the park, with much of the power remaining in Washington. While the commission carried on the day-to-day work, the secretary of war retained authority over the commission and approved all monuments, inscriptions, locations of tablets, and disbursements. Most importantly, Congress retained budgetary control over park finances; Shiloh National Military Park depended on an annual appropriation to exist.

Thus, the enabling legislation set the future course of Shiloh National Military Park. Not only did the legislation establish the preserve, but it also set rules and regulations concerning how the park would operate for decades to come. Unfortunately, some errors and miscalculations within the bill created future problems for the park. Perhaps most importantly, congressional debate on the bill had introduced another major theme, typical of United States government activities, that would continue to affect the history of the park—a lack of adequate funding to operate the federal facility. The House cut the original appropriation in half, and the park commissioners and superintendents were forced into a continual fight for additional appropriations. In the ensuing years, Shiloh often faced financial shortfalls.

By 1895, however, Congress had established the park, and the War Department was carefully completing the task of organizing a commission to build and operate it. Decisions about personnel that were made early in 1895 would affect the park for all time, and Secretary Lamont, very much in favor of the military parks, realized the importance of able appointees. He thought long and hard about whom to include on the Shiloh Battlefield Commission. The commissioners Lamont appointed would have to overcome the developing problems of minimal appropriations and geographical isolation. They would also have to deal with yet another, more vexing problem they actually helped to create—the display of massive egos and pride.[46]

The enabling legislation establishing Shiloh National Military Park not only provided the essential basis to preserve the battlefield, but it also marked a larger phenomenon taking place on a nationwide level. By the 1890s, the United States had entered a period of nationalism, patriotism, and sectional healing, all of which manifested themselves in a country-wide memorialization of the honor and heroism of Civil War soldiers. Few still argued about the morality of slavery or about racial issues; instead, most focused on the bravery of the soldiers themselves, an angle of remembrance on which both sides could agree. Thus, the isolated tract in rural west Tennessee became a national treasure, with veterans from all over the nation talking about Shiloh, even in the very halls of Congress itself.

CHAPTER 3

The Shiloh Commission

Secretary of War Daniel S. Lamont not only directed an international power's growing military forces, but he also made decisions concerning the nation's remembrance of past military actions. Enabling legislation called for Secretary Lamont to appoint commissioners for Shiloh National Military Park, and whether he realized it or not, Lamont's choices would forever affect the park and also, perhaps, help decide the national memory of the Civil War. An avid supporter of the military park idea, Lamont considered his choices carefully, and they generally proved to be sound.[1]

Congress had called for the appointment of veterans of the battle of Shiloh to hold the important positions of commissioners and historian-secretary. Lamont also had other mandates to meet, such as appointing a commissioner from each of the three armies that had fought at Shiloh. Of course, Lamont also wanted competent commissioners who could accomplish the work in an efficient and cost-effective manner. As it turned out, he had little trouble finding such men. As soon as word was released about the establishment of the park, office seekers began to send him their résumés. For example, A. W. Wills, builder of the national cemetery at Pittsburg Landing, inquired about a position. He reminded the War Department of his former service and touted his familiarity with the area. Then, there were those who had the powerful backing of congressmen or bureaucrats. They received special consideration. Fortunately, individual work experience also played a major role in consideration for inclusion in the developing workforce at Shiloh.[2]

Several prominent figures quickly came to the forefront. The elderly John A. McClernand was already involved with the Shiloh Battlefield Association and was one option, as was E. T. Lee, who actually expected an appointment because of all his land-purchasing activity at the battlefield. Don Carlos Buell, retired general and former commander of the Army of the Ohio, was also available. For the Confederate army representative, any number of distinguished former officers seemed appropriate, including Colonels Robert F. Looney and William Preston Johnston and Generals Alexander P. Stewart, Basil W. Duke, and Joseph Wheeler. In the end, Lamont named Colonel Cornelius Cadle to head the commission, assigning the other commissioner positions to Buell and Looney.[3]

Born on May 22, 1836, in New York, Cadle had moved with his parents to Muscatine, Iowa, in 1843. There, he attained a limited education and entered the workforce as a bank cashier. When the war broke out, he enlisted and served in Company H, 11th Iowa Infantry. The twenty-four-year-old clerk, carrying the straps of a first lieutenant, did not serve with his company in the ranks at Shiloh but was on detached duty at brigade headquarters. There he served as adjutant on the staff of Colonel Abraham M. Hare of the 11th Iowa, who briefly commanded the brigade at Shiloh in the absence of the original brigade commander, Brigadier General Richard J. Oglesby. Cadle accompanied Hare throughout the battle and earned his colonel's praise. Hare reported that Cadle "rendered me efficient service, and during the whole action, by his promptness, energy, and activity, exhibited all the best qualities of a soldier." Cadle even won the commendation of his division commander, Major General John A. McClernand.[4]

Promoted to captain and assistant adjutant general on May 1, 1863, Cadle remained with the 11th Iowa through the Vicksburg Campaign, where he gained some notoriety by raising the United States flag over the Mississippi capitol building. Later in the campaign, however, he received a flesh wound in the cheek and ear. In July 1863, he mustered out of the 11th Iowa, only to accept an appointment as captain and assistant adjutant general on the staff of Brigadier General Marcellus M. Crocker of the Army of the Tennessee. After attaining the rank of major later in the war, he received a brevet promotion to colonel on March 13, 1865.[5]

Cadle remained in the army until September 1866, serving in the Freedmen's Bureau in Alabama. He remained in that state after his discharge, accepting an appointment from the secretary of the treasury as receiver of the First National Bank of Selma. He then became interested in mining operations and soon became general manager of a large coal mine in Blockton. Later in his mining career, he moved to Birmingham. After decades in the mining business, Cadle moved to Cincinnati, Ohio, around 1893.[6]

When Lamont began organizing the Shiloh Battlefield Commission, Cadle received support for commissioner from several important people, one of whom was D. B. Henderson. E. C. Dawes, a Shiloh veteran who was very influential in postwar veterans' activities, also recommended Cadle for the commission. Dawes assisted in the publication of the *Official Records* and served as commander of the Ohio Commandery of the Military Order of the Loyal Legion of the United States, which placed him in the company of such luminaries as William T. Sherman, Jacob Cox, Rutherford B. Hayes, and Benjamin Harrison. Considering all the glowing recommendations he received about Cadle, the secretary of war made his appointment official on March 12, 1895. Cadle readily accepted the position of commissioner as representative of the Army of the Tennessee with a salary of $250 a month, a substantial sum for those days.[7]

Fig. 5. An elderly Cornelius Cadle, first chairman of the Shiloh National Military Park Commission. Attaining the rank of brevet colonel during the war, Cadle later entered the mining business before being appointed to the commission in 1895. Cadle would direct the work of building the park from his headquarters in Cincinnati. Courtesy of Shiloh National Military Park.

While Cadle had been a minor officer at Shiloh, the secretary of war's second appointment to the commission was a well-known leader, Don Carlos Buell, the commander of the Army of the Ohio. His appointment was dated the same day as Cadle's, March 12, 1895.[8]

Born on March 23, 1818, Buell had graduated from West Point in 1837 and served in the Mexican War. Early in the Civil War, he gained command of the Army of the Ohio, which captured Nashville and reinforced Grant at a critical moment at Pittsburg Landing. Later, Buell took part in the spring 1862 operations against Corinth, but his army soon marched eastward to threaten Chattanooga. At the October 1862 battle at Perryville, Kentucky, Buell proved lethargic, and this slowness cost him his command. Although he survived a military investigation, he never received another command, and he resigned from the army in 1864. After the war, he was involved in mining operations and then became a United States pension agent.[9]

To round out the three-man commission, Lamont chose a well-known Confederate veteran of Shiloh, Colonel Robert F. Looney, commander of the 38th Tennessee Infantry. Born on August 5, 1824, Looney was a lawyer by profession before the Civil War. When he entered Confederate service, the men of the 38th Tennessee elected him colonel. After he gave excellent service at Shiloh, several of his men recommended him for promotion to the rank of brigadier general, but the appointment never came. Looney remained a colonel for the duration of the conflict and spent some time as a prisoner, having been captured while recruiting near Collierville, Tennessee. After the war, he became involved in Tennessee politics and was a delegate to the 1884 Democratic National Convention.[10]

Lamont realized that this three-man commission could not by itself perform all the necessary jobs required to build a park. The original enabling legislation, in fact, provided for additional workers including a historian, engineer, clerk, and laborers. Consequently, Lamont had further appointments to make.

The secretary of war made the first of these second-tier appointments even before the commission took final shape. To locate deeds and acquire land legally and easily, Lamont appointed Captain James W. Irwin, a local lawyer from nearby Savannah, to be land agent. Irwin was born in Savannah on April 13, 1835. He had served as a second lieutenant in the 1st Confederate Cavalry in April 1862 and had acted as commander of a special group of escorts and guides for General P. G. T. Beauregard during the battle. Later he attained the rank of captain. After the war, Irwin returned to Savannah and operated the family store. While engaged in merchandising, he read law and was admitted to the bar. He later practiced law in Savannah as well as Sparta, Tennessee, before becoming a deputy United States revenue collector in McMinnville, Tennessee.[11]

When news of the creation of Shiloh National Military Park spread, Irwin sought an appointment. He contacted Senator William B. Bate of Tennessee for help in securing a position. Bate obviously came through, for Lamont appointed Irwin as land purchasing agent on February 11, 1895, even before the commission was named. Irwin subsequently moved home to Savannah and began his work of tracking down the owners and titles to the land.[12]

To process speedily the vast amount of correspondence that was sure to follow, the War Department hired J. M. Riddell to serve as commission secretary. Riddell was a young, energetic man from Cincinnati who studied law and passed his bar exam in 1899. He also served as a sergeant in the Ohio National Guard. In addition to Riddell, a park policeman called a "Range Rider," F. A. Large, maintained law and order within the federal reservation. Large was a veteran of the 12th Iowa Infantry and had been captured at Shiloh. After parole and exchange, he had been discharged for disability, the result of shooting himself in the hand on a hunting trip. He later reenlisted as a veteran volunteer, however.[13]

Lamont made two other appointments that would have an extremely important effect on the formulation of Shiloh National Military Park policy and procedure, indeed even more important than the appointment of Cadle's two fellow commissioners. In order to survey and map the field correctly, the War Department transferred an engineer from the Chickamauga and Chattanooga National Military Park to Shiloh.[14]

Fig. 6. A member of the 12th Iowa who surrendered after defending the Hornet's Nest, F. A. Large would return to Shiloh as "Range Rider" and would later serve as assistant superintendent. Large poses here at the place where he was captured on April 6, 1862. Courtesy of Shiloh National Military Park.

Atwell Thompson was a lively man. Born in Ireland, he received an education in engineering at Oxford University in England (with the highest honors, as he was fond of reminding people) and worked in various jobs in that field, including railroad construction and maintenance, city engineering, and topography. In 1892, he migrated to the United States "with a recommendation from the English Crown." Just after arriving in America, he joined the staff of Chickamauga and Chattanooga National Military Park as road engineer. There he oversaw the building of more than forty miles of park roads. With that job almost completed by 1895, Thompson was looking for work elsewhere. When news reached him that a park was planned at Shiloh, Thompson applied for the engineer-in-chief's position.[15]

Thompson asked for recommendations from his employers, the park commissioners at Chickamauga. All gave him glowing reviews despite his fiery and combative personality. Resident Commissioner Alexander P. Stewart wrote to Chairman Cadle that Thompson was a "high toned, honorable gentleman, capable and educated, and a very competent engineer." The other members of the commission agreed with Stewart's recommendation. Cadle received these endorsements along with Thompson's own application, in which he deemed himself "as well equipped as almost any other man in my profession." As a result, Thompson received the position, with his appointment dated May 1, 1895.[16]

Thompson's appointment was not without conflict, however. The Grand Army of the Republic complained that both the Chickamauga and the Shiloh battlefield commissions hired Thompson—not even an American citizen, much less a veteran of the Civil War—when they should have hired veterans who had become engineers. Because of the Panic of 1893, the Grand Army of the Republic argued that many such veterans needed work. Cadle responded that Thompson was very good at his job and that he had sworn his intention of becoming a naturalized citizen very shortly after reaching the country in June 1892. He also pointed out that the majority of the workers were indeed veterans or sons of veterans.[17]

For the position of historian and secretary, the one who would have to wade through the massive piles of historical documentation on Shiloh, Lamont appointed David W. Reed. A veteran of Shiloh and historian of the famed "Hornet's Nest Brigade," a veterans' organization of the regiments that had defended that position, Reed would spend the rest of his life working for the park. Indeed, Reed laid out the troop positions and much of the interpretation seen today at Shiloh National Military Park.[18]

D. W. Reed was born in Cortland, New York, on April 2, 1841, but moved to Iowa before the Civil War. When the conflict broke out, he was a student at Upper Iowa University in Fayette. He and his colleagues formed a company, which later became Company C, 12th Iowa Infantry. In this unit, Reed began his association with D. B. Henderson, who after the war became an influential Iowa politician.

Henderson took a deep interest in his friend and monitored Reed's welfare for the remainder of his life.[19]

Like Henderson, Reed first saw combat at Forts Henry and Donelson in February 1862, but it was his participation in the battle of Shiloh as a member of Colonel James M. Tuttle's brigade, which defended the position later known as the Sunken Road and Hornet's Nest, that would forever change his life. In the action of April 6, a fragment of an artillery shell hit Reed in the right knee, and a bullet struck him in the right thigh. The Confederates captured the wounded Reed but abandoned him on the field the next day.[20]

Reed recovered and remained in service throughout the Vicksburg Campaign. In December 1863, his company elected him second lieutenant, and in January 1865, he became captain. He served on various staff assignments and gained a brevet major's commission for heroism at Spanish Fort near Mobile in April 1865.[21]

Fig. 7. David W. Reed, the Shiloh National Military Park's first secretary and historian. After Civil War service in the 12th Iowa, in which he attained the rank of brevet major, Reed returned to Shiloh and became the driving force behind the park's historical interpretation. After Cadle's resignation, Reed became chairman of the commission. Reed's work at Shiloh earned him the title "Father of Shiloh National Military Park." Courtesy of Shiloh National Military Park.

Reed joined the Iowa bar in 1868. Through the years, he held numerous government posts, including commissions in 1867 as a notary public and as a deputy collector of the Internal Revenue Service for the Third District of Iowa. He acquired the latter position with the help of his friend D. B. Henderson. Reed's fellow citizens elected him county recorder in 1868. In 1878, Reed became captain of Company E, 9th Iowa National Guard Regiment, and in 1880, President Rutherford B. Hayes appointed him postmaster of Waukon, Iowa. He later held other notable positions. In 1888, he became the Department of Iowa assistant inspector for the Grand Army of the Republic, while in 1890, he was named national aide-de-camp for the Grand Army of the Republic, as well as supervisor of the census for the Second District of Iowa.[22]

In 1891, Reed moved to Chicago, Illinois, but maintained his contacts with prominent Iowa friends. One of the most important was D. B. Henderson, then in Congress and soon to be Speaker of the House. Henderson, the man who pushed through the bill establishing Shiloh National Military Park, could very well have had Reed in mind when he wrote a provision in the bill calling for "some person recognized as well informed concerning the history of the several armies engaged at Shiloh." Reed had spoken extensively about the battle and was well known as the historian of the "Hornet's Nest Brigade." Henderson worked to get Reed the historian position, calling for documentation of Reed's record to aid "in making the fight for the Secretaryship of the Shiloh Commission." Reed received the position and was appointed on March 26, 1895.[23]

Any analysis of Lamont's choices leads to the conclusion that he made his appointments carefully and with a purpose. None of the original members of the Shiloh Battlefield Association, for example, became members of the new commission, not even E. T. Lee, who had put so much effort into the venture. Lee's defiant ways and controlling personality no doubt turned Lamont away from him.

Just as Lamont passed over Lee, who might have made trouble for him, the secretary likewise did not seem to want any opposition to his control from the commission members. As a result, the commission consisted of an aged Buell, who held definite ideas but had little political clout, and Looney, whose appointment ultimately mattered little, perhaps because of his Confederate ties. Buell's war record was not that of a hero such as Grant or Sherman, and his power base within the government, particularly in Congress, was not great. Looney also had little influence, and Lamont may well have appointed him simply to meet the law's requirements. Indeed, it appears from a study of available correspondence that Looney never played a significant role in any of the decisions concerning the park. His primary assignment, it appears, was as liaison with the State of Tennessee, his home state. He only appears in any important capacity when the state ceded title of the battlefield to the War Department in 1895.

Fig. 8. The park commission and laborers gathered for this photograph in front of the commission's tents, situated in the cemetery near Pittsburg Landing. This photo was taken between 1895 and 1899. From left to right are: Will Pride, laborer; F. A. Large, range rider; J. W. Irwin, land agent; Cornelius Cadle, chairman; D. W. Reed, secretary and historian; J. R. Duncan, laborer; Robert F. Looney, commissioner; J. T. Curtis, laborer; Atwell Thompson, chief engineer; and M. A. Kirby, laborer. Note J. T. Curtis's peg leg. Courtesy of Shiloh National Military Park.

With no appointments of potential troublemakers and with the supporting roles filled by passive members such as the aged Buell, the real authority behind the Shiloh National Military Park became evident. Cornelius Cadle organized the work along the lines to which he and his trusted associates, Reed and Thompson, agreed. Second in authority was Reed, who dominated the historical work of the park under the steady but unobtrusive eye of Cadle. Last in influence was the engineer, Thompson, who actually ran the affairs of the park on a day-to-day basis.[24]

There was also a strong political force behind the commission. Congressman D. B. Henderson did not end his association with Shiloh once his bill passed Congress and the commission appointments were complete. He remained actively involved in all manner of park issues, including the appointments that took place and those that did not. Henderson was heavily involved in defeating E. T. Lee's attempt to become a member of the commission. Henderson also successfully petitioned Lamont for Cadle's and Reed's appointment, as he did for others such as Range Rider F. A. Large.[25]

Henderson and some members of the commission had obvious connections. The congressman was from Iowa and had fought at Shiloh in Company C, 12th

Iowa. Cadle, the commission chairman, had been a member of Company H, 11th Iowa. Reed had served as a member of Henderson's own company. F. A. Large, whom Henderson backed strongly, had been a member of Company E, 12th Iowa. T. J. Lewis, masonry foreman at the park, had fought with Company D, 12th Iowa. Even if there was no behind-the-scenes collaboration among these Iowa veterans, the appearance of packing the commission with Iowans did exist.[26]

With the appointments complete, Secretary of War Daniel Lamont ordered Cadle and his colleagues to assemble at Pittsburg Landing on April 2, 1895, to meet, to organize themselves, and to be on-site for the thirty-third anniversary of the battle. War Department officials had already inspected the area in March, when Major George B. Davis had toured the site in order to make recommendations to the commission. The arrival of the commissioners in April, however, marked the first official act of park development.[27]

Thus, some thirty-three years after the conflict had raged around Pittsburg Landing, the Shiloh National Military Park Commission met on that hallowed ground to transform the battlefield into a preserve of remembrance and honor for those who had fought there. As the commission began its work the next day, April 3, they inaugurated the long process of shaping the isolated battlefield into a gathering place for Civil War veterans and their families, their descendents, and other interested Americans. They also, perhaps unknowingly, contributed to producing a national memory of the Civil War.

Once at Pittsburg Landing, the commission found very little infrastructure to support its needs. Based on his recent visit to the site, Major George B. Davis had warned the commission that the "present outlook for offices and quarters at Pittsburg Landing is not promising." When Cadle and the other commissioners arrived, they found that he had been correct. A few structures stood at the landing itself, most importantly a group of buildings associated with the national cemetery. There they met Superintendent Clayton Hart and his staff, who cared for the facility. The commission also got a taste of why they were there: legions of visitors had traveled to the site of the battle, and their numbers had almost certainly increased because of the anniversary date. As they arrived on the battlefield, the commission no doubt relived many memories at such prominent points as Pittsburg Landing and Grant's headquarters tree.[28]

Just inland from the landing, Cadle met the first of a number of local inhabitants whom the commission would deal with for the next decade and a half. Sam Chambers owned a small tract of land atop the bluff. On that small parcel sat a house, a hotel, and a large store. Chambers, however, was actually the largest landowner in the area, possessing 543.42 acres in seven plots. Chambers owned much of the land where the battle had begun, including Fraley Field, where the first shots had been fired. Other landowners also possessed large tracts in the area. The Tilghman, Cantrell, and Fraley families

Fig. 9. David W. Reed (right) and Marcus J. Wright stand beside the "Grant tree" in Shiloh National Cemetery. General Ulysses S. Grant made his headquarters under this tree on the night of April 6, 1862. Unfortunately, the "cyclone" of October 14, 1909, destroyed the tree. Wright was a member of the War Department commission publishing the *Official Records*. Courtesy of Shiloh National Military Park.

owned multiple plots of hundreds of acres, each holding deeds to land the commission needed. As chairman, Cadle would need to make every effort to gain their support and friendship.[29]

Cadle realized that the commission would have the difficult task of building a park with only meager resources. What the commission first needed were offices, living spaces, furniture, and sundry smaller items that would help it operate effectively. One important aid was the War Department's successful request to the Post Office Department to increase mail service to Pittsburg Landing. Mail now arrived six days a week.[30]

War Department officials had also begun the flow of money to the commission. Cadle was thus immediately able to begin the paperwork for payrolls and to buy needed items. He bought stationery to carry on correspondence, furniture to facilitate the work, and horses to allow travel over the battlefield and to nearby localities. For correspondence, Cadle also bought a typewriter, a new technological device at the time and certainly an amazing machine in the isolation of Shiloh.[31]

Unfortunately, the commission did not have a place to house all these purchases. Finding a site for the commission headquarters became a major problem, because little space existed anywhere nearby. The second story of Chambers's store was vacant but inadequate. There was some talk of taking over Chambers's house, but this idea likewise never became a reality.[32]

Cadle decided to erect tents for housing but realized that the only government land in the area was the cemetery. The Quartermaster Department gave the necessary permission, and the commission erected its tents along the western edge of the burial ground. Eventually, Cadle had these tents equipped with wooden roofs and floors, making life more comfortable. Reed made his quarters seem more homey by nurturing a large rose bush that grew up the posts supporting his roof. The War Department, trying to make the dismal facilities more comfortable, provided wooden bins full of sawdust, in which ice was kept. Cadle also found temporary office space in the cemetery lodge. A more stable structure for the commission lay in the future, however, and War Department officials told Cadle to begin drawing up plans for the type of building the commission desired.[33]

The lack of adequate housing and workspace helped create an awkward system of administration, but it also fostered the growth of Cadle's, Reed's, and Thompson's authority. Unable and apparently unwilling to live permanently at Pittsburg Landing, Cadle established commission headquarters in his hometown of Cincinnati, Ohio, where he and clerk J. M. Riddell tended to the official business of the park. D. W. Reed maintained his home in Illinois and later Iowa, continually poring over the massive number of historical accounts of the battle. At Pittsburg Landing itself, Atwell Thompson controlled the everyday work of park building. Visits to the growing park by both Cadle and Reed were numerous, as were those by Buell and Looney for commission meetings. Correspondence was even more

Fig. 10. Looking northwest, a view of the hotel at Pittsburg Landing that was destroyed in the 1909 "cyclone." In the foreground are rows of cannon and shell used to mark the battlefield. Courtesy of Shiloh National Military Park.

Fig. 11. D. W. Reed (*left*) and Cornelius Cadle and their wives wait for river transportation to arrive and carry them to their homes in Illinois and Ohio. J. H. Ashcraft is in the rear at right. Plainly seen are the commission's tents. Reed planted and nurtured a rose bush in front of his tent. Courtesy of Shiloh National Military Park.

Fig. 12. A view of the north side of the Cemetery lodge. The building was so damaged in the October 1909 tornado that it had to be razed and replaced. Courtesy of Shiloh National Military Park.

frequent. There emerged a three-way communication between Cadle, Reed, and Thompson, each heading their own distinctive areas, with Cadle, of course, in contact with the War Department in Washington. Such unwieldy circumstances produced delays and problems in correspondence, but the lack of housing and facilities at Pittsburg Landing left the War Department no choice but to allow them.

Thus emerged early in the commission's history the dominant figures who led construction at the park. The disjointed administrative network proved to be the key to allowing Cadle and Reed, more so than even Thompson, to guide the building and marking of the battlefield. Even the War Department viewed Cadle and Reed as the major actors at Shiloh, sending only these two men on an information-gathering trip to Antietam and Gettysburg in 1895. Of course, Thompson was already quite familiar with park policies, having served as an engineer at Chickamauga. Cadle, Reed, and Thompson would soon be making minor decisions regarding their respective duties, apparently without consulting other members of the commission. Most importantly, this system of organization affected the interpretation of the battle, allowing Cadle and Reed to make their understanding of Shiloh's history the dominant interpretation. As a result, the original appointments and the decisions these men made, by choice as well as by necessity, loomed large in establishing the park that visitors now enjoy.[34]

CHAPTER **4**

"The Work of Converting Mere Land into a Park"

Once the Shiloh Battlefield Commission arrived at Pittsburg Landing, its members realized both the magnitude of their task and the paucity of their resources. Undaunted, they began the work of transforming an isolated locale into a national park. But they were also participating in a movement that was transforming a nation. Just as engineers surveyed the ground around Pittsburg Landing, so did America as a whole survey its past. White America was refining its national identity, and Shiloh National Military Park was a part of it. Yet, before the park could come to fruition and take its place in the growing national memory of the Civil War, the site had to be developed.

The first order of business was to purchase land, and many problems emerged. Cadle had no maps of the area showing land ownership or topography. Numerous landowners were unhappy about losing their property, some of which had been in their families for generations. Owners willing to sell sometimes asked exorbitant prices, which the congressional appropriation could not cover. Most disconcerting of all, E. T. Lee and the Shiloh Battlefield Association still had options on much of the land. Cadle realized that his task of acquiring land, much less that of locating troop positions and placing monuments, would be difficult indeed.

The Shiloh Battlefield Association initially proved to be the major obstacle. What had begun as a noble cause soon degenerated into petty bickering. E. T. Lee, secretary of the Shiloh Battlefield Association, a Shiloh veteran of Company I, 41st Illinois, and a postwar newspaper reporter and relic collector, began to create problems within the organization. These difficulties soon infected the association's relationships with other veterans' organizations and then caused major problems for the War Department commission. Seeing himself as originator of the idea of a park at Shiloh, Lee was angry that he had not received an appointment as a park commissioner. Displaying petty jealousy, Lee created problems over land ownership that severely hampered the commission and, ironically, delayed his original goal of establishing a park and memorializing those who had fought there.[1]

When dealing with veterans' organizations, for example, Lee assumed more responsibility than he actually had. The Society of the Army of the Tennessee organized a committee to aid the Shiloh Battlefield Association, and Lee told them bluntly that he was in charge. "Mr. Lee's reply . . . was, in effect, that his association did not need any aid of the kind I proposed, but that it was in great need of money," reported the society's committee chairman, who added that the "tone" of Lee's letters was condescending. Nevertheless, the Society of the Army of the Tennessee passed a resolution at its 1895 meeting stating that they "heartily favor[ed]" making Shiloh a park. Significantly, they made no statement supporting Lee's association.[2]

In the summer of 1895, President John A. McClernand called a meeting of the Shiloh Battlefield Association, which Lee and treasurer J. W. Coleman, also a veteran of the 41st Illinois from Lee's hometown of Monticello, Illinois, refused to attend. McClernand immediately contacted the two men and asked why they had shunned the meeting. He lectured them on the need to give the land options to the government by March 1896, or else speculators would invade and buy the land, thus causing the government to pay exorbitant prices. Lee and Coleman responded that they planned to hold on to the land options until they were treated with more respect. McClernand contacted commission chairman Cadle and apologetically informed him of the problem with Lee and Coleman. Indignant, the elderly McClernand even contemplated resigning his position.[3]

Cadle and the War Department Commission refused to bow to such pettiness. They examined various ways to circumvent the association's possession of the land options. They inquired about the association's status of incorporation and the legality of its options. Failing in that attempt, the commission appealed to Coleman's patriotism. If Coleman joined McClernand in agreeing to give the options, they could outvote Lee. Coleman almost gave in but ultimately sided with his hometown partner, Lee.[4]

The situation grew worse when, behind McClernand's back, Lee took his case to the public. He began to write letters to veterans on behalf of the association. He also began a war of words in the press, most notably in the *Cincinnati Commercial-Gazette*. His whining words brought sharp reaction from all around the nation. Some writers said that he was holding the land claims until the government reimbursed him for his personal expenses and that he was blackmailing the War Department for a position on the commission. Others said that Lee had not received permission from many of the association's "vice-presidents" to use their names and that he called himself a colonel when he had only reached the rank of corporal. He was accused of once stating that he hoped the government "will have to pay the people there [Shiloh] fifty dollars an acre for the land," an exorbitant amount in the 1890s. One particularly harsh critic, H. V. Boynton, a newsman known for creating controversy, said Lee was "ignorant, illiterate, and cannot write six lines of decent English." He wondered in amazement how Lee could even imagine being commission historian.[5]

Clearly, Lee had alienated everyone, including McClernand, the park commission, the War Department, and many others. McClernand wrote Cadle regarding Lee's "lack of manners, modesty, grammar and intelligence." In another letter, the general declared that "he deserves no quarter." D. W. Reed, commission historian, put it even more bluntly. He wrote that "one would think the fool would get enough [humiliation] and quit. . . . He will try to pose as a martyr." Even Lee's colleagues tired of him. The Shiloh Battlefield Association reacted swiftly when Lee went so far as to try to cancel the reunion at Shiloh on April 6 and 7, 1896. They voted Lee out of the organization. One observer gleefully reported to Chairman Cadle that the association had "disposed of" Lee. Perhaps most telling of all, the Grand Army of the Republic, the most powerful and respected of all veterans' organizations, expelled Lee from its membership.[6]

Despite the expulsions, Lee and Coleman still held options to the land. Major George B. Davis of the War Department wrote of Lee as "that blackmailing humbug . . . who should be disposed of in some way." Still, the War Department advised patience. Davis called the entire episode the "nearest nonsense" and encouraged the commission that all would turn out for the good because Lee would find it "difficult to compete with the government." The official War Department stance was to wait until Lee's land options ran out and then buy the land; until that occurred on March 4, 1896, the commission should concentrate on gathering the remainder of the land allowed in the establishment bill.[7]

In all fairness to Lee, he had worked tirelessly in the Shiloh effort, writing letters and whipping up veteran support. His fall came when his ambition caused the War Department to bypass him in its appointments and he lashed out in anger. By the time Lee passed from the scene, the effort to establish a park no longer needed his help. Congress had taken up the effort, and new leaders had emerged to drive it forward. But the entire episode demonstrated that even the desire to memorialize the dead and wounded at Shiloh was not immune from pettiness and ego.

With almost half the land designated in the enabling legislation under option until March 1896, land acquisition and the work of the commission went forward slowly. Since they could neither postpone building the park for a year nor force Lee to give up his options, Cadle and the commission decided to turn their attention to other matters. Cadle's workers drew maps, located battle lines, and purchased land not optioned to Lee. In this manner, the commission produced results even while a majority of the most important land tracts remained out of its possession for a year.[8]

Cadle especially needed an accurate map showing topography, boundaries, and landowner tracts. Only then could the commission begin "the work of converting mere land into a park." The secretary of war had given approval to employ the county surveyor for any needed work, but it soon became apparent that the magnitude of the task required a full-time engineering staff. After the commission met at Pittsburg Landing, Secretary of War Lamont authorized hiring an engineer, two transit men, a level man, four chain men, one level rodman, two back rodmen, and four axemen. Consequently, Cadle and the commission hired an experienced engineer and staff to oversee the work at Shiloh. Atwell Thompson entered the picture.[9]

As engineer in charge of the park, Thompson's duties included road building, monument placement, topographical work, and map making. To aid Thompson in his work, the War Department at first hired only three additional engineers: M. A. Kirby as a transit man, W. M. Pride as a rodman, and J. R. Duncan as an axeman. All three would become long-time fixtures at Shiloh National Military Park. Later, William S. Keller, a brother of Helen Keller, was hired as assistant engineer.[10]

On May 1, 1895, Thompson began work on the site by dividing his laborers into two separate transit teams. Each team began surveying the field, establishing east-west and north-south lines, which would provide an efficient grid system for marking the field. Thompson surveyed an east-west line at the extreme southern boundary of the park, as specified in the enabling legislation. He took extreme care in surveying this line, checking the distances and measurements "both by chain and transit." Every two hundred feet along this standard line, Thompson drove stakes into the ground. From this standard line, Thompson and his transit parties surveyed north-south lines. These lines lay two hundred feet apart, corresponding with the stakes set in the original line. The north-south lines were as long as three and one-half miles in length. Thompson also placed stakes every two hundred feet on these north-south lines, from which he then surveyed east-west lines. Thompson cleared sight paths along all these transit lines, so that each stake could be clearly seen from its neighbor.[11]

The local inhabitants quickly realized the magnitude of the work progressing at Shiloh. They watched as Thompson and his crews worked, some remarking on the accuracy required and the amount of work performed. Some, however, complained of trespassing on their property. S. M. Rogers, for example, protested that Thompson's men had devastated his cornfield and requested payment for the damages. When told he would not receive any reimbursement, Rogers wrote tersely that "you will greatly oblige me by keeping off my land." In those days of Jim Crow racism, he continued: "I want to be treated like a white man, also an American Citizen." No doubt others similarly looked with disdain on the government's actions on their private lands.[12]

Most did not complain, however, and benefited from the park's establishment. The majority of the residents on the battlefield sold their land for fair prices, around thirteen dollars an acre. Others cut free firewood from the trees felled by surveying parties. Local businesses saw an upsurge in activity, as when Armpy Johnson's sawmill, located near Owl Creek, received orders for thousands of wooden surveying stakes. Perhaps most importantly, the park eventually provided jobs for residents of the area, making it one of the highest per capita income regions in the county. Workers stuck in hard farming jobs on terrible soil welcomed a set routine of government work for a dollar a day. The arrival of government checks every month created visible excitement. Displaying graphically how destitute the economy of the area was, however, local businesses could not cash the many federal checks that locals presented to them.[13]

Thompson continued his work throughout the summer and fall of 1895. Once enough surveyed lines had been marked, he added a level team to determine and measure topographical relief. A few delays resulted from accidents such as broken surveying transits, one of which was caused by a runaway team of horses. Nevertheless, Thompson soon completed his grid of lines every two hundred feet apart, which, he explained, was done with "as near perfect accuracy as can be obtained." The workers finished the transit survey on September 12, 1895, and accomplished the task of determining relief several weeks later, allowing Thompson to lay off one transit team and the level team.[14]

Thompson then surveyed other areas. He mapped the land between Crump's and Pittsburg Landings over which Lew Wallace had marched and countermarched on April 6, 1862. He surveyed the Brown's Landing Road and the main Corinth Road as far south as Shiloh Church. In consultation with Buell, Thompson also decided to map the area south of the battlefield as far as the Bark Road.[15]

Once Thompson completed these basic surveys, he turned his attention to creating maps of the battlefield. He produced a large blueprint showing not only the topography and water courses but also the roads in the vicinity. Included in the sites placed on the map were buildings, natural features, and, once the remaining transit party located property lines, the actual land holdings on the park.[16]

By December 1895, the commission had an accurate topographical map that showed land ownership, as well as individual maps of each resident's property compiled from deeds in the Hardin County Courthouse. This advancement sped up the process of building the park. For example, the surveyed lines allowed the commission to mark prominent positions on the field by taking careful measurements from the surveyed lines. Buell became very interested in mapping, and he and Thompson created, to the best of their ability, an April 1862 map. Historian and secretary Reed also began his work, laying out troop positions on a copy of Thompson's map. Perhaps most importantly, Thompson's map greatly aided J. W. Irwin's work of acquiring land.[17]

Irwin began his task with zeal but soon learned just how difficult a job he had. While E. T. Lee held his options, Irwin mapped out a survey of the original boundary as detailed in the enabling legislation and then compared that with

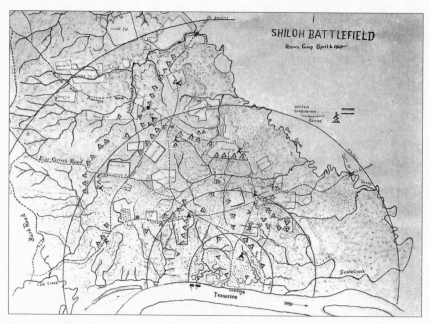

Map 2. An example of the many battlefield maps produced by the park commission. Courtesy of Shiloh National Military Park.

what Reed and Cadle viewed as the necessary land needed to establish the park. The commission determined that outright acquisition of the 6,000 acres originally contemplated was not needed; 3,650 acres would adequately preserve the battlefield. Congress had set an appropriation limit of $20,000 for land purchase at Shiloh, but if the commission only bought the 3,650 acres deemed necessary at the low price of $10 an acre, that would still amount to $36,500. The commission clearly faced a serious problem and lobbied Congress for more money.[18]

These problems did not deter Irwin and the commission; they pushed forward despite the obstacles. They faced the time-consuming process of weeding through documentation and negotiating with some two dozen landowners. First, Irwin and Thompson had to survey the land and determine the actual tract boundaries. Then, Irwin had to locate deeds for the land, making sure the owners owned what they said was theirs. Landowners in the Pittsburg Landing area were not the most careful record keepers and determining property ownership required much research. Afterwards, legalities such as the payment of taxes remained to be checked. After Irwin determined that the owners were in good standing, he had to negotiate a price. Papers then had to be drawn up, including such legal documents as an index to the abstract of title, the abstract of title, and the opinion. Once all this paperwork was accomplished, the deeds could then be compiled, signed, and registered in the Hardin County Courthouse. Finally, the

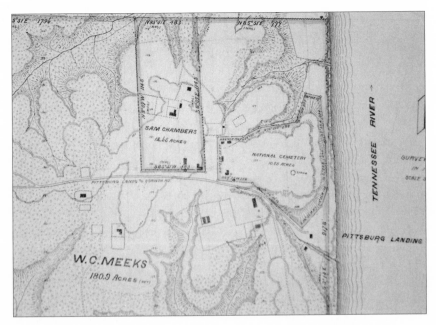

Map 3. In preparation for buying an individual owner's land, Atwell Thompson drew maps of each land plot. Here is a section of Thompson's map containing Pittsburg Landing, the National Cemetery, and the hotel and headquarters area. Courtesy of Shiloh National Military Park.

government paid for the land, although many landowners grew impatient with the government's bureaucratic vouchers and slow-arriving checks. Irwin clearly earned his salary as land purchasing agent.

Irwin waded through this process one tract after another. At one point, he admitted that "we find it very tedious work getting up abstracts." Disputes over boundaries emerged, prompting Cadle to complain about titles "being found very imperfect." Thompson had to take time out of his map-making and land-clearing duties to resurvey boundaries and clear up discrepancies. If the process could not be settled peaceably, Irwin implemented condemnation procedures, which added dramatically to the amount of time and paperwork required.[19]

Slowly but surely, the work of acquiring land progressed, particularly after March 4, 1896, when E. T. Lee's options expired. The first purchased tract of land was George W. L. Smith's 85.18 acres lying on the western edge of the battlefield. This tract, through which ran the Hamburg-Purdy Road, contained the headquarters site of one of William T. Sherman's brigade commanders, John McDowell. On September 28, 1896, the commission bought Smith's property, originally optioned to Lee, for $851.80, or $10 an acre.[20]

In the first four months of 1897, the commission purchased five more tracts of land, totaling some 797.25 acres, at $10 an acre. Thomas Walker owned four separate areas, most notably two tracts in the center of the battlefield. His land included the site of Sherman's headquarters as well as the position of Ruggles' Battery. The 206.05 total acres plus improvements cost the government $3,184.70, or $15 an acre.[21]

To this point, Irwin had found the land owners eager to sell their land and, despite the earlier option problem, not generally exorbitant about price. W. C. Meeks was not so amiable, however. He owned 180.90 acres fronting on the Tennessee River, including Pittsburg Landing. Not in any mood to sell for $10 an acre, Meeks asked $25,000 for his land. The commission would not pay such a sum and ordered the case to condemnation. The lawsuit went to trial, and the court rendered a decision on April 27, 1897. In Cause No. 2274, *The United States* v. *W. C. and O. C. Meeks*, the Eastern Division of the Western District of Tennessee, District Court of the United States, awarded the United States title to the land for $6,000, thus bringing the price down from $138 per acre to $33, still a very good price.[22]

Cadle believed the results of the condemnation proceedings, as well as the precedents set by purchasing inland tracts for around $10 an acre, gave the government leverage in future land deals. Most owners readily sold their land for around $10 an acre. They realized that they could not fight the government in court and expect to win. In Cadle's view, they also believed that the government was not trying to cheat them.[23]

By February 1897, Cadle and Irwin had spent $18,675 of the $20,000 limit for land on 1,390 acres, at an average of $13.43 an acre. Much more land was needed, however, so a further appropriation was necessary. Cadle reported to Representative Joseph G. Cannon (Republican) of Illinois, chairman of the House Appropriations Committee, and received a new limit of $50,000 in the Sundry Civil Bill of 1897. Using this new money, Irwin continued buying up property. Between 1897 and 1903, Irwin and the commission bought twenty-four more tracts with no threats of court action. These purchases included many of the famous sites on the battlefield. On December 1, 1897, Irwin finished the deal with Samuel Chambers for Fraley Field, where the battle had begun. On January 8, 1898, John R. Duncan sold Duncan Field and the Hornet's Nest–Sunken Road tract. Also on that date, Irwin secured George H. Hurley's 43.50 acres, which included a portion of Bloody Pond.[24]

By 1903, the vast majority of the battlefield was in the United States government's possession. Irwin had secured 3,313.76 acres at a total price of $48,318, at just under $15 an acre. The majority of the money spent had gone for land, but the government also paid small sums for improvements on several of the tracts, such as Pittsburg Landing, houses, and other structures. Despite earlier concerns, Lee's options apparently did not raise the ultimate prices.[25]

Throughout the acquisition process, a good relationship developed between the federal park and the local residents, most of whom chose to remain in their homes with the option of life tenancy. A tactful Cadle made sure that they remained satisfied. Indeed, the government provided many new services for the people living on the battlefield, including modern wells at each site and material to keep the grounds clean and attractive. A vast majority of the tenants went to work in the park as laborers. Likewise, as a result of the park's establishment, the standardized arrival of mail and steamboats at the landing opened this secluded and isolated area of west Tennessee to future development. No one was cheated, no one was ejected out of a home, and most were better off economically than they had been before the park's establishment.[26]

After making the initial land purchases, the commission later acquired only isolated and small pieces of property, usually those surrounded by the earlier purchased park lands. This resulting slowdown in land acquisition necessitated eliminating Irwin's position as land agent. Such a move had been contemplated as early as 1900, but Cadle had stood by Irwin and kept him on beyond that time. In 1902, Secretary of War Elihu Root, wanting to cut all unneeded workers from the War Department payroll, once again focused on Irwin. While Cadle could not deny that he could get by without Irwin's services, he tried to keep him anyway. Senator William Bate of Tennessee provided critical support in this effort. By 1906, however, very little land purchase was taking place, so the War Department finally took Irwin off the payroll. His discharge was dated July 19, 1906, effective July 31. As records became unkempt or new acquisitions took place in later years, however, Cadle periodically requested and received permission to bring Irwin back on the payroll for several days at a time.[27]

By surveying and buying land, Atwell Thompson and J. W. Irwin laid the foundation for the park. As the engineer in charge, Thompson was present in the park at all times and coordinated the work in preparation for marking the historically significant places on the battlefield. Working with J. W. Irwin, Thompson provided the commission and the nation with a park of some thirty-five hundred acres, on which they could effectively preserve the history of the important battle of Shiloh and, in the process, help advance a national memory of the Civil War.

CHAPTER 5

"Preserved on the Ground"

The main functions of Shiloh National Military Park were, from its beginning, physically preserving the battlefield, interpreting the battle historically, and marking the grounds to explain that interpretation. The Shiloh Battlefield Association began the process, and Congress added official legitimacy to that effort. Congressional committees provided a number of reasons for setting this historic ground aside, while the enabling legislation itself spoke of having the history of the battle "preserved on the ground." In this context, Cadle and the commission began the process of erecting monuments, tablets, and artillery pieces to mark the field, continuing in the isolated region around Shiloh the larger national effort of remembering Civil War veterans and honoring their sacrifice.[1]

By 1894, physical preservation and a historical consensus on the interpretation of the battle could not wait much longer. After thirty years, nature and human activity had changed the appearance of the battlefield dramatically. In the mid-1890s, however, clues to troop positions and other locations paramount to understanding the battle still existed. But these physical reminders would not last forever, and important links to the past would soon be lost if action was not taken quickly.

Similarly, many more years would see the drastic thinning of veterans who had participated in the battle. The young soldiers of 1862 were now aging veterans with graying beards. In time, these men would lose their faculties and forget what they had done on that memorable field; or, worse still, as was already happening, they would increasingly mix their adventures at Shiloh with experiences in other battles, thereby distorting history altogether. The numbers of veterans would only continue to dwindle, and in a short time they would be gone, depriving those seeking to understand the battle of important first-hand accounts.

Almost as detrimental as the loss of the field and death of the participants was the proliferation of the argumentative historical publications that appeared in the thirty years after the battle. Even during the war, major controversies had erupted, and these only swelled in furor as time passed and egos grew. Many Northerners, even during the war, blamed Ulysses S. Grant and William T. Sherman for having been surprised and not fortifying the camp, while these generals and their supporters angrily defended the generals' actions. Other wartime disputes emerged between Grant and Lew Wallace over the latter's all-day countermarch on April 6. Grant was also involved in a nasty wartime debate with Buell over the effect the Army of the Ohio's arrival had on the battle. These wartime controversies over precisely what happened where and when, as well as over individuals' motives for particular actions or inactions, spilled over into the participants' postwar writings.[2]

The Confederates outdid the Federals in debating the battle. Many Southerners argued over Albert Sidney Johnston's role in the fight, but by far the most castigated man on the Southern side was P. G. T. Beauregard. Braxton Bragg and William J. Hardee particularly blamed defeat on Beauregard's calling off the Confederate attacks on the evening of the first day. Beauregard vehemently defended his action.[3]

The result of such controversy was a confused history of Shiloh, prompting no less a person than Ulysses S. Grant to remark that the "Battle of Shiloh . . . has been perhaps less understood, or, to state the case more accurately, more persistently misunderstood, than any other engagement." In addition to the tangled units and widespread tactical chaos that Shiloh had become famous for, historians trying to understand the battle had conflicting historiographical views to contend with, no preserved battlefield to rely upon as a source, and, until the government published all of the *Official Records,* no after-action reports to offer contemporary evidence. The need to produce an official history of the battle was thus at a critical stage when Congress established the park.[4]

The effort to meet the historical need at Shiloh centered on one man: David Wilson Reed. The park, to be sure, was not a one-man effort because Reed worked closely with veterans, particularly state commissions appointed to erect monuments. He also worked closely with Chairman Cadle. Reed did, however, have more of an effect on the historical interpretation that the park ultimately presented than any other American. He became the chief historian of the battle and probably knew more about the tactical movements of troops at Shiloh than anyone before or since. Once the commission had purchased the land, Reed began the process of marking the battlefield.

Reed followed the commission's rules that covered a variety of matters from commission conduct to monument placement. Cadle, Looney, and Buell met monthly to work out these guidelines, but controversy soon developed. Feeling left out and shunned by the Iowa contingent on the commission (Cadle and Reed), Buell complained directly to the War Department. He offered "slight but polite exception" to Cadle's making decisions without the commission's vote. Cadle "confidentially" admitted to Reed that he had acted this way, but he insisted that he had the approval of the War Department to do so. Buell more forcefully questioned the practice of keeping all commission records closed to the public and, amazingly, even closed to Commissioner Buell himself. He believed that closed records prevented supervision, and he felt such supervision was needed, considering the not-so-hidden Iowa monopoly on the historic work. Buell called for a meeting of the commission to work out procedures and then successfully challenged a set of earlier rules written by Cadle and Reed. Buell offered a substitute set of regulations, which he made sure included open files. This controversy even gained the notice of the secretary of war, who lectured Cadle on the need for "entire unanimity in the Commission."[5]

The commission unanimously accepted most of Buell's suggested regulations on July 20, 1896. These included a majority vote of the commission for any action, a move clearly aimed at diluting Cadle's power to act alone on behalf of the entire commission. The new regulations also stipulated that when two commissioners wished to meet, they could call a meeting and they would constitute a quorum. Of course, the critical regulation concerned keeping the files open to public view. No longer could Cadle make decisions in sole consultation with Reed; a vote of at least two commissioners was now required, with Buell apparently believing that the Southern member of the commission would more often than not side with him. Cadle was not worried, however. In a letter to Reed about the new regulations, Cadle said, "There is nothing that will limit our work or make any trouble."[6]

Since the first order of business for the commission was to create accurate battle maps for subsequent memorialization of operations on the field, the commission first passed "Rules to be Observed in Preparing the Battle Map." The commission instructed Reed to locate the lines of battle on Thompson's topographical map, indicating all geographical features, unless they had appeared after the battle. Reed was also to locate creeks, ravines, woods, and thickets, as well as houses, roads, and fences, where they were at the time of the battle.[7]

Secondly, the commissioners established approved sources for Reed to consult. They allowed the use of two highly regarded maps of the battle: the "Thom map," made by Colonel George Thom of Major General Henry W. Halleck's staff, and the "Michler map," made by Captain Nathaniel Michler of Buell's staff. The commission likewise authorized the use of reports in the *Official Records,* as well as oral evidence from veterans and even evidence remaining on the field. Finally, the commission prohibited any marking of the field until Reed had completed the map.[8]

The commission then produced a third set of regulations, specifying the process to be used in marking the field. These regulations authorized marking general lines of battle "as described in the official reports," as well as other points "worthy of identification" or interesting to the visitor. The commission thus called for the marking of successive Union positions on both days of battle, with Confederate units located to show the positions the Confederate army took to attack those successive Union lines. Finally, the commission ruled that, before anyone could erect a monument on the battlefield, that individual or group had to get commission approval first.[9]

Volume 10 of the *Official Records* proved to be Reed's most helpful source. Part 1 of this volume contained all available contemporary reports of the battle written by unit commanders. These firsthand primary sources gave Reed a magnificent, if somewhat jumbled, view of the tactical movements on the battlefield. Part 1, containing some 229 different detailed reports, gave Reed insight into different unit movements. Part 2 included officers' correspondence surrounding the battle. The War Department had published the Shiloh volumes of the *Official Records* in 1884, only ten years before the park's establishment. Without these published reports and correspondence, the task of marking Shiloh National Military Park would have been much more difficult, indeed nearly impossible.

Large veteran turnouts at reunions provided Reed with the oral evidence he needed to clarify any confusion in *Official Records* reports and letters. From privates to generals, emotional veterans who returned on the anniversary of the battle frequently found their old positions and reminisced about their actions. The majority of these veterans were, of course, of lower rank, so they could describe only a small portion of the battle as they had seen it from their limited viewpoints, but these remembrances were invaluable.[10]

Higher-ranking officers were particularly helpful to Reed in locating positions and clearing up misunderstandings. When generals could not travel to Shiloh, Reed went to them. He visited John A. McClernand in Illinois and A. P. Stewart and James R. Chalmers in Chattanooga. At various times, senior officers of both armies, such as Lew Wallace and Isham G. Harris, returned to the battlefield. Often, the return of these well-known officers brought a feeling of excitement to the area, particularly when a veteran had become a celebrity, such as Senator William Bate. On one occasion, a crowd of veterans wanted to hear a speech from Confederate General A. P. Stewart, but he could not be found because he was "off locating places in the battle." Buell, of course, was especially active in locating positions.[11]

Such excitement clearly surrounded the return of Lew Wallace, commander of the Army of the Tennessee's 3rd Division at Shiloh. Wallace had gained the ire of his commander, U. S. Grant, by spending the battle's first day in confused countermarching while the remainder of the army fought for its life. Wallace never overcame the ridicule resulting from his error-filled march, even when some later credited him with saving Washington, D.C., at the Battle of Monocacy. After the war, Wallace served in a number of positions, including ambassador to Constantinople and territorial governor of New Mexico. While governor, Wallace wrote *Ben-Hur*, published in 1880 and destined to become one of the most popular novels in American literary history.[12]

Fig. 13. Members of the War Department staff, along with staff members from other parks, at Shiloh. From left to right are Shiloh commission members J. H. Ashcraft, Cornelius Cadle, and D. W. Reed. Next to Reed is John C. Scofield of the War Department, followed by Frank G. Smith and H. V. Boynton of the Chickamauga commission. Next is John P. Nicholson, chairman of the Gettysburg commission, followed by F. A. Large, the Shiloh Range Rider. Courtesy of Shiloh National Military Park.

Wallace returned to Shiloh on November 19, 1901. With several former officers and D. W. Reed, he landed at Pittsburg Landing on board the steamer *Tennessee* and stayed at Chambers's hotel, where the group took meals. For several days, Reed led Wallace across the land that they had fought over some forty years earlier. It took several days for the party to retrace the route Wallace had taken to the battlefield from Crump's Landing and they spent additional time locating the positions his division held on the second day. The trip was successful, with one member of the party later remembering that "Gen. Wallace seemed to recognize the ground perfectly." Some lower-ranking officers questioned the location of houses and troop positions, but when told that clearings and timber lines had changed, they seemed satisfied.[13]

The survey of Crump's Landing proved successful. Wallace pointed out the site of his headquarters and Reed placed a stake to mark the spot, intending to return later and place a headquarters monument there. Likewise, Wallace located the camps of his brigades, as he did a persimmon tree, which "the whole party engaged in devouring . . . as the various conditions of their several anatomies would permit." The group also found "a young cadaverous looking resident" who stated that he had a journal from the war. Reed and Wallace read several pages and commented on its valuable content. The boy, however, refused to donate the document to the park, and nothing further was ever heard of it again. After lunch at the new hotel in Adamsville, with Wallace paying for the whole party, the group continued its survey of Wallace's route, passing the Overshot Mill and crossing Snake and Graham Creeks. As if repeating his wartime confusion, Wallace became turned around in the thick woods. Finally, he regained his bearings and located the point where he had ordered the countermarch. In so doing, he admitted that his cavalry had not covered as much territory as he had always insisted. After this enlightening episode, the group returned to the landing and had supper, after which Wallace entertained everyone with tales of his adventurous life.[14]

The group spent the next day in more exploring. Wallace retraced his march again, but he still had some questions as to specific locations, such as where his division had actually left the main road. After Wallace was satisfied with his own remembrances, Reed erected a sign that read, "By this road General Wallace's army marched to Shiloh April 6, 1862." Rain precluded further exploration, and Wallace once more entertained the group. There was a minor glitch, however, when a member of Buell's army made a comment about stragglers from Grant's army. This remark, one observer remembered, "produced considerable but suppressed irritation on the part of the members of Grant's army present." The competitive feelings between the Union armies that had fought at Shiloh were still evident. Veterans were determined that the history of the battle would not minimize their unit's role in it or emphasize what they believed were inaccuracies.[15]

After several more days of tramping the battlefield and establishing troop positions, Wallace departed on November 24, 1901. His visit had been extremely helpful to Reed. He had verified locations that Reed and individual state monument commissions had already identified.[16]

While the return of famous officers and authors created excitement, other visits were more somber. In 1896, Senator Isham G. Harris returned to Shiloh for the express purpose of locating the site of General Albert Sidney Johnston's death. During the war, Harris had been Confederate governor of Tennessee and had served as a volunteer aide to Johnston. He was now a senator from Tennessee, and he and Senator Bate had sponsored the Senate legislation establishing the park. Harris, however, had never become involved in Shiloh's physical development. To him, Shiloh was the epitome of loss and defeat. A major portion of his state had been all but lost at Shiloh, and the Confederacy had never recovered. Most of all, Harris had witnessed at Shiloh the death of his close friend Albert Sidney Johnston. It was understandable, therefore, why Harris supported creating a park yet remained aloof from it.[17]

The exact location of Johnston's death had been in question ever since the battle. Reed and Thompson had identified several possibilities, with Reed locating one site north of the Peach Orchard and Sunken Road, just west of Bloody Pond. Colonel Looney and others of the senator's friends impressed on

Harris the need to locate accurately Johnston's death place. Looney informed Reed in 1896 that Harris planned a return to the field and requested that Reed accompany him during the visit.[18]

Reed and Harris arrived at the battlefield in April 1896. Reed tried to make conversation about the battle, but Harris rebuffed him. "Please do not ask me to say anything about that. The whole subject of Shiloh is a bitter memory which I do not allow myself to talk about or think about when I can help it. I have never visited the field since the battle and would not now except at the urgent request of the friends of General Johnston," Harris responded. At Pittsburg Landing the two men found many of the senator's friends waiting for their arrival. Harris repelled everyone, including Buell, who offered him a ride in his carriage. "You will please excuse me, General, for until the matter I have in hand is disposed of I desire to be alone," Harris said. He then called for a horse and, turning to Reed, told him to do the same.[19]

Harris told Reed to take him to a stream with very high banks on the Confederate right. Reed immediately thought of Locust Grove Branch and took the senator past Prentiss's headquarters and down the valley of the stream. Once in place, Harris asked if a Union camp had been situated to their right rear, and Reed informed him that the 18th Wisconsin had camped in that direction. Harris then rode up the bluffs alone, gained his bearings, and called for Reed. The senator had located the point where Johnston had sat for some two hours, deploying his reserve corps. He remembered a small stream where orderlies fetched water and also nearby Union campsites. "Everything is perfectly natural just as I remembered it," Harris muttered.[20]

Buell and others followed at a respectful distance while Harris and Reed pushed forward. Harris told Reed to take him about a half-mile due north to a large field on the left. Knowing the lay of the land, Reed conducted him to the southeast corner of Sarah Bell's cotton field. Harris rode alone into the field, then east across the Hamburg-Savannah Road. He stopped near a large oak tree, then drifted into a large ravine to the south. Soon, Harris reappeared at the tree and motioned for Reed to join him.[21]

Almost with amazement, and no doubt with tears in his eyes, Harris declared that everything was just as he remembered it. "This is the place," he remarked, "I cannot be mistaken." Reed recommended that Harris tell his story to the large crowd that was now following the two men. He reminded the senator that locals had a "tradition" that Johnston had fallen north of the Peach Orchard, on the front lines. A simple retelling of his story, according to Reed, would forever convince local residents of the location of Johnston's death. Harris agreed, and Reed called the crowd forward. They listened attentively to Harris's story.[22]

Harris's visit ended with several important results. The official place of Johnston's death was no longer a matter of controversy. Reed also had seen the depths of Confederate emotion regarding Shiloh. Most importantly, Harris had a change of heart. The senator had remarked to Reed on the way to the battlefield from Corinth that he had very little sympathy with those preserving battlefields. He preferred to forget about all that had happened there. After his experience at Johnston's death site, however, Harris congratulated Reed and said, "I have changed my mind about your work here, and say that I am pleased with your plans and will take pleasure in doing anything I can, in Congress or out, to assist you in the work." Unfortunately, Harris had little time left to participate in Shiloh's establishment; he died in July 1897.[23]

But Harris, Lew Wallace, and countless other veterans had contributed important information to the collective history of Shiloh. The veterans played a crucial role in the memorialization of their own exploits on those April 1862 days. And, as the brief flare-up between Grant's and Buell's veterans indicate, every group was determined that its contribution to the battle's history be remembered accurately—at least according to its own perspective. Personal attitudes clearly helped determine the historical memory of Shiloh, and these differences in remembrance were definitely not merely North versus South.

Reed accompanied many more veterans to the field and then verified their stories in the *Official Records*. He also spent countless days wandering the battlefield alone, looking for signs of action and militarily advantageous positions. He found much physical evidence, such as tent rings and sinkholes. In Cloud Field, remnants of mud ovens used by Hurlbut's Division still dotted the countryside. Somberly, too, physical evidence of regimental burial grounds also still existed.[24]

Once Reed located the major troop positions, he began the process of marking the field. That in itself was a major task, requiring the cooperation of many people. Taking its cue from other battlefield parks, the commission determined that tablets would "mark, in letters of iron, the history of the battle." Additionally, cannon would locate artillery positions. State monuments would add to the scene. Reed and Cadle had to get the secretary of war to approve all the tablet inscriptions and wording; once that was done, the tablets and artillery carriages had to be ordered. When they arrived, workers under Thompson had to erect them.[25]

Realizing that this process would take years, Reed placed temporary wooden signs on the field to offer some interpretation while the park was being developed. In the spring of 1896, Reed placed some one hundred wooden signs at prominent points on the field. Painted white with red letters, these poplar boards usually located prominent natural features such as fields, springs, and houses. In several instances, however, Reed marked the locations of prominent battle sites such as Bloody Pond, the Peach Orchard, the Sunken Road, and the Johnston oak tree. These wooden boards gave the visitor locations to visit and something to look at before the monuments and markers could be completed. Indeed, Reed and Cadle had visitors in mind when they placed the boards and wanted these signs to be posted "before the spring excursion parties begin to arrive." More importantly, the commission had in mind establishing Shiloh's part of the historical memory of the Civil War.[26]

As was the case with all too many matters, controversy erupted within the commission concerning the type of tablets to be used. Buell once again found himself at odds with Reed and Cadle. He favored a scheme of coloring for the tablets, which included painting first-day tablets yellow, second-day tablets green, Confederate tablets red, Army of the Ohio tablets white, Army of the Tennessee tablets blue, and camp tablets black. Reed and Cadle had their own scheme, which they ultimately used. The tablets would be painted white and trimmed for the Confederates in red, the Army of the Ohio in yellow, and the Army of the Tennessee in blue. The camp tablets would be black. Later, Cadle, Reed, and Thompson talked of changing the background color from white to silver, which Thompson viewed as "the prettiest we have: my old university colors." Shape also mattered. The first-day tablets would be square with ornamental corners, while the second-day tablets would be oval. Camp tablets would be pyramidal, signifying a cross section of a wall tent. Large rectangular signs would describe the movements of large organizations of men (armies, corps, and divisions), as well as post laws governing the field. Finally, smaller signs would denote roads or historical points that Reed deemed interesting, such as the Peach Orchard, Bloody Pond, the Johnston death tree, the Hornet's Nest, and Water Oaks Pond. [27]

Cadle requested permission from the War Department to hire an "expert iron master" to cast the tablets without having to let bids. When he received approval, he contracted the Chattanooga Car and Foundry Company. With models of the required tablets, Atwell Thompson traveled to Chattanooga to oversee the casting process personally and to answer any questions concerning appearance. Many details, including letter size, capitalization, and spacing on each tablet had to be worked out after Reed wrote the text and the secretary of war approved it.[28]

The commission tackled the massive task of ordering and erecting tablets in an orderly fashion. Reed concentrated on the camp tablets first, and Thompson placed all eighty-three on the field by November 1900. A number of permanent road signs also went up during this time. Reed then turned to the more complicated process of erecting position tablets. To mark sufficiently the first day's action, Reed needed 199 square tablets with ornamental corners. These arrived from the Chattanooga foundry on May 23, 1901, and Thompson immediately placed them on the field. Some controversy emerged as to the relation of each to its neighbor, prompting Reed to order that if three or more tablets were in line, they should point in the same direction, parallel with one another. Other controversies emerged, mostly regarding placement of tablets on privately owned land, most notably T. J. Hurley's land along the Hamburg-Purdy Road just west of the park. One entry in the commission's "Daily Events" diary reads, "Hurley is mad but can't

Fig. 14. An early view of the Johnston tree, showing the temporary signage placed on the battlefield by the commission. This early signage transformed battlefield areas—such as the Hornet's Nest, Bloody Pond, and this tree—into popular landmarks. Courtesy of Shiloh National Military Park.

help himself." Another states, "Hurley wants to fight." Over the next two years, however, the second day's tablets, as well as division, corps, army, and law tablets, were also placed on the field. Tablets marking the action of the Union gunboats and the small engagement at Pittsburg Landing on March 1, 1862, also went up. By 1908, Cadle was able to report that the work of erecting tablets on the battlefield had been completed. There were 651 tablets: 226 Union, 171 Confederate, and 254 road signs and explanatory markers. The cost of these tablets totaled $11,726.14.[29]

Reed dominated the decisions on the design and placement of the tablets. It was he who decided on colors, inscriptions, and positions, even making the foundry correct several errors. Once the tablets arrived at Pittsburg Landing and Thompson's crews erected them according to Reed's notes, he returned frequently to inspect them. He found tablets facing in the wrong direction and ordered the laborers to point them the appropriate way. In this process, Reed established the first permanent interpretive scheme at the park. He worded the text in such a way that a visitor could "follow easily the movements of each organization from the morning of April 6, 1862, to the close of the battle." Each tablet pointed the visitor to the unit's next location.[30]

At the same time that the commission was erecting tablets, it was also placing artillery pieces on the field. Cadle had ordered 215 cannon tubes from the War Department on November 14, 1896. The secretary of war, with many obsolete pieces of ordnance filling arsenals, had already turned over hundreds of pieces to other parks. Now, he approved the guns for Shiloh, and Cadle worked out the details of the shipment. On March 3, 1897, 188 cannon tubes arrived at Shiloh aboard the steamer *City of Paducah*. Other tubes arrived in following days, and Cadle later requested even more. In all, the park received some 250 cannon tubes from five different arsenals: Allegheny Arsenal in Pittsburgh, Pennsylvania; New York Arsenal in New York City; Rock Island Arsenal in Rock Island, Illinois; Watervliet Arsenal in Watervliet, New York; and Indianapolis Arsenal in Indianapolis, Indiana.[31]

Reed and the commission were not yet ready to place the cannon, however. The guns needed carriages, and bids would have to be let for this construction. In the meantime, Cadle and Reed opted for "a platform of crib work" to house the guns. Cadle ordered five thousand feet of lumber to build these stacks, which sat just south of Chambers's store, atop the bluff overlooking the landing.[32]

Cadle first began investigating which foundries should build the carriages in early 1897. He requested that two firms, one in Gettysburg and another in Chattanooga, send him a carriage as an example of their work. The two foundries had made carriages for Gettysburg and Chickamauga, but the commissioners at those parks did not highly recommend either foundry. The Gettysburg Commission chairman, John P. Nicholson, even asked Cadle not to buy anything from the Gettysburg foundry because of problems his commission had experienced with that company.[33]

Cadle finally began the process of letting bids for the carriages in late 1900. He placed advertisements in several newspapers around the nation, including the *Cincinnati Commercial-Tribune, Chattanooga Times,* and *Birmingham Age Herald*. The advertisements ran between early January and February 1901 and asked for bids on 150 cast-iron Civil War type carriages to be delivered to Pittsburg Landing. The commission accepted bids until February 11, 1901. Nine foundries responded to the request for bids. The commission then sent additional requirements to each company and awaited their responses. Five of the nine responded with final bids, ranging from $65 to $254 per carriage. The commission eventually awarded the contract to the lowest bidder, the Ross-Meehan Foundry Company of Chattanooga, Tennessee.[34]

Fig. 15. Cornelius Cadle (left) and D. W. Reed stand in front of the crib work that housed the park's artillery tubes. Acquired before the commission was ready to place them, these cannon lay near the landing for some four years before being positioned on the battlefield. The two guns in the background were the only erected pieces before 1901; they were mounted on sample carriages bought for test purposes. The cemetery lodge is in the background. Courtesy of Shiloh National Military Park.

Some of the carriages had to be sized proportionately to the guns they mounted and could not be uniform. Cadle had to have larger carriages for the thirty-pounder Parrott siege guns, of which he wanted to mount six. He also called on the War Department to transfer to the park two naval guns similar to those used on the gunboats. He and Reed planned to erect them at Dill Branch ravine in order to commemorate the navy's actions at Shiloh. These, too, would require different carriages.[35]

The government paid $9,750 to the Chattanooga foundry on June 14, 1901, without a single carriage having been delivered. The first shipment did not arrive for a month. When Thompson began erecting the guns, he found the cheek plates too narrow and immediately complained to the carriage makers. The foundry apparently then remade several carriages, and the next shipment did not arrive until January 2, 1902. The foundry delivered all 150 by February 10, 1902, but they were in varying states of corrosion.[36]

Thompson had many questions concerning spacing and length. He asked Reed for an accurate description of a battery's correct deployment. Reed told him to place the guns in a battery covering one hundred feet, with the guns sixteen feet apart. He also told Thompson to place the guns in front of the tablet marking the unit's position. Reed also specified that the butt of the guns should be in line with the tablet post. With these instructions, Thompson soon placed each gun on the field, bolting them down firmly to concrete bases for both support and security.[37]

Thompson also painted the carriages with primer and olive green paint, trimmed with black. He was finished by November 17, 1902. Cadle also exercised an option in the contract with Ross-Meehan. He requested seventy-seven more carriages on December 12, 1901. These began arriving on December 27, 1902, and filtered in as late as August 1, 1903. Thompson and his crews finished placing the additional seventy-seven cannon, excluding the siege guns and two steel guns, on September 17, 1903.[38]

While this artillery positioning was going on, Cadle asked the Chickamauga and Chattanooga Park Commission to exchange several guns with Shiloh, a swap to benefit both parks. In another transfer, one of the original guns that arrived at Shiloh was labeled "The Ladies Defender, Columbus, Georgia," so the commission arranged for its return to that city, where it still remains today.[39]

While Reed was the dominant force in locating troop positions and marking them on the field, he was also involved in other important historical work. He used the expertise gained in his studies of the battle to produce two documents that still stand as basic sources for understanding the battle of Shiloh: the Reed maps of the battle and the official commission history.

In preparation for marking the field, Reed completed two large troop-position maps in 1900, one for each day. Combining Thompson's topography map and his own knowledge of troop movements, Reed produced very accurate maps of the battle. The diagrams show the action as it unfolded, demonstrating to the viewer the successive positions of the armies.[40]

More descriptive than the maps was Reed's prose. He had long been involved in historical scholarship, having written pamphlets for veterans' organizations. He would also later publish a history of his regiment, the 12th Iowa. In 1902, Reed published, under the auspices of the Shiloh National Military Park Commission and through the Government Printing Office, a volume entitled *The Battle of Shiloh and the Organizations Engaged*. The book quickly became the standard treatment of the battle and would remain so for seven decades.[41]

This book was a slim volume filled with details. After a short history of the commission and a listing of several documents, Reed gave an overview of the campaign and battle. Then, he fulfilled his title by detailing the units engaged. He described the movements of every brigade throughout the battle. Various detailed tables of casualties and organization of the armies filled out the volume.[42]

One of Reed's purposes in writing this history was to provide veterans with a documented account of the battle, so that they in turn could make recommendations and correct any faulty statements. Once Reed published the book, he sent it to a variety of veterans and their families free of charge. At the same time, he sold it to non-veterans. In return, he received corrections and new eyewitness

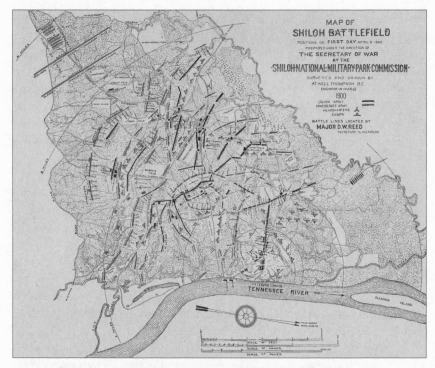

Map 4. Map depicting the battlefield on April 6, 1862, drawn by Atwell Thompson with troop positions located by D. W. Reed. This map and the one for the second day are probably the most accurate maps of the battle ever produced. Courtesy of Shiloh National Military Park.

accounts. By and large, Reed's scholarship withstood this test, but a few corrections prompted the commission to request a second edition. Reed issued this new edition in 1909.[43]

Reed's marking of the battlefield and the publication of his history created the dominant historical interpretation of the battle of Shiloh. In 1896, Reed had placed the temporary wooden board signs at prominent places on the field, such as Bloody Pond, the Peach Orchard, the Sunken Road, and the Johnston oak tree. These easily assessable battle sites, so marked, quickly became accepted as the dominant attractions on the battlefield and thus became the center of Shiloh interpretation even after the field was marked with monuments and tablets that actually told a different story.[44]

For example, Reed marked the Bloody Pond, which today is one of the most popular sites in the park. No after-action report mentioned the pond, and the account of bloodstained water came only from a local resident walking the field after the battle. In addition, other people reported similar instances of bloodstained water at other locations. But Reed marked this pond, and it has become known to history as Bloody Pond. Similarly, Reed seems to have overstated the effect and organization of Ruggles' Battery. Few Union or Confederate reports even mentioned the barrage of sixty-two cannon. The best recent research has concluded that because of attrition, the Confederates were only able to gather about fifty-three cannon at the site, and these did not fire in concert, contrary to the impression the visitor gains at the park. Likewise, the Johnston tree, located by Senator Harris, became the tree under which Johnston allegedly fell.[45]

Most importantly, the Sunken Road seems to have been a creation of Reed's historical activities rather than the reality of the battle. No Federal report of the battle mentions a "sunken road," and only a few postwar accounts even referred to the old road. Reed's 12th Iowa defended the area, however, which no doubt played heavily in his mind when he emphasized the importance of the position. Battle veterans tend to view the operations they are involved in as more important than events that happened elsewhere. During the thirty years between the war's end and the founding of the park, Reed became convinced of the importance of the Sunken Road. A veterans' organization called the "Hornet's Nest Brigade" had come into being with its first reunion at Des Moines in 1887. Reed served as its historian. Supporting Reed's thesis, Benjamin Prentiss, who surrendered in the Hornet's Nest, had made dramatic claims in his battle report that he had saved the day for the Union. The result of Reed's conviction that the Hornet's Nest was the pivotal action at Shiloh is subtly seen in the monumentation and historical writing on the battle. Reed's book suggests that the Hornet's Nest was the key site in the battle, and the veterans took this cue and placed three state monuments in the area, more than any other grouping on the battlefield. Ruggles' Battery, therefore, took on larger-than-life status for Reed as a result of the alleged importance of the Hornet's Nest. In his book, Reed made the assertion that the Confederates had to assemble a massive line of artillery to break the Hornet's Nest line and then only succeeded in driving away the supporting Union artillery.[46]

Despite the emphasis on the Hornet's Nest's importance, a different story probably took place. Several pieces of evidence offer insight into the Sunken Road and Hornet's Nest in the context of the battle as a whole.

The number of dead and wounded in the area shows that the Hornet's Nest did not see the heaviest fighting at Shiloh. An 1866 document produced by laborers locating bodies on the battlefield stated that the heaviest concentrations of dead lay on the eastern and western sectors of the battlefield and that the dead were fairly light in the center, where the Hornet's Nest was located. That document in itself states that casualties were fewer in the center, where, according to legend, the heaviest and most important fighting took place. Supporting this point are casualty figures for the units engaged in the Hornet's Nest. Colonel James M. Tuttle's brigade of four Iowa regiments, which held the Hornet's Nest and the Sunken Road in front of Duncan Field, reported a total of 182 killed and wounded in the battle—a number far less than some individual regiments sustained on other parts of the field.[47]

Troop positions also show that, for most of the day, the critical area on the field was not the Hornet's Nest and Sunken Road. When they went into action, Colonel Thomas W. Sweeny's Union brigade of six regiments, positioned in Duncan Field north of the Corinth Road, did not have ample room to deploy. As a result, only two regiments went on line; Sweeny held the other four in reserve for most of the day. Once the Union line began to fall apart on either side of the Hornet's Nest, Sweeny began to send his reserve regiments as reinforcements for the other more critical areas. He sent two Illinois regiments to the Peach Orchard sector and one to the north to aid McClernand's division. Only one regiment went to aid the Hornet's Nest. Had the Hornet's Nest been a critical point with severe fighting, Sweeny probably would not have sent his regiments away from the area. Furthermore, troop-position tablets show that very little action took place in Duncan Field. Confederate officers, knowing what would happen to their men in charges across open ground, chose to seek cover while making their attacks. Duncan Field, where myth states that so many Confederate charges took place, has no Confederate tablets denoting troop positions.[48]

Fig. 16. D. W. Reed at the monument to his regiment, the 12th Iowa, in the Sunken Road. Reed's interpretation of the battle was no doubt influenced by his role in defending the Hornet's Nest. Courtesy of Shiloh National Military Park.

On similar questions, Reed may also have let his pride guide his memory. In response to arguments by Army of the Ohio veterans that they had saved Grant's army from destruction, Reed downplayed the significance of the Army of the Ohio's arrival on April 6, arguing that the Army of the Tennessee had the battle in hand and that the arrival of the Army of the Ohio had had little effect on the late afternoon fighting on April 6. Likewise, he refused to admit that the Army of the Tennessee had been surprised on the first day and vociferously argued that the commanders had been aware of the Confederates' approach.[49]

Despite Reed's undoubted quest for accuracy and commitment to tell the truth, his subjectivity and desire to create tangible points of interest for visitors caused him to create myths that are taken as gospel truth today. Reed's Hornet's Nest–based interpretation of the battle became the dominant explanation that has stood for decades. Only recently have historians begun to look at the placement of units, casualty lists, and time and space considerations to conclude that the Hornet's Nest may not have been the decisive factor at Shiloh.[50]

Reed did his best to create a park that told the true story of Shiloh as he understood it. This process, however, opened the commission to attacks from those who did not fully agree with this interpretation, causing controversies over the positioning of tablets and monuments. The placement of tablets and artillery pieces was strictly a government action, however, and few veterans had the power to change Reed's account or his decisions about the placement of troops.

Trouble would erupt, however, as time passed. When Reed's work became well known through his maps and book, veterans began to challenge him. Most notably, controversy emerged when state governments began to erect monuments on the field. The state commissions, wanting to tell accurately the story of their troops, did not always agree with Reed's version. Thus, the Shiloh National Military Park Battlefield Commission, relatively non-confrontational to this point, soon found itself embroiled in several major disputes as it defended its creation of memory at Shiloh National Military Park.

In all these monumentation activities at the battlefield, the commission was taking part in the larger, national effort to honor the courage and sacrifice of the soldiers who had fought in the Civil War. The markers and tablets at Shiloh exemplified the national phenomenon being carried on elsewhere in the nation. The veterans' fixation on courage and honor not only allowed white America to agree on the need and use of these battlefields parks, but it also pushed to the background the highly charged issues that had actually caused the war. Reed's placement of troop positions at Shiloh was a classic demonstration of how individuals in the postwar years constituted the collective memory of the Civil War.

CHAPTER 6

Conflict and Consensus

In the early years of the 1900s, D. W. Reed oversaw the location and placement of tablets and artillery pieces that commemorated troop positions at Shiloh National Military Park. The result was an impressive array of markers on the battlefield, allowing visitors to locate and study the movements of the armies as they related to one other. In the process, Reed developed the first embryonic efforts at interpretation, pointing visitors toward what he considered important positions on the field. The placement of tablets and artillery pieces, however, was only half of the monumentation effort at Shiloh. More impressive than even the hundreds of cast-iron tablets were the stone monuments that soon covered the field. Numbering 156 in all, these monuments of varying types of stone not only marked additional troop positions, but they also grandly honored the units. This flurry of monument placement at Shiloh corresponded with the general trend of 1890s-era nationalism and consensus, portrayed not only on battlefields but also on courthouse lawns and famous avenues all across the nation.

The 1894 enabling legislation stated "that it shall be lawful for any State that had troops engaged in the battle of Shiloh to enter upon the lands of the Shiloh National Military Park for the purpose of ascertaining and marking the lines of battle of its troops engaged there." Many states enthusiastically responded. In the early 1900s, state after state began appointing battlefield commissions to locate troop positions and to erect monuments. The enabling legislation required that, while the individual states could place monuments of any size and shape at any location, the process had to be done with the approval of the secretary of war, who acted on the approval of the commission, which in turn acted on the approval of Reed.[1]

The monuments at Shiloh represented the best the nation had to offer. The speeches at the various dedication services spoke of reunification and forgiveness, and the memorials themselves commemorated glorious acts of bravery performed long ago, but with the understanding that the Civil War that had divided the nation was in the past and that the nation was one again. As beautiful and elegant as the monuments were, however, they caused much controversy in their own right. But these controversies were different from those that had divided the nation decades earlier. These new battles over monumentation were waged with much less at stake, but they were nevertheless prosecuted with determination.

Thus, in analyzing the monumentation at Shiloh National Military Park, a paradigm of conflict and consensus emerges, one in which monuments intended to bring the nation together tore veterans apart.

Egos and reputations were on the line in the early 1900s as these monuments went up. Unit pride from regiment to army level often caused heated controversies, with each participant believing that his own unit was the most important. Reed was an adamant individual who would not back down when convinced he was right. The state commissioners and others proved just as persistent, however, and the result was a series of confrontations overshadowing even the E. T. Lee controversy over control of the Shiloh Battlefield Association. The seeming ease of erecting artillery and tablets had perhaps spoiled Reed and Cadle, who were taken aback by the ferocity of the attacks that emanated from some of the state commissions concerning Reed's interpretation of the battle.

Reed and the commission itself erected four different types of memorials at Shiloh: the headquarters monuments, the mortuary monuments, the Confederate burial trenches, and the monuments to the regular army units that had fought there. Each of these entities (generals, fallen leaders, regular army units, and Confederates) had no organization to look out for their commemoration, so the duty fell to the commission.

In order to mark the headquarters of general officers of the Army of the Tennessee, which had camped at Pittsburg Landing for some three weeks before the battle, the commission opted for a pyramid of cannonballs set atop a concrete base. Designed by Atwell Thompson, these monuments sat on the spot of each headquarters as located by Reed, and they bore the name of each officer whose headquarters they denoted. Thompson built fourteen headquarters monuments in 1902 and 1903, each costing two hundred dollars.[2]

For both division and brigade headquarters, Thompson designed a square concrete base formed in steps, painted white with black letters displaying the commanding officer's name on the front. Atop the concrete base sat a four-sided pyramid of eight- or ten-inch cannonballs secured in cement. In all, Thompson built five large division-headquarters monuments, along with nine smaller brigade monuments. The smaller brigade-headquarters monuments contained a bronze plaque in "somewhat of a star shape" atop the pyramid of cannonballs, telling the details of the encampment. Perhaps hoping to forestall controversy, Cadle was careful to remind everyone that the star "does not represent anything in the heavens or under the earth." Reed originally intended to place a large bronze plaque directly on the cannonballs of the larger division-headquarters monuments, but he settled for a full-sized, descriptive iron tablet to give the detailed information about each division's actions at Shiloh.[3]

Just as with the condemned cannon brought in to mark artillery positions, the commission had to request condemned shells in order to create these monuments.

In 1897, eleven thousand shells arrived from the Allegheny Arsenal in Pittsburgh, Pennsylvania. Like the artillery pieces, however, the commission was not immediately ready to begin using them in the monuments. As a result, Thompson placed the shells in pyramids near the stacks of cannons at the landing. He had to keep souvenir seekers away from the shells, but apparently he had more trouble from little boys who enjoyed seeing the round shells roll down the long hill to the river, creating a large splash. Wanting to keep account of every projectile transferred to his possession, Thompson systematically retrieved the shells from the water. No doubt the hot-tempered engineer also scolded the youngsters.[4]

Some mystery exists regarding the placement and description of the headquarters monuments. Thompson built only fourteen of them. These included all five division headquarters at Pittsburg Landing but only nine of the fifteen brigade-headquarters sites. Many possibilities exist as to why Thompson did not build the other six, such as the chance that Reed could not accurately locate all the brigade headquarters. This possibility, however, seems improbable, given Reed's success at finding all eighty-three Union campsites and their reported near-pristine condition in the 1890s. Perhaps because of budget constraints, the commission probably decided to place these large monuments only on major roads for public viewing. The missing brigade-headquarters monuments were off the beaten path in the 1890s. However, even this scenario does not make sense, given the determination of Reed and the commission to mark the battlefield correctly and given their placement of tablets and artillery far off roads. No one will ever know why the remainder of the brigade headquarters were not commemorated.[5]

Of similar design were the five mortuary monuments, commemorating the locations where unit commanders above the regimental level fell on the field. Three Union officers (Colonels Everett Peabody and Julius Raith and Brigadier General W. H. L. Wallace) and two Confederate officers (Brigadier General Adley Gladden and General Albert Sidney Johnston) fell at Shiloh, and their elaborate memorials presented the circumstances of their respective deaths. Each monument contained the Thompson concrete base with steps and the officer's name on the front. The centerpiece was an upright thirty-pounder Parrott with a bronze plaque giving the details of the mortal wounding or death. Surrounding the shaft were four small pyramids of eight-inch cannonballs. Thompson erected each monument in 1902 at a cost of $250 each.[6]

All of these monuments were of uniform shape and size, with only minor modifications. The Peabody monument was square with no rounded corners and steps. Since Peabody fell at his headquarters, the mortuary monument also contained his brigade-headquarters star. The W. H. L. Wallace monument also had a unique appearance, with a surrounding apron of cannonball-laden concrete and steps leading up the embankment to the monument. These features have since been removed.[7]

The third major monumentation activity taken on by the commission was to mark the burial sites on the battlefield. Most of the Union dead had already been removed from the field and taken to the national cemetery, but the commission nevertheless marked the original burial grounds. In the case of Confederate dead, who remained on the field, Reed and the commission went to great lengths to preserve their resting places.

Problems quickly emerged. After nearly forty years, many Confederate burial trenches were no longer visible. At least in this case, it seems preservationists had waited too long. Nevertheless, Reed could locate some of the trenches. Cadle noted in his 1903 annual report that the commission had located nine such trenches, six within the boundaries of the park and three outside. Cadle and the commission marked five of the six within the boundaries of the park with a concrete wall twelve inches high, with ten-inch cannonballs spaced every three feet. Also denoting the positions were road signs labeled "Confederate graves."[8]

In the early twenty-first century, only the five mass graves are marked and the mystery of the lost burial trenches remains a major topic of discussion among park officials. The locations of the sixth trench in the park and the three outside the field are lost. Cadle reported that these trenches would be marked with a tablet, but like many other projects (such as Lew Wallace's campsites), such monumentation never came to pass. Nevertheless, there is at least one more trench on the battlefield and no doubt others. Today, four of the five marked mass graves rest on the western edge of the battlefield. Severe fighting raged in the center

Fig. 17. Veterans gather at a Confederate burial trench. From left to right are Cornelius Cadle, Marcus Wright, J. H. Ashcraft, and D. W. Reed. Courtesy of Shiloh National Military Park.

and particularly the eastern portion of the field, but the commission marked no Confederate burial trenches in that area. Common sense indicates that Federal soldiers, who drew the dubious duty of burying the Confederates, would not have dragged the enemy bodies across the battlefield to bury them on the western side. Documents resulting from the exploration of the battlefield by grave locators and cemetery builders in 1866 also speak of many burial trenches on the eastern half of the field, particularly one northeast of Sarah Bell's cotton field. Unfortunately, the locations of these missing trenches will probably remain a mystery forever. If Reed could not locate them in the 1890s, any chance of finding them in 2004 is small, even with space-age technology.[9]

The final group of monuments erected by the commission commemorated the activities of regular army detachments at Shiloh. With no state organization to develop plans and place such monuments, the task fell to the federal government. Cadle first asked that the general staff be tapped for the job but then pushed for a commission of regular army veterans who had served at Shiloh. When informed that the War Department would not pay these men, Cadle finally admitted that he and Reed would have to "get up the matter ourselves."[10]

Cadle let out bids for the monuments and, after consultation with the commission, chose the Hughes Granite Company of Clyde, Ohio. They were not the lowest bidder, but the commission liked their design and knew the quality of their work since Hughes had erected the Ohio monuments some years earlier. Nevertheless, the War Department vetoed the action, forcing Cadle to hire the lowest bidder, the Hodges Granite Company of St. Louis.[11]

In the end, Cadle and Reed placed three regular army monuments, one for each arm of the service. They were identical, except for the inscriptions and insignia. For the regular infantry, of which three battalions fought at Shiloh, the commission erected a monument adorned with the crossed-rifles insignia and the units' names. The regular artillery had three batteries in action at Shiloh, and only the crossed cannon and a listing of the engaged units differed from the regular infantry monument. For the cavalry, made up of two companies, crossed sabers and a short inscription denoted their service. All of the monuments contained shields and laurel wreathes, with the initials "U.S." clearly cut.[12]

When William R. Hodges won the bid to build the monuments, he immediately began construction and delivered all three by December 9, 1910. Made of Barre granite, these monuments cost a total of $5,750. The artillery monument went up just north of Bloody Pond, between two positions the regular artillery had held. Reed placed the infantry monument near the northeast corner of Duncan Field, where the regular infantry had fought on the second day as members of Brigadier General Lovell H. Rousseau's brigade of Buell's army. The cavalry monument went up at their campsite on the Hamburg-Savannah Road in the Russian Tenant Field.[13]

While Reed continued to be the major power behind the erection of commission monuments, he met his match when dealing with the state commissions sent to erect memorials to their state's units. Stern and accustomed to acting as the supreme decision maker in locating troop positions, Reed had a good deal of trouble with these veterans, who tended to be as passionate as he was. The result was a series of controversies over locations of monuments, inscriptions, and procedures.

As soon as Congress had allowed states to erect memorials, the state-appointed commissions had begun to research their units' role in the battle, spending many days on the field locating the best positions for the monuments. The arrival of these commissions tended to shake up the usually docile environment at Pittsburg Landing. Even the naming of these commissions caused some trouble. Most states named their group the "Shiloh Battlefield Commission," prompting Cadle to seek permission from the secretary of war to change the national commission's name to "Shiloh National Military Park Commission." More importantly, Cadle and Reed and the other commissioners met each group at Shiloh, not only to offer advice and council but also to make sure that the state commissions followed the park's many laws and regulations. These commissions, made up entirely of veterans, brought a feeling of nostalgia as they returned, and a festive atmosphere usually attended their visits.[14]

State monuments quickly began to go up all across the battlefield. These state memorials were of differing shapes and sizes, adding personality to the battlefield. Indeed, the states acted on their own accord. Some states, such as Wisconsin, Minnesota, and Michigan, placed large central monuments while others, such as Indiana and Ohio, opted for individual memorials to commemorate each unit. A third group, including Illinois and Iowa, erected large central monuments as well as individual unit memorials.

The Northern states by far erected the most monuments at Shiloh. The Union had won both the battle and the war, and many veterans wished to honor that victory. Northern states also had ample money to spend on these memorials. Southern states were still reeling economically from the war in which Shiloh had played such an important part. A less-than-spectacular agriculture policy of sharecropping and excessive reliance on cotton was also a problem in the South, leaving these states with little unencumbered money to spend on memorializing Confederate defeat. As in the case of Senator Isham G. Harris, the Southern states wanted to forget what had happened.

Eight Northern state legislatures erected varying forms of monuments at Shiloh while not a single Southern state legislature (in the War Department administrative period) appropriated any money for such memorials. Only two former Confederate states, Arkansas and Alabama, eventually built monuments in

Fig. 18. Many state commissions placed monuments on the battlefield. Here, the Illinois Commission gathers at Shiloh. Cornelius Cadle, Robert F. Looney, Atwell Thompson, J. W. Irwin, and D. W. Reed are the first five from the left. Major General John A. McClernand is on the far right with his arm outstretched. Courtesy of Shiloh National Military Park.

this period, but even these were the work of the United Daughters of the Confederacy (UDC). The UDC also placed a large Confederate memorial on the field. Similarly, two wealthy Confederate veterans paid for regimental monuments themselves. Accordingly, proud Northern states, dominated politically by veterans, preserved the memory of Shiloh while Southern legislatures, also made up of veterans and sons of veterans, seemingly ignored the battlefield, allowing their past to slip quietly away.[15]

While the state commissions and UDC groups did the majority of the work for these monuments, the commission was nevertheless heavily involved. The commission, as well as the secretary of war, had to approve each monument. Similarly, Reed had to check each inscription to insure that it complied with regulations; each inscription had to be historically accurate according to the *Official Records* and could honor no individuals. Reed also had to coordinate with each group to find the best location for every monument. For states that erected only one monument, this issue posed no problem, but Reed spent countless hours with the commissions from Ohio, Indiana, Iowa, and Illinois. Placing monuments to individual units, these states picked the point of each unit's most significant action as the location for its monument.

Perhaps the most important part the commission played in the process was in the actual erection of the memorials. Workers from the various stone companies

traveled to Shiloh to erect them, but Thompson and his engineering staff had
to oversee the entire affair. Regulations such as weights on park roads and standards for government bronze had to be taken into account, and Thompson was
just the man to do this necessary, detailed work.

Thompson also oversaw the building of tools to unload the monuments at
Pittsburg Landing for transportation to their permanent locations. Everything
from cannon tubes to completed monuments arrived at Pittsburg Landing, and
for the very large monuments, new unloading and building procedures had to be
invented. The big obstacle was to get the stones from the barges on the river to
the top of the bluff. The steep roads up the bluff proved a problem for heavier
stones, so engineers developed an ingenious system, certainly revolutionary for
rural west Tennessee. Four hundred yards south of the cemetery, engineers
placed a rail line down the almost perpendicular bank. These tracks matched
tracks built on the barges. A winch and engine hauled the stones, once loaded on
small rail cars, up the very steep bank. It occurred to one astonished onlooker
that this was the first railroad in Hardin County.[16]

Once the stones were on the tableland west of the landing, large wagons with
twelve-inch-wide tires and strong teams of oxen, horses, and mules hauled them to
their specific locations. With the stones on location, workers placed them on concrete foundations, paid for by the federal government and built by Thompson.[17]

Placing the smaller memorials posed no major problems, but building the
larger monuments necessitated additional new procedures. To erect the Illinois
monument near Woolf Field, Thompson cut large trees from the surrounding
virgin forest and created a large frame structure over the base of the monument.
A small crane built atop the scaffolding and run by a small engine placed the
stones in position. Because it was taller by some twenty-five feet, the seventy-five-
foot Iowa monument, placed just atop the bluff at Pittsburg Landing, proved to
be a particular challenge. Engineers placed a large "A" frame over the base, from
which workers and stones were hauled to the top. Finally, Thompson had to
inspect the completed monuments for soundness and to insure that all bronze
work met government specifications. Only after the engineer's approval did the
commission accept the monument on behalf of the government.[18]

The commission was also heavily involved in dedication ceremonies.
Thompson built stands and speakers' platforms for many of the dedications. Cadle
and Reed had to act as hosts for the visiting commissions as well as for the many
veterans who returned. These dedications brought a feeling of festivity, and veterans and visitors alike seemed to enjoy the events. Huge crowds attended the dedication ceremonies, such as the fifteen thousand who viewed the Confederate
UDC monument's unveiling. Visitors to these dedications witnessed programs full
of prayers, patriotic songs, and addresses by influential men of the time. It was not
extraordinary to see governors and senators at the park for these dedications.[19]

Such major monumentation at Shiloh in the first decade of the 1900s resulted in a battlefield covered not only with tablets and artillery but also with permanent stone markers commemorating the actions of April 6–7, 1862. The money spent by the federal government, as well as the individual states (some $217,172 just for monuments, tablets, and artillery through 1910), demonstrated the esteem in which the public held veterans and their actions. Indeed, visitors flocking to Shiloh agreed that the park, adorned with monuments, tablets, and artillery, was a thing of beauty. Unfortunately, the process by which those monuments were erected also caused many heated controversies, somewhat diluting the festivity of the dedications. Amid the joy of placing and dedicating monuments in the park, severe arguments erupted between Reed, veterans, and the state commissions over Reed's interpretation of the battle.[20]

A number of Shiloh veterans questioned the emerging history of the battle. Allen C. Waterhouse, who commanded a Union battery at the battle, informed Cadle that he was "all wrong at Shiloh" and wanted a meeting with Reed. Similarly, a member of the 64th Ohio complained that his regiment's monument stood amid a group of others commemorating units that had not actually fought at Shiloh.[21]

T. M. Page, a member of the 4th Tennessee, vehemently argued with Reed over the position of his regiment's attack on the Federal line near Review Field. Page tried to "manifest . . . by mathematical demonstration" that Reed had incorrectly placed two Federal brigades. Page concluded that the Union men engaged in the fighting could not possibly fit into the space shown by Reed and that the resulting position of the 4th Tennessee was wrong. Reed responded that the numbers used by Page to determine the length of line were incorrect because Page had included officers, as well as men assigned to batteries deployed in the area. As Reed wrote to Cadle, "I see nothing in this letter to tend to show any error." Cadle, however, took the matter to the full commission, which wholeheartedly backed their historian. The matter disappeared once Reed wrote a lengthy rebuttal to Page's arguments, a trademark response by Reed to such controversies.[22]

Members of the 32nd Illinois made a similar complaint. Veterans of that regiment faulted Reed for his placement of the camp tablet and position markers for their regiment. The major issue was the location of the camp, which H. G. Keplinger, the leader of the dissatisfied veterans, stated was labeled as the 41st Illinois camp. Also in doubt was the midday position tablet for the regiment. Keplinger appealed to the secretary of war, William Howard Taft, but did not produce enough evidence to warrant a change. Reed explained that veterans of the regiment and the Illinois commission both agreed with him and that any change of campsites would cause an adverse reaction by veterans of the 41st Illinois. Keplinger lost his appeal, but veterans continued to mutter about errors, later alleging other inaccuracies in Reed's publications.[23]

Members of the 81st Ohio had more success in combating Reed. As placed by the Ohio commission and Reed, the 81st Ohio monument was to sit near the crossing of the Corinth–Pittsburg Landing and Hamburg-Savannah Roads. This position denoted a first-day engagement, in which the regiment had taken part late that day, having spent the earlier hours guarding the bridge over Snake Creek. Members of the regiment, led by W. H. Chamberlain, wanted the monument to commemorate what they believed was its more important engagement, which occurred on the second day. As Reed and the commission had it, the monument would honor an "insignificant action," and the inscription did not even mention the action of April 7. The 81st Ohio veterans appealed to Secretary of War Elihu Root, who ordered a cessation of work on the monument until the controversy was cleared up.[24]

Three entities were involved in the dispute: Reed, the Ohio commission, and the 81st Ohio veterans. The Ohio commission sided with Reed against the 81st Ohio's veterans but in another controversy asked for a movement of the 20th Ohio's and 78th Ohio's positions. Nevertheless, the major confrontation was with the veterans of the 81st Ohio. T. J. Lindsey, chairman of the Ohio commission, wrote to Reed that W. H. Chamberlain, leader of the dissatisfied 81st Ohio veterans, "certainly got some other battle mixed with Shiloh," for none of the veterans' contentions agreed with official reports.[25]

Work was stopped on the foundation for the monument and the inscription changes until the secretary of war could rule on the matter. No real hurry existed, however. Cadle informed the War Department that, during transportation of the monument to Pittsburg Landing, the ropes placing it onto the barge had broken, and it had fallen into the Tennessee River. Some time would pass before the river fell to a sufficient level to allow retrieval of the massive granite memorial.[26]

Swayed by testimony of the 81st Ohio's veterans, the secretary of war ordered a change in position and inscription for the monument. A flurry of disapproval resulted. Cadle was concerned about the park's having to pay for the change out of funds that were already short. Likewise, the Ohio commission gathered a petition of other 81st Ohio veterans stating that they wanted the monument to remain at the original position. Another appeal thus went to the secretary of war, requesting a reversal of the first appeal decision.[27]

When Chamberlain wrote a new inscription, Reed would not approve it, and the matter remained deadlocked for several years. The continual delays in changing the inscription caused the new secretary of war, William Howard Taft, to revisit the issue, however, and Cadle could stall no longer. Finally, Reed and Chamberlain worked out a compromise inscription, but Reed would not budge on the new location. Ultimately, Taft brought the matter to a close by siding with the veterans. The monument now sits where Chamberlain and the secretary of war placed it. Grudgingly, the Ohio commission reported that the

Fig. 19. The heavy granite and limestone monuments had to be hauled from the landing to their positions on the battlefield. Here, ten oxen are used to haul an Illinois monument to its position. Courtesy of Shiloh National Military Park.

secretary of war was heavily affected by "influential friends" of the 81st Ohio veterans who desired the change.[28]

A much more heated controversy raged over the positions of the 15th and 16th Iowa on the first day of battle. The argument erupted over Reed's objection to the Iowa commission's inscriptions on the monuments in relation to their positions in Jones Field. Reed maintained that the records did not bear out the occurrence of any fighting at that location at the time specified. Reed delivered an ultimatum, saying that the Iowa commission had to change either the monuments' locations or the times from 10:00 A.M. to 1:00 P.M. The stage was set for a major controversy.[29]

Reed said he had no problem with the locations, but the times were wrong. In an effort to make amends, Cadle even sent Reed to meet with the dissatisfied veterans at Dubuque and again at Des Moines, Iowa. Ultimately, however, the Iowa commission agreed with the veterans, and the matter grew more contentious. The Governor of Iowa, Albert B. Cummins, appealed to Secretary of War Elihu Root for an investigation. The secretary sent the correspondence to an arbiter, Brigadier General F. C. Ainsworth, who ruled primarily for Reed and Cadle, forcing the inscriptions on the monuments to state no times. This victory was only short-lived, however.[30]

Governor Cummins and the Iowa commission, armed with letter after letter from veterans confirming their case, promptly appealed the decision of the arbiter and demanded that the War Department change the inscriptions back to the original forms. Cadle spent many days in Washington trying to work out a time for a hearing with the Iowa delegation, but because Governor Cummins was busy with legislative activities, no agreeable time could be set. Finally, legislative matters allowed Cummins to travel to Shiloh, and a hearing occurred before the commission on May 20, 1904. Cummins offered a very lengthy argument, which Reed rebutted in an equally lengthy statement. The "Conclusions of the Commission," issued on August 9, 1904, completely sided with Ainsworth and Reed's position.[31]

Undaunted, Cummins again appealed to the War Department. He asked for another hearing before the department accepted the verdict. Acting Secretary of War Robert Shaw Oliver granted the request, but Cummins could not work out a time for the hearing until after the fall elections. At that time, the governor offered a compromise, which Reed and Cadle rejected. The controversy intensified.[32]

After "the most elaborate investigation and consideration of the matter," the War Department found the two sides' inscriptions basically the same, except for the times the regiments went into action. The acting secretary of war returned to the practice of using the *Official Records* as the basis of inscriptions, not the testimony of veterans after forty years. Once again, the War Department approved Reed's original inscriptions.[33]

Still undaunted, Cummins appealed to the new secretary of war himself, future president William Howard Taft. Once again, work was stopped on the bronze tablets. After so much time and debate, the matter had become personal. Ironically, although Reed and Cadle were Iowans, they thought that the Iowa commission had completely disregarded the *Official Records* out of ignorant stubbornness. The Iowa commission blamed Reed for similar peevishness. "Major Reed could scrap for years, ridicule us beyond endurance and pose as a defender of War Department figures but where personal interests were concerned his acts belie his words," one of the Iowa commissioners complained. This time, however, a clearly fatigued Taft ruled firmly. On March 10, 1906, arguing that the matter had been "most thoroughly considered and investigated," he ordered that the Iowa commission inscriptions and times be used. He also directed that "no further hearings or consideration in the premises will be granted." The result was a ruling against Cadle, Reed, and the Shiloh commission. Defeated, Cadle and the commission nevertheless prepared for dedication activities, which they carried out with no animosity.[34]

A somewhat more humorous but equally irritating controversy arose with Lew Wallace. The former commander of the 3rd Division of the Army of the Tennessee was not satisfied with many of Reed's conclusions, which he deemed "detrimental to the credit of my division and in violation of the truth of history." As early as 1896, Wallace had viewed preliminary maps prepared by Thompson and Reed and found fault with many parts of them. He disputed the claim that

Sherman's men had rested on his left on the night of April 6 and in the battle of April 7. He also disputed Reed's positioning of his division on its march from Crump's Landing. He even argued over particulars of what the famous missing order from Grant had said. Wallace requested a hearing before the commission in 1896 and again in 1903, the latter even after he had returned to the field in November 1901 and admitted that he did not know where he had marched.[35]

Wallace went on to make other accusations, asserting that Reed had incorrectly positioned monuments (particularly Thompson's 9th Indiana Battery), misrepresented field and wood lines, and inaccurately located 1862-era roads. But Reed's rebuttals, always very lengthy and full of facts from the *Official Records*, caused the old general to backtrack. By 1903, the commission had evidently become tired of his stubbornness. On one occasion when Wallace requested a hearing, Cadle advised Reed to prepare thoroughly. Cadle somewhat exasperatedly counseled, "[The] interview if it comes off in October, which I doubt, will simply be a rehash of what has been said before. But still I suppose you had better write out your views and have them ready for the meeting in October."[36]

The nastiest controversy, by far, concerned Don Carlos Buell and the Army of the Ohio's representation on the commission. Buell's pre-appointment correspondence spoke of anxiety over this issue of representation, and subsequent actions bore out his fears. Early in the history of the commission, it had become very apparent that Reed and Cadle, and to a lesser degree Thompson, ran the park. Buell was seemingly left out, as was the Confederate representative, Robert F. Looney, who complained bitterly to Buell of Cadle's usurpation of authority. The Southerners on the Shiloh commission, as well as on other military park commissions, had very little bargaining power with the federal government, but Buell believed that he did. His resulting actions, as well as those of his army's defenders, soon created a controversy of immense proportions.[37]

The defenders of the Army of the Ohio, namely the Society of the Army of the Cumberland, claimed that there were errors in many of the army's monuments and tablets at Shiloh. One of the chief spokesmen for the society was Whitelaw Reid, no stranger to past controversy. It was Reid, a reporter for the *Cincinnati Gazette*, who had penned a famous April 1862 newspaper account alleging that Grant's men had been surprised and bayoneted in their tents. Now, in 1904, Reid was again attacking the modernized form of Grant's army, the Shiloh commission. He charged that the errors of Reed and Cadle were at best a result of incompetence and at worst a part of a vast conspiracy to make the Army of the Tennessee and its leaders look better at the expense of the Army of the Ohio. "Whether this [monument error] is due to a blundering effort to shield names which need no such treacherous props to their solid renown, and to do it at the expense of the Army of the Ohio, or whether it is due to mere incompetence, the effect is the same," ran Reid's blistering synopsis.[38]

Reid's major argument was that historian Reed had incorrectly labeled the times of engagement for the Army of the Ohio. Reed contended that Buell's forces had not engaged the enemy until eight o'clock on the morning of April 7 and that Grant's Army of the Tennessee had taken the fight to the enemy much earlier that morning. Reid and the Society of the Army of the Cumberland believed that the Army of the Ohio had actually led the advance and at a much earlier hour. The War Department sent the matter to arbiter F. C. Ainsworth, the same individual who had decided the 15th and 16th Iowa controversy in Cadle's and Reed's favor. Ainsworth again sided with the Shiloh commission. After extensive research, Ainsworth concluded that the complaint could only come from "the lack of information on his [Whitelaw Reid's] part." Enthused by the result, Cadle wrote Reed that "we are sustained and that is a pleasant thing."[39]

More controversy was soon to come, however. Other influential men arrayed themselves against what they believed was an Army of the Tennessee cabal running Shiloh National Military Park. The next person to fire a volley at Reed and Cadle was their old friend Henry V. Boynton, a veteran, former newspaperman and writer, and now commission chairman at Chickamauga. Boynton, who in 1875 had carried on a debate with William T. Sherman over the general's memoirs, had not served at Shiloh but had been a member of the 35th Ohio and a Medal of Honor winner for gallantry at Missionary Ridge. As a former member of the Army of the Cumberland, Boynton felt it his duty to defend his army's precursor, the Army of the Ohio.[40]

In 1905, Boynton took issue with Reed's book, stating that gross inaccuracies existed in regard to the Army of the Ohio. In Boynton's view, notable among the errors were the allegations that the Army of the Tennessee had not been surprised on the morning of April 6. Boynton also railed against Reed's failure to recognize the positive effect of Buell's arrival on the evening of April 6, his failure to state truthfully when the Army of the Ohio engaged the enemy on April 7, and even Reed's small stylistic lapses. In fact, Boynton's attack on Reed's book was an attempt to improve the reputation of Buell's army at Shiloh. In what had by this time become a custom, Reed produced a very lengthy rebuttal to every allegation, complete with extensive quotations and supporting evidence from the *Official Records*.[41]

Boynton was not finished, however. He leveled an even more sustained attack against the commission, complaining outright to the secretary of war that the Shiloh commission was conspiring to discredit Buell's army during the battle and had ignored Buell as a commission member. In a scathing letter to the secretary of war, Boynton asserted that Buell was "constantly ignored by the Chairman of that Commission, acting with its Historian." He further argued that Cadle and Reed had purposefully destroyed Buell's maps and notes of the battle's second day and had even denied their existence. Boynton further stated that, although a majority of the commission (Buell and Looney) voted that the question of surprise was outside the commission's realm of activity and thus should not be treated, Cadle and Reed had nevertheless defended Grant's army against accusations of surprise. Finally, Boynton argued that Cadle ignored correspondence and protests from Buell and even Looney. Boynton asked Buell's stepdaughter, Nannie Mason, for information on this alleged conspiracy against Buell and his army. Mason obliged and offered damaging testimony against Cadle and Reed, citing inaccessible park files and allegations of the destruction of Buell's maps.[42]

Later in 1905, the controversy grew messier. Boynton penned another harsh letter to the secretary of war, this time with the sole purpose of "further discredit[ing] the historical work of the National Shiloh Commission, and its Historian, Major Reed." Once again, Boynton attacked Cadle and Reed's insistence that Grant's Army of the Tennessee had not been surprised on the morning of April 6, 1862. In an effort to support a thesis that Reed had done shabby historical work, Boynton and the Society of the Army of the Cumberland argued that the non-surprise position "tends to cast serious doubt upon the historical methods adopted, and the historical accuracy of the rest of the work." Taking a page out of Reed's book, Boynton compiled a very lengthy argument that Grant's army was indeed surprised but that Reed had "wholly ignored" the issue and that Reed's book and his positioning of tablets and inscriptions "have been used to keep that controlling fact out of sight."[43]

A somewhat aggravated Reed responded to Boynton's "very discourteous" attacks. "I see no need of argument or explanation over this matter," he fumed. Nevertheless, he responded at length and again refuted Boynton's entire thesis. While the affair did not elicit a critical response from the War Department, Assistant Secretary of War Robert Shaw Oliver reminded Reed that he had invited criticism in his 1902 publication and requested that he submit a revised edition encompassing pertinent corrections. Reed obliged and, exhibiting animosity toward Boynton, remarked on his "well known proclivity to attack everything that is not the product of his own brain and ready pen." The new edition of Reed's book appeared in 1909 but incorporated few changes brought to light in the Buell controversy.[44]

The griping continued, however, as Boynton next alleged that the commission misrepresented the Army of the Ohio in placing tablets. He stated that Reed erected almost 200 tablets for the Army of the Tennessee and more than 160 for the Confederate army. By contrast, the Army of the Ohio had only 41.[45]

Finally tiring of the dispute, Assistant Secretary Oliver submitted the entire matter to a "specially constituted Committee of the War College for consideration and report." The special committee made no formal report but did recommend that "the changes suggested by the National Military Park Commission be adopted." Reed had won.[46]

Other smaller disagreements also occurred during the years of monumentation at Shiloh. Like Reed, Atwell Thompson always seemed to be in the middle
of such controversy, with his short temper and fiery personality often causing
him to become angry. On one such occasion, Thompson tangled with the Iowa
monument designer, Frederick E. Triebel. The bronze work for the monument
did not meet government standards, and Triebel blamed Thompson. The Shiloh
engineer had already tired of Triebel's micromanagement and his inclination to
change his mind, most notably when he switched the statue of Lady Fame from
the west to the east side during construction. Finally, Thompson snapped. "I
concede my temper was a little ruffled while his was decidedly brisk," Thompson
reported to Reed. Yet, the two men worked through their differences, even if
they did not exactly enjoy one another's company.[47]

In all these controversies, discernable patterns of behavior are clear. Almost
all those opposing the commission's decisions began their work with a heartfelt
feeling of duty and honor. Yet, as time passed, these noble feelings turned to
frustration as they ran up against the firmly entrenched duo of Cadle and Reed.
Another pattern existed, that of Reed's careful documentation of the evidence.
In each instance, Reed heard the accusation and responded with a detailed and
lengthy rebuttal, using many sources but most notably the *Official Records*. In
almost every attempt, Reed was exonerated, showing fully that he was the expert
historian of the battle and that his carefully calculated conclusions were the most
accurate that anyone had produced some forty years after the fact.

Throughout all the disputes, Cadle and Reed maintained control over all the
affairs of the park, most notably the positioning of markers and the interpretation
of the battle. Opponents regularly confronted a deeply entrenched commission
run by Cadle and advised by Reed. At least some of Boynton's allegations were
true. Cadle and Reed firmly controlled the operation and in most cases had the
War Department, except for Taft, on their side.

It must be said in Cadle and Reed's defense, however, that they never allowed
their power to turn to corruption. They were legally appointed and charged to
work closely together. In fact, placing these controversies in context shows just
how little disagreement actually took place. Over 270 different units served at
Shiloh, totaling more than 109,000 men. Well over half of these individuals were
still alive at the turn of the century. The fact that only ten major controversies
erupted was a testament to the commission's fairness. Likewise, the massive private correspondence between the two men, in which they told each other the
facts as they saw them, demonstrated that they ran the commission the way they
saw fit but that they always did so within the context of truth and accuracy. In his
heart, Reed always believed in the historical validity of his conclusions, and he was
almost always proven to be correct. Yet, some Shiloh veterans did not agree. Representative Joseph H. Outhwaite's 1894 statement that the establishment of the

park would "put at rest once and for all time to come the uncertainties and mis-representations surrounding the battle" proved inaccurate.[48]

As the monuments went up, the proverbial smoke cleared. When over, these controversies faded from memory as the beautiful park setting suddenly appeared, as if out of nowhere. In only a matter of years, Cadle, Reed, and Thompson had created a reserve full of position tablets, artillery, and graceful monuments. In addition, almost everyone agreed with the accuracy of the positions, and visitors reveled in the beauty of the park.[49]

The emergence of the completed park, however, symbolized another great phenomenon occurring around Shiloh and, indeed, all across the nation. When the park was established, the United States was still being torn by accusations of blame for the Civil War. The North blamed the South for slavery, secession, and firing the first shot. The South blamed the North for trying to run its affairs and retreated to the Lost Cause mentality (martyrdom, honor, courage, constitu-tional correctness, defiance, and defeat only because of massive Union numbers) to defend its section. By the time Shiloh was completed as a park around 1908, however, animosity and hatred were dwindling away, caused in part by the feeling of nationalism that had such an effect on the establishment of the park but also by a further reconciliation of veterans who dismissed the radicalism of the Lost Cause and proudly formed a consensus as Americans, not as North-erners or Southerners.[50]

This consensus was clearly seen in the monuments at Shiloh National Military Park and in the addresses that dedicated them. None of the symbolic monuments themselves portrayed any evidence of placing Shiloh in the context of the Civil War and the big questions of slavery and secession. Likewise, they made no state-ments concerning the causes of the war or the correctness of either side. Rather, the monuments pointed inward, giving the viewer a sense of what had happened at Shiloh and the meaning of specific military actions. Many of the Northern monuments contained symbolism of glory and honor. Another dominant theme of Northern monuments was the watchful eye. The lady atop the Illinois monu-ment looked toward the direction from which the attack came. The soldier atop the Michigan monument also peered toward the south. Others, such as the artilleryman on the Minnesota monument, watched anxiously for the enemy. The Confederates similarly included this style of symbolism, as illustrated, for example, by the soldiers crowning the Arkansas and 2nd Tennessee monuments. They both gazed steadily toward the enemy lines, their goal. Additionally, many of the monuments contained lists of dead and wounded at Shiloh.

Perhaps most symbolic of all the monuments was the UDC's. Even the loca-tion was important, standing at the Confederate high-water mark where the Southerners captured the defenders of the Hornet's Nest. The three figures in the center represented the South, death, and night. The South was symbolically

handing the laurel wreath of victory over to death, which took their commander
Albert Sidney Johnston, and night, which ended the victorious Confederate
attacks on the first day. The figures on the right and left symbolized each branch
of the army. The infantryman and artilleryman stood gazing through the smoke
of battle toward the north, while the cavalryman and officer corps figures were
seemingly exasperated because of the wooded terrain and their inability to act.
Finally, the row of heads on the face of the monument denoted the first and
second days of battle. The uplifted row on the right represented victory and
hope on the first day, while the fewer dejected heads on the left, bowing in sub-
mission, represented defeat on the second day and the loss of life.

While this and the other monuments were filled with such symbolism, they
were based firmly on the tactical actions at Shiloh and made little attempt to get
involved in the Lost Cause myth or the arguments over the war itself. Even the
interpretation of the field, such as the Johnston death site and the Hornet's Nest,
offered insight into the Confederate reasoning as to why they lost at Shiloh but
spoke very little of the war itself. Southerners took Reed's concentration on the
Hornet's Nest and developed the idea that brave and heroic Confederate
charges failed because of faulty leadership, most notably that of Braxton Bragg,
who, they said, launched so many piecemeal attacks. Similarly, many Southerners argued the importance of Johnston's death. Confederate veterans would
for years insist that victory was theirs but perished with their leader. The arrival
of the Army of the Ohio on the night of the first day also fueled Southern arguments that the Confederates would have won had not all these Union reinforcements changed history. As a result, some strands of Lost Cause myth (honor,
defeat by massive numbers, martyrdom) emerged in the monumentation and
interpretation, but these references were oblique and made no effort to explore
the larger issues of the war (slavery, race, freedom) or to make any statement
about the legitimacy of the Confederacy's actions.

Similarly, the dedication ceremonies exuded reconciliation and harmony, not
constitutional correctness or Lost Cause mentality. At the Ohio dedication in
June 1902, Cadle spoke of the Confederate and Union veterans in attendance "as
more than friends now—they are blood brothers." Former Confederate officer
Josiah Patterson, formerly a congressman and one of a series of Confederate
representatives on the commission, addressed the crowd and spoke of reconciliation, asking "with common traditions, a common language and a common
origin, where is the citizen of the Republic who does not rejoice we have a
common flag and a common country?" He then declared that the "sectional animosities have been swallowed up in the patriotism and magnanimity of a
common country." Luke W. Finally, a former Confederate colonel representing
the Governor of Tennessee, addressed the crowd and stated, "It is a matter of
rejoicing that we now have a common flag that represents a common country."[51]

Josiah Patterson also spoke at the Indiana dedication in April 1903 and admitted that the way to heal animosity was not to forget but to show "mutual respect and forbearance." He further said that "it was fitting that the work of reconciliation and rehabilitation should begin with the old soldiers." At the Pennsylvania monument dedication seven months later, Cadle spoke of the battle and the war that "convinced the Nation, both North and South, that it was a war between Americans that could only be ended by courage, blood and time."[52]

At the Illinois dedication in May 1904, Confederate General Basil W. Duke, another in the series of Confederate representatives on the commission, stated that "we, who once confronted each other on this field in 'stubborn opposition,' now meet with friendly intercourse—meet with no thought of the past conflict, save to wish to honor its heroes on both sides." At the dedication of the Wisconsin monument in April 1906, Duke spoke to the crowd with equal eloquence and seriousness. He argued that the South had been constitutionally right in its efforts but morally wrong to secede and fight. A Confederate victory, he said, would have divided a strong nation, and he thought the Confederacy would not have stood because of the precedent of secession. In the end, Duke admitted he was glad that the two sides were now one. Many Confederate veterans attended the dedication, which further lent a feeling of camaraderie to the proceedings. Duke also spoke at the Iowa dedication in November 1906, stating, "In that terrible ordeal we learned that we were truly the same people, and must remain the same nation."[53]

The Confederate dedications exhibited the same patriotism and reconciliation. Duke spoke at the 2nd Tennessee monument dedication in 1905, stating that "the dead who lie here, Federal and Confederate, all distinction between them forgotten, all enmity buried in the grave, shall be held in equal honor as American soldiers." Duke also spoke at the Alabama dedication in May 1907, returning to his theme of reconciliation. "But out of all that ordeal [war] we have come a stronger and a wiser people," he thundered amid the pouring rain. In applauding the establishment of the park, Duke spoke of a place "where citizens of a common and reunited country, all former enmity forgotten, may meet in amity to recall with proud remembrance the deeds of a sad but glorious past and witness equal honors paid to all the dead."[54]

At the UDC monument dedication in May 1917, the principal speaker, Bishop Thomas F. Gailor, the Episcopal bishop of Tennessee from 1898 to 1935, said that "the time has long since passed when a gathering like this in honor of the Confederate soldier could be in any way or degree construed as an occasion to revive outworn political controversies or reargue the questions that were at issue among our people fifty years ago." In dedicating the monument, he sent a message "to all our young men, not only in the South, but throughout the United States, to rejoice that they are Americans."[55]

Thus, the monuments themselves, the veterans dedicating them, and the early interpretation of the park spoke inwardly of noble sacrifice and courage at Shiloh, not the Lost Cause of the Civil War. What Lost Cause mentality that exists at Shiloh National Military Park is not easily recognized and exists only as a veiled link to the larger issues of the Civil War. The absence of any developmental-era monuments erected by Southern state legislatures supports this point. No Southern legislature allocated funds for a monument at Shiloh, and this lack of support can only argue that Southern legislatures, made up of veterans and sons of veterans, were not interested in commemorating some Civil War battlefields, particularly isolated Shiloh. Rather, the United Daughters of the Confederacy, which placed the Arkansas, Alabama, Joseph Wheeler, and UDC monuments, provided what Lost Cause mentality that does exist on the field. What *was* strongly and forcefully portrayed in the monuments at Shiloh was a sense of nationalism, reconciliation, and honor, which was clearly a sign of the times.

CHAPTER 7

"These Here Sticks"

The period from the park's establishment in 1894 to 1909 serves as the dominant and most important stage of Shiloh National Military Park's history. The decisions and actions made and taken in these first years produced the park and the interpretation that still dominates the site in the twenty-first century. It was also in these formative years that the organizational structure of the park crystallized, with Cadle delegating engineering control to Thompson and historical preeminence to Reed. Most importantly, it was during this stage that veterans tangibly paid tribute to their comrades with a collective national memory of the Civil War built around the heroism, bravery, courage, and sacrifice of the common soldier. Amid this stage of constructing a park, locating troop positions, erecting tablets and monuments, and dedicating them, however, a distinctive lifestyle and work process emerged in the isolated region Atwell Thompson described as "these here sticks."[1]

After the creation of the commission and establishment of the park, matters settled down into a busy routine. Veterans still came and went and work continued, but the major tasks of mapping, marking, and turning the land into a park slowly faded away while a structured operation of maintaining the park emerged.

Actions taken during the waning years of this first stage, however, had a particularly distinct effect on the park. Major changes to the organizational structure of the commission took place. Several original commissioners died, only to be replaced by other aging veterans. A continual cycle of replacement soon emerged. More importantly, as park life settled into a routine, the dominant leaders began to fade away. By 1905, Atwell Thompson would leave the park, cutting the active leadership down to two: Cadle and Reed. This development proved critical to the park's history in that it further consolidated power in the hands of Cadle and Reed.

Chairman Cadle dominated the building process. Carrying on the work of the commission from his office in Cincinnati, Cadle ran the operation with as much smoothness as the long distances and fragmented organization allowed. In Cincinnati, he and his trusted clerk, J. M. Riddell, carried on a massive correspondence with Thompson at Shiloh, Reed in Iowa, and the War Department in

Washington. Likewise, Cadle corresponded with the various commissioners who came and went, but such communication was never on the same level as his communication with Thompson and Reed.

Cadle stayed particularly busy traveling. He made frequent trips to the park for commission meetings, special events, and monument dedications. He also frequented Washington in official and unofficial capacities, often testifying before congressional committees regarding appropriations but also becoming involved in such efforts as erecting the Sherman statue on Pennsylvania Avenue. Cadle served as secretary of the "General Sherman Statue Committee" of the Society of the Army of the Tennessee. A good Republican, Cadle also attended several presidential inaugurations, participated in the inaugural parades, and even acted as what he called a "floor manager" at President William McKinley's inaugural ball. Cadle made other unofficial trips during his tenure, including travels in the West to visit his family, a trip to Rhode Island to bury his mother-in-law, and even a tour of Europe between March 5 and April 15, 1901.[2]

Cadle kept his clerk, J. M. Riddell, busy with the park's correspondence. He also tapped Riddell's clerical ability to type many of Reed's lengthy responses to alleged errors in interpretation or monument placement. Although Riddell stayed busy, he also became involved in a number of extracurricular activities. He studied law at night for three years before passing the bar examination in March 1899. An obviously proud Cadle reported to Reed that Riddell was "now a full fledged lawyer." Riddell also served as regimental quartermaster sergeant of the 1st Ohio National Guard, which forced him to spend at least some time away from his work.[3]

While Cadle consistently served on the commission in the early years of the park, his associate commissioners did not. As time passed, aged veterans died. This slimming of the ranks affected the commission especially hard because most of the commission members had been commanders during the battle and thus had been middle-aged men during the war. These older veterans, of course, died away before the younger generation of enlisted personnel, mere young men at Shiloh, passed on. The relative youth of Cadle and Reed facilitated their dominance of the commission for two decades.

The first commission member to die was Don Carlos Buell. Born in 1818, Buell was eighty years old when, after a lengthy illness, he died on November 19, 1898, at his home in Kentucky. Considering the stormy relationship he had had with Cadle and Reed, the two men did not miss him. Letters between Cadle and Reed discussed Buell's death matter-of-factly and then moved on to other park affairs, as if nothing significant had happened. Neither Cadle nor any commission representative attended the funeral, something they routinely did for others during Cadle's tenure as chairman. Buell was buried in Bellefontaine Cemetery, St. Louis, with no one from Shiloh present.[4]

Displaying an obvious lack of mourning, Cadle remarked to Reed that "there will be a lively scramble for his place [on the commission]." Soon, however, the secretary of war filled the void by appointing J. H. Ashcraft of Kentucky as the representative of the Army of the Ohio. Ashcraft had served at Shiloh as a first lieutenant in the 26th Kentucky Infantry and later, in 1864, received a wound at Brandenburg, Kentucky. His appointment was dated January 12, 1899. Apparently, Ashcraft fit in better than Buell had. On numerous occasions, such as Cadle's trip to Europe, he acted as commission chairman in Cadle's absence.[5]

Shortly after Buell's death, Robert F. Looney also passed away. Born on August 5, 1824, Looney was seventy-five at the time of his death, a year to the day after Buell died. After several months of failing health, he died of heart failure on November 19, 1899, at his home in Memphis. Although Cadle and Reed showed none of the coolness toward Looney they had felt for Buell, they probably did not miss his atrocious handwriting, which made reading his prose a difficult chore.[6]

Despite Cadle's support of land agent J. W. Irwin, the secretary of war appointed Tennessee politician Josiah Patterson to replace Looney as the Confederate representative. Born on April 14, 1837, in Morgan County, Alabama, Patterson had practiced law in Alabama before the Civil War. Serving as a first lieutenant in the 1st Alabama Cavalry at Shiloh, Patterson remained in service throughout the war, eventually becoming colonel of the 5th Alabama Cavalry. After the war, he practiced law in both Alabama and Memphis, Tennessee, where he entered politics. He served in the Tennessee state legislature and three terms in the United States House of Representatives. His appointment to the Shiloh National Military Park Commission came on January 1, 1900.[7]

Patterson seemed to participate in the affairs of the commission only rarely, surely no more than Looney had. He certainly did not cause any problems for Cadle and Reed. Cadle even wrote Reed to applaud Patterson's appointment, stating that he "will be in accord with us." After a short and uneventful term, Patterson himself died on February 10, 1904, and was buried in Forrest Hill Cemetery in Memphis.[8]

To replace Patterson as the Confederate representative, the secretary of war appointed General Basil W. Duke. Duke was born on May 28, 1838, in Scott County, Kentucky. He practiced law in St. Louis before the war and enlisted as a private under his brother-in-law, John Hunt Morgan. At Shiloh, Duke served as acting adjutant for Morgan's unit. He later became colonel of what came to be called the 2nd Kentucky Cavalry. He participated in Morgan's spirited raids and was captured in Ohio. Paroled and exchanged, he became a brigadier general on September 15, 1864. After the war, Duke practiced law and entered politics. His appointment as commissioner of Shiloh National Military Park came on February 20, 1904, and Duke served a long but uneventful term. He had no startling effect on the commission, although he spoke at numerous monument dedications.[9]

Not only death but also congressional action shuffled the makeup of the commission. New legislation attempted to change not only the Shiloh commission but also all military park commissions. There was a distinct effort in Congress to limit the number of commissioners at each park and even to create one national commission to oversee all the military parks. This consolidating effort was, of course, the result of the completion of the initial establishment of each park. Reorganization would save funds, especially since there were some thirty-four new park bills then pending in Congress. A separate commission for each battlefield would cost entirely too much money.[10]

Because of the need for fiscal frugality, as well as for coordinated effort, talk of combining the commissions emerged as early as 1900, but it did not take organized form until 1902, when it suddenly appeared in the Sundry Civil Bill of that year. The powerful Joseph G. Cannon (Republican) of Illinois wrote new legislation authorizing only two commissioners per park. The House Military Affairs Committee held several important hearings on the issue, at which time the obvious issue of costs came to the forefront of the discussion. The bill failed, primarily because of the five commissions' opposition, but it highlighted again the congressional doubts about the expensive military parks. The debate also emphasized the lack of a central policy governing the military park system. [11]

Although this effort to consolidate the commissions failed, it did produce other results. Because of the obvious costs discussed in the hearings, Congress began implementing the "Antietam Plan," which established a process of buying only lines of battle and a few significant historic sites, not an entire battlefield. Implemented at Antietam and later at sundry other battlefields, such as those of the Wilderness and Atlanta campaigns, this plan soon became a major policy of the War Department. Meanwhile, the efforts to combine the park commissions continued to emerge periodically, and a form of such legislation ultimately passed in 1912.[12]

While Cadle handled the affairs of the commission and the changes in its organization, Thompson continued his engineering work on the park, actually serving as resident director for a number of years. He settled into his work, overseeing his engineers and laborers, most notably his chief assistants, M. A. Kirby, Will Pride, F. A. Large, and Simpson Keller. A native of Tuscumbia, Alabama, Keller was the brother of the famous Helen Keller, who actually visited Simpson on several occasions. The two could be seen riding their double-seated bicycle through the park. Thompson loathed the meager accommodations at Pittsburg Landing and continually tried to get better facilities. He developed plans to build a small two-room office building for his use, which he built "near the center of the park." Likewise, he pushed for a residence of his own, finally settling his family into Thomas Walker's old residence in Review Field. Other members of his engineering staff also resided at the house.[13]

Thompson oversaw the physical building of the park despite frequent health problems, such as a severe sickness that required surgery, absence from work for a month, and a cocaine prescription. His men, meanwhile, worked to clear underbrush from the timber, which made the battlefield more historically accurate. They were always careful, however, to leave undergrowth where reports mentioned heavy foliage. Thompson's men likewise worked to return field lines to their actual place at the time of the battle. The workers also placed foundations for the state monuments, built the mortuary and headquarters monuments, and placed the tablets and artillery pieces. Perhaps the most important construction was building roads. At a cost of $83,983.18, Thompson's crews had by 1906 quarried gravel from local pits and surfaced some twenty-five miles of roads within the park, most twenty feet wide and "thoroughly ditched and drained." Most of the time Thompson took extreme care to maintain the historical accuracy of the April 1862 roads, and his men did little grading. Total accuracy could not always be attained, however, because of increased road construction carried out by Union troops after the battle in preparation for their advance on Corinth. Thompson could with certainty locate all the April 1862 roads, but he may have missed the exact dating concerning pre- or post-battle thoroughfares. Thompson did straighten several "ugly kinks" in the roads but for the most part maintained their historical accuracy. Work crews also built stone gutters and wooden bridges to facilitate travel in inclement weather and filled gullies and planted grass to stop erosion.[14]

Other physical improvements occurred throughout the years, including telephone service to the area in September 1896. The government funded a warehouse at the landing in 1901. Hardin County placed a steel bridge across Snake Creek in 1904, which required park work to connect the road and bridge. Thompson dammed Dill Branch to create a swimming hole and placed a wooden bridge across the creek in 1905. Workers fenced Bloody Pond in 1908 to keep out "hogs and cattle that were making it a nuisance." Other projects never survived past planning stages, including an electric railroad to offer access to the park and a ninety-foot concrete tower at Pittsburg Landing. The commission also recommended building a first-class road to Corinth to offer accessibility to the park. This project, however, did not take place until the 1920s.[15]

Thompson's laborers, at times as many as one hundred, worked hard and received a day's wage of one dollar. Cemetery workers went on strike in 1904 over their dollar-a-day pay, but park employees seemed to be satisfied. Over time, particularly during the Progressive Era, their work hours were reduced with the continual advancement of civil service rules, such as a half-day's work on Saturdays and eight-hour work days. Originally, laborers toiled twelve hours a day. Frequent work delays also resulted when quarterly appropriations ran out. On other occasions during summers, Thompson gave his workers two hours off in the heat of

Fig. 20. Much gravel had to be hauled to build park roads. Here laborers pose at one of the many gravel pits located at the park. Courtesy of Shiloh National Military Park.

Fig. 21. Bloody Pond around 1908, showing some of the renovations such as the encircling fence. Courtesy of Shiloh National Military Park.

midday. Likewise, workers had several days off during each year's Thanksgiving and Christmas holidays.[16]

Some fatal incidents took place during park construction. As the last wagons of the day were being loaded just before quitting time on March 31, 1899, a cave-in occurred at one of the gravel pits, killing three men. Two left wives and small children, while the third was a minor who left a widowed mother. Two more injured persons lost legs to amputation in this "deplorable accident." The pit later became known, somewhat morbidly, as "Dead Man's Gravel Pit." Another fatal affair occurred in September 1901, when a smallpox epidemic broke out. At least one small child died, and Thompson stopped work for several weeks. An unspecified accident also occurred in March 1905, killing one man.[17]

By 1905, Thompson's work at Shiloh seemed to be slowing. He had built most of the roads and drainage systems, and he had also completed the vast majority of the monumentation. Thompson apparently tired of his purely bureaucratic job of overseeing laborers and performing maintenance on the almost-finished park. As a result, he informed Cadle in October 1905 of his desire to find "private work in his profession" and bought a house in Columbia, Tennessee. Not knowing what to do about Thompson, Cadle simply labeled him as "absent on leave without pay." Thompson did return periodically thereafter, however, to perform some skilled engineering work.[18]

In 1907, War Department officials realized that Thompson had never officially resigned. In an effort to clear their rolls, which also included the land agent, J. W. Irwin, the War Department requested a proper resignation from him. He submitted one in January 1907 but dated it December 30, 1905, the actual date he had left the park.[19]

In reality, Thompson left in a huff, writing in the commission's "Daily Events" ledger book, "Left Shiloh National Military Park this afternoon for good–Atwell Thompson." When he left his residence, he even went so far as to dig up the yard's bushes, shrubbery, and an asparagus bed. Cadle was obviously angry at this behavior, stating to Reed, "I think we can get along without his services in the future." Reed likewise seemed to be glad Thompson was gone. Years later, he wrote of Thompson with obvious derision, stating that the engineer "took great pride in road work and would sacrifice any tree rather than make a false curve in the road."[20]

When Thompson departed, Cadle and Reed had a decision to make. They could not legally leave the park without a resident director to oversee work and answer the vast correspondence. Reed and Cadle discussed placing F. A. Large, E. R. Underhill, or T. J. Lewis in charge, but both believed that none of the three could handle the task. The only option left was for Reed himself to move to Shiloh, which he did in 1905. Reed and his family settled into Thompson's place in Review Field, commonly known as "Review Place."[21]

Now living in the park, Reed continued to direct its historical arm. In 1909, he reissued his book, incorporating within it the corrections that veterans had pointed out to him. He also became the chief preservationist, tending to relics such as a complete musket Dr. W. J. Petty found in Shiloh Branch. "It is remarkably well preserved, is loaded, and has a cap on it," one employee confirmed. Reed also fought efforts to destroy or alter the battleground. Senator William Bate, a friend of the park, wanted to dam up Shiloh Branch and create a lake just south of the proposed monument near Shiloh Church. Such a lake would, according to him, provide a beautiful setting in the area where he and his men had fought. Amazingly, Bate believed the lake "essential to the proper or[na]mentation of that noted point" and convinced himself that Cadle and Reed were supportive. He wrote of "the lake we contemplate." In reality, Reed and Cadle never supported the idea. Cadle in fact wrote that "the scheme is entirely out of the question and will never be carried out" but nevertheless had surveyors map out the proposed lake to assuage "Bate's insistency." The lake would alter the historical ground, which the enabling legislation prohibited, and Union veterans also fought the idea. The pressure for damming the creek, however, only ended with Bate's death in 1905.[22]

In his historical work, Reed also became involved in a Shiloh exhibit that toured the nation. He and Cadle put together a sampling of Reed's work that

Fig. 22. A view of Review Field looking east along the Hamburg–Purdy Road. At left is the 77th Pennsylvania Monument. In the background at left is "Review Place," Atwell Thompson's residence until his resignation and afterwards D. W. Reed's residence. Courtesy of Shiloh National Military Park.

included tablets (Cadle sent the 11th Iowa tablet—his regiment's), artillery pieces, Reed's maps, inscription books for each monument and tablet on the field, copies of Reed's book, and twenty-four "photographic views of scenes on the park." Workers built frames for the maps and the enlarged photos from walnut trees cut in the park. This example of Shiloh monumentation and interpretation appeared at the 1904 Louisiana Purchase Exposition in St. Louis. In 1905, the maps and photographs appeared at the Lewis and Clark Exposition in Portland, Oregon. Cadle and Reed were not pleased with the idea of taking park property and sending it away, especially without a park employee accompanying it. They did so, however, "at the insistence of Mr. John C. Scofield, representative of the War Department." Fortunately, Cadle was able to send employees to look after Shiloh's possessions at the St. Louis event. Later, Cadle somewhat humorously included in his annual report the fact that "a commemorative diploma has been awarded to the Commission for its exhibit."[23]

In a day before modern museum techniques and interpretation, Reed made no apparent effort to place Shiloh in the context of the war, much less the political, economic, and social context of the period. What interpretive effort Reed made in these early years was strictly confined to tactical troop movements. No interpretive visitor center existed. His large maps hung on office walls and a few relics existed for visitors to view, but Reed made no concerted effort to give people a hands-on experience. Adding to the disjointed nature of interpretation, uninformed locals gave guided tours for twenty-five cents.[24]

Such a policy made sense given the effort at reconciliation between North and South and since the main audience in these early days consisted of veterans and their families. As noted earlier, old soldiers returned to see the places where they had fought. Consequently, Reed marked the field first with wooden signs and then with iron road markers, locating for the visitor important positions. Likewise, Reed concentrated on giving veterans a tour of the field by unit, placing within the text of the tablets the location of the specific unit's next position on the field. Other interpretive efforts similarly pointed visitors to the field itself. Reed's book, *The Battle of Shiloh and the Organizations Engaged*, was strictly a tactical study, as were Reed's maps. Often, Reed and the veterans on his staff gave tours of the field, continuing the tactical interpretation in that way. Even the broader interpretive efforts, such as the exhibits at the two world's fairs, were inward-looking, giving the viewer mostly an idea of the monumentation at Shiloh.[25]

Reed, of course, became even more closely involved when he moved to the park after Thompson's resignation. Settling his family into Thompson's former residence in Review Field, Reed and his family (including everyone's favorite—Reed's daughter Minnie) created a home. He discovered the easygoing lifestyle Thompson and the many residents had enjoyed in the park. Leisurely evenings filled with sounds of fox hunters (fox hunting was the exception to the no-hunting rule) or casual strolls throughout the park offered a haven from a hectic lifestyle. Also offering entertainment were the animals of the park, such as Pat, a "mischievous harness horse" left behind by the company building the Iowa monument. Pat became a favorite at the landing and "was closely associated with Park affairs for several years." Other forms of amusement included swimming in Dill Branch. Returning veterans also provided entertainment, as did inquisitive visitors. Holidays offered special festivities for visitors and veterans alike, including amenities such as lemonade stands on Memorial Day.[26]

The center of activity was Pittsburg Landing, where almost all visitors arrived by boat. Roads around the turn of the century were still very poor, even forcing the commission on occasion to delay visits in order to get to the park. At the landing itself was the park's headquarters office, as well as that of the cemetery. Sam Chambers ran a small store and hotel just inland from the landing. After the government bought the land and buildings, Chambers remained at the head of the store on contract. Later, W. P. Littlefield ran the store and hotel, along with the ferry, under a similar contract. Thousands of veterans returned to the landing on each anniversary of the battle and on Memorial Day, although rain usually attended the May memorial services. Almost each entry in the park's "Daily Events" diary speaks of the "usual rain" or "customary rain" on Memorial Day. Another haven of activity was Shiloh Church, which remained an active congregation. In the years after the park's development, Confederate veterans would meet at the church rather than at the cemetery. The Rea Springs picnic area was also a popular area near the church.[27]

Politics offered a lively pastime for Shiloh residents and employees as well. Inhabitants closely watched national and local elections while Cadle became actively involved in inaugurations and other political actions. The war with Spain in 1898 caused a stir at Pittsburg Landing. Cadle himself offered his services to the secretary of war, saying, "I am ready for such service as you may direct." Residents of the park received periodic updates on the war, but the park's isolation, of course, delayed most reports. With the victory won, residents applauded the effort. Even Atwell Thompson, born in Ireland, ended a letter to Reed with "Hurrah for the army and navy." The military did not use Shiloh as a troop staging area like Chickamauga, most likely because of its isolation. There were, however, troops in the park during the conflict, including "regulars" and at least "one regiment of volunteer Cavalry."[28]

Because of the community atmosphere that developed in the park, sickness and misfortune affected the entire neighborhood. A "slight but distinct earthquake shock" sent fear through the area on February 13, 1901. The previously mentioned smallpox epidemic broke out in September 1901, causing a work stoppage for several weeks. Neighborhood care went to the sick, most of whom worked together at the park. When a young boy became ill in September 1898 with a 105-degree fever and congestion, the neighborhood immediately showed its concern for the young man, with one employee reporting to Cadle that "by placing mustard all over his body the doctor pulled him thro."[29]

A community spirit also emerged between the park and the cemetery, the other governmental facility at Pittsburg Landing. Until 1933, when government reorganization placed both under the National Park Service, the two agencies coexisted as separate entities. The cemetery superintendent and his laborers, however, worked in close cooperation with park officials, even allowing tents and offices in the cemetery. The two entities regularly worked together for the common goal of honoring and preserving the battlefield and dead of Shiloh.[30]

Other examples of small but beneficial cooperation occurred in the years after the park commission took form. When Thompson ran out of surveying markers, the cemetery superintendent, John W. Shaw, loaned small gravestones for use in marking the battlefield. When the commission found it was out of cement, cemetery officials gladly loaned part of their supply. Battle relics, including the drum long on display in the visitor center, changed hands frequently between the cemetery and park officials. Even War Department officials took notice of the teamwork, commending both on the "splendid spirit of helpfulness that exists between the Park and Cemetery activities at Shiloh." As one official said, "Cooperation of this sort was and is in the full interests of the Government."[31]

While a spirit of cooperation generally existed throughout the decades, there were also moments of disagreement. One source of minor contention resulted over use of the cemetery lodge and the erection of commission tents. Cadle had wanted to get out of the cemetery as early as 1898, but he could not get the appropriation to build an office and quarters. The problem emerged again in 1905 when the cemetery superintendent declared the need to use the lodge for cemetery purposes. The park commission complied with the War Department ruling in favor of the cemetery, which of course owned the building in the first place. Cadle now searched for other facilities to house the commission's office. Local houses were an option, but the commission had to settle on a room in the nearby hotel at Pittsburg Landing.[32]

The two sides exchanged more controversial words when the cemetery superintendent requested that the commission remove its "very unsightly" tents. Cadle had his workers move the tents to a position near Chambers's store, which was now park property. Laborers aligned the tents facing east, but Cadle warned them to wait before aligning Reed's tent so that the picky historian could place it where he wanted it. Reed lived in his tent until he moved permanently to Review Field. The commission inhabited the tents until 1909.[33]

More serious disputes periodically broke up the community spirit at Pittsburg Landing. Acts of violence and unlawfulness, common in such secluded and isolated areas, seemed to be the norm at Shiloh. Reed called the rough people of the

Fig. 23. The second Shiloh Church, built in the 1880s. Courtesy of Shiloh National Military Park.

area "lawless characters that invest the region." Offenses ranged from throwing mud on park signs to murder. Park officials prohibited gambling in the park and also enforced laws banning alcohol. On Memorial Day, May 30, 1901, for example, Mrs. Chambers found a box of beer and a jug of whiskey in a storeroom above her store. Cadle confiscated the alcohol and "destroyed [it] by pouring it upon the ground." Often, Range Rider F. A. Large arrested drunks on the park grounds.[34]

Worse offenses also took place. One individual was caught in Nashville selling relics from the battlefield. He sold four hundred dollars' worth before being apprehended. In February 1897, thieves robbed a nearby post office, delaying mail to Pittsburg Landing for several days. There was even a murder when, on January 14, 1899, Perry Jones, a park employee, got into a family disturbance with "one of the Wicker boys." Wicker shot and killed Jones, whereupon Jones's son stabbed Wicker four times. Atwell Thompson reported, "I presume that some of the Wicker relations will kill young Jones, and the two families [will be] 'wiped out' before they get through." He continued, "I wish our neighbors . . . were more civilized." Later in the year, in June 1899, vandals shot thirteen times into G. W. Moore's house in Cloud Field and set it on fire. Moore emerged from the house only to be a target again. He lived through the affair and was able to put out the fire. Thompson informed Reed of the matter, stating, "I regard this with some concern." He continued, "It concerns us as it was a deliberate attempt to destroy U.S. property."[35]

Despite such occasional lawlessness, life at Pittsburg Landing was normally quiet. By 1909 the park was almost totally marked with monuments and tablets. The founding commission had met the challenges of isolation, lack of funds, poor roads, inadequate office and housing space, and historiographical disputes to produce a first-rate park. The commission had indeed done a remarkably good job of making a park out of nothing and doing so despite recurring controversy.

The park, however, was at a crossroads. By the end of this first phase, the dominant group of Cadle, Reed, and Thompson was beginning to break apart, setting the stage for a new phase of park history. More importantly, this next stage would include a shift from commemoration and monumentation by veterans in this collective national memory to a management-and-perpetuation mentality by sons of veterans. The memory of the Civil War was alive and well, but it was passing from veterans to a younger generation. Although life at Shiloh was quiet and enjoyable for the most part, underneath lay tremors of broad changes that would forever affect the park. The result, by 1909, was a completed park that was passing into the hands of men and women who had not fought there. Now the real test would come. No doubt many veterans wondered and worried over the question of whether this younger generation would maintain a passionate memory of the Civil War as the old soldiers, now slipping quietly away, had done. Would Shiloh continue to serve the function for which the battlefield founders, and indeed the nation, had established it?

CHAPTER **8**

The Changing of the Guard

"At 5:26 P.M. a cyclone visited the Park." So began the October 14, 1909, entry in the Shiloh National Military Park Commission's "Daily Events" ledger book. The destruction that resulted was severe, heavily damaging the park's most important area, the Pittsburg Landing sector. The storm, as past Shiloh historian Charles Shedd has described it, "placed a tragic period at the end of the first stage of development." Indeed, the initial phase of park development, that of veterans promoting a national memory of the Civil War built upon reconciliation, had ended. By 1909, the park was almost complete, with only scattered dedications of monuments in the decades to come. The next years began the period of consolidation, which would continue throughout the twentieth century.[1]

The tornado of 1909 actually produced some beneficial results at Shiloh. The commission had concentrated before 1909 on building the park and its monumentation, often doing so at the expense of infrastructure, such as offices and living quarters for the commissioners and workers. Once the park was completed, however, time and money became available for development of this infrastructure. Yet, just because the funds existed did not mean that offices and quarters would be built quickly. Cadle, Reed, and Thompson had already discovered Congress's slow appropriation process on everything that was not absolutely critical. It was the 1909 tornado, however, that highlighted the need for the replacement of the destroyed, mediocre support structures, as well as for the building of new facilities. The storm quickened their needed construction at Pittsburg Landing and thus proved to be an important watershed in the history of Shiloh National Military Park.

The tornado reached Pittsburg Landing around sundown on October 14, but local residents had noticed strange weather patterns all day. One reported that "all day the elements seemed to be disturbed, and an electric storm and general upheaval and disturbed, unbalanced weather conditions had been noticed." As the storm approached, locals noticed that "the clouds were seen to clash, boil together, spew with electricity, suddenly fall, rapidly whirl . . . with intense velocity and [a] deafening roar."[2]

The storm tore a swath of destruction two hundred yards wide and a mile and one-half long through the eastern edge of the park. It entered the grounds from the north through Snake Creek bottom, destroying many "large and valuable trees." The tornado then ascended the hills north of the park and destroyed much of the Hagy family's property, "plowing up the ground for many yards." Once in the park, the storm's course changed to a southeasterly direction, which took it straight toward Pittsburg Landing.[3]

At the landing itself, life was going on as usual in the minutes before the storm struck. Hotel operator W. P. Littlefield had left the area with one of his children en route to Adamsville. His wife, remaining at the landing with the other five children, went about her tasks of running the hotel and livery stable. Soon, she and the children noticed the black cloud forming to the north. Mrs. Littlefield remembered that "we gave very little attention to it at first." Becoming more alarmed, however, she "hurried the preparation of supper."[4]

Two guests arrived at the hotel about this time. John Godwin and R. W. Lemmon had traveled from Kossuth, Mississippi, to tour the battlefield and arrived just as the Littlefields finished supper. One of the Littlefield sons was checking them into a room at the hotel when the tornado hit the building. Over in the cemetery, Superintendent George Dean and his wife sat in the office of the lodge. Mrs. Dean remarked about the roar and, approaching a window, saw the storm looming. She ran upstairs to close another window but never made it. Glass began to pepper the couple as they ran for safety to the inward portion of the lodge.[5]

When the storm struck, the buildings at Pittsburg Landing almost ceased to exist. Death reigned in the hotel. The two guests from Mississippi were killed instantly, as was the Littlefield son, Luther, who was checking them in. All were blown some fifty to seventy-five feet away. Another Littlefield son, Otis, having just told his mother not to "get excited," also perished in the storm. The park's masonry foreman, T. J. Lewis, was not killed but had to dig himself out of the debris that had once been the hotel. The surviving members of the Littlefield family did likewise, as did schoolteacher Bertha Hardin, who boarded in the hotel. Hardin had run into the cookroom with the Littlefields and could only think, "Lord save me." She remembered that "everything was moved from over, around and under us, we were moved a few feet from where we were standing."[6]

Just as quickly as it appeared, the storm vanished, leaving an eerie calm. Survivors began to emerge from the rubble as they quickly gathered their wits about them. Bertha Hardin awoke to find herself in the cookroom under the brick chimney, which had fallen on top of her. She was trapped by brick lying on her hair, with her "head fastened down so that I could hardly move." Her foot was also pinned beneath a beam; she struggled to get up. Meanwhile, Lewis unearthed himself and "began to wander, but everything was so dark and everything was so changed." In the cemetery, Superintendent Dean awoke to find his office gutted, one wall missing, and the building on fire. Flames also destroyed what was left of the hotel.[7]

Terror reigned as night fell on the tragic scene. Survivors soon put out the fires, and the heartbreaking task of locating those who had perished began. Cadle later reported that "the entire park force was employed all night in rescuing and caring for the injured." Local physicians arrived from as far away as Adamsville. There was jubilation when a survivor emerged, but extreme sadness attended the location of a dead body.[8]

W. P. Littlefield in Adamsville spent suspenseful hours wondering about his family. He tried to telephone, but the lines were down. He received news of the loss of his sons at 10:00 P.M. and immediately began the torturous journey home, arriving near midnight. There, he found his surviving family at the cemetery lodge, "bleeding and bruised almost from head to foot." He then faced "the saddest of all sad scenes ever witnessed by parents"—his two lifeless sons lying in the undestroyed blacksmith shop. "I kneeled between them and caressed their cold cheeks, and bade them a long farewell," he remembered. His only solace was the "hope to meet them in Beulah land, and bask in the sunshine of God's eternal grace." In all, seven people were killed, including the two Littlefield sons and the two guests from Mississippi. Two more perished at John W. Jordan's home and one at the Hagy residence. Thirty-three people were injured, including two who later died of their injuries—a baby who died the next morning and an adult who died some two weeks later.[9]

The long night finally ended. "The sun rose to cast its gentle rays over the darkened and gloom casted scene," remembered one survivor. The shaken residents then saw the magnitude of the destruction. Almost everything in the path of the storm had been swept away, totaling thirteen government buildings. The hotel and livery stable were destroyed, with the loss of several horses. The store was toppled and burned. The small house occupied by T. J. Lewis was "deposited . . . in the ravine north of the cemetery." Other park facilities were destroyed, including the warehouse at the landing and various stables and sheds. Similarly, the commission tents near the hotel had been no match for the storm and were completely leveled. The national cemetery also suffered significant destruction as the storm blew toolhouses and barns away. Only the lodge remained, but it sustained heavy damage. The south wall was blown out and many records lost. The storm likewise destroyed all the trees, and many headstones were broken or made to lean, as was the 9th Illinois monument, which was blown down the terrace. Perhaps more importantly, the storm blew away the Grant tree and left only small pieces of wood, one of which cemetery superintendent Dean retrieved in order to make a cane. Viewing the destruction some days later, Cadle observed that "the wreckage from all the other buildings seemed to lodge in the tree tops of the Cemetery['s] down[ed] trees."[10]

Damage was severe in the cemetery, but the tablets and artillery pieces near the landing suffered only minor destruction. The major devastation came to the

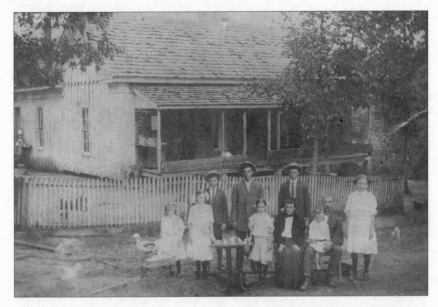

Fig. 24. The Shiloh "cyclone" destroyed the Jordan house on October 14, 1909. Two were killed, including Rubye Jordan, shown here on the extreme left, and John Marshall Jordan, in the center back row. Wife and mother, Julia Marie Sowell Jordan, seated fourth from right, died of injuries two weeks later. Courtesy of Jordan Descendants Collection, Shiloh, Tennessee.

three-year-old Iowa monument. The top portion fell to the east, breaking the arm of the statue of Fame and cracking the stones below. Many of the park's trees were also uprooted, including many in the ravines north and south of the cemetery. The storm also destroyed many old trees in Dill Branch ravine.[11]

Perhaps most damaging was the loss of official records collected since the park's establishment. Housed in the hotel room used as an office, these records were scattered or burned beyond use. Viewing the destruction days later, Cadle lamented the loss of "all the records, notes or surveys, maps, original drawings, orders, correspondence, supplies, heavy furniture, office desks with roll tops (2), large table, office chairs, files cases, library of 300 volumes, stove, valuable relics, *everything* has disappeared completely." The storm also carried away many valuable relics from the Indian mounds, including bones, wood pieces, and ear ornaments. Cadle bemoaned the loss, stating that "not one thing has been found but a few penalty envelopes, still in a heap on the place occupied by the office." In the days after the storm, reports of discovered Shiloh material came from far away. In Nixon, five miles across the river, residents found a penalty stamp and a few leaves from the Shiloh library books. Perhaps most amazing, a resident of Florence, Alabama, forty-five air miles away, found General Basil W. Duke's blanket, which had been kept in his tent near the hotel. Cadle marveled that it

Fig. 25. The cemetery lodge, showing the damage done by the tornado of 1909. Courtesy of Shiloh National Military Park.

was "without rent or damage except the mud." Residents of Florence also found several flags that had been flying in the cemetery when the storm hit, and a nearby farmer found one of Cadle's mining business cards as well as several letters that had been in his tent.[12]

Quickly, Cadle and the commission began the process of rebuilding at the landing, while the families who lost loved ones began the much harder process of beginning life again. Cadle and Ashcraft arrived on October 20, with Duke following later. Once at the landing, they began to take stock of what was left and what could not be used. Because of the storm's wide destruction, Cadle, Duke, and Ashcraft had no place to stay and had to make pallets on the floor of Reed's undamaged house at Review Field. There, Cadle found Reed taking care of five of the injured.[13]

Workers were able to preserve some of the materials. The shop where laborers stored tools and supplies was blown over but not destroyed, thus saving much of the material contained inside. Likewise, the blacksmith shop was "moved on its foundations but not destroyed." Perhaps helping the feelings of many shocked by death, the surviving animals also showed their resilience. Everybody's favorite horse, Pat, was in the barn when the storm tore it down. Touring the destruction during the night, T. J. Lewis located the remnants of the barn and was cheered when Pat was able to "nicker" when he called for him. Lewis also noticed that the chicken coop was intact and that the chickens "walked out next morning ready for their feed, as though nothing had happened."[14]

Fig. 26. The damaged Iowa Monument. The state would repair the memorial and rededicate it on the fiftieth anniversary of the battle in 1912. Courtesy of Shiloh National Military Park.

The destruction at Pittsburg Landing was more severe than what the workforce or the annual appropriation could handle, thus necessitating help from Congress. Cadle halted all unnecessary work in order to repair the damage. For example, he delayed work on a new bridge at Dill Branch and also on the regular army monuments. Fortunately, the War Department told Cadle to submit a list of needs, and Congress responded with an emergency appropriation of $19,500 for the park, $8,000 for the cemetery, and $15,000 for repair of the Iowa monument. Congress delegated the money for the Iowa monument with the understanding that the state would reimburse the federal government.[15]

Rebuilding began immediately. The entire park's workforce of around twenty laborers began cleanup the next day, and they cleared out much of the damage within several weeks. In all, Cadle estimated that the storm uprooted ten thousand trees, most by the roots. Laborers turned the stumps over to fill in the holes and made lumber out of the bulk of the downed trees, which they used to rebuild outbuildings such as barns, warehouses, and storage sheds. By July 1910, Cadle reported that all the buildings except commission quarters and offices had been replaced. There was even a new store and hotel. As of June 30, 1910, the rebuilding disbursements totaled $10,092.32.[16]

Reconstruction also took place in the cemetery. Fallen trees were removed and the entire area relandscaped. Workers repaired or straightened headstones, and the 9th Illinois monument was restored. More noticeably, a massive building program began. A new lodge, finished in 1911 and sitting just north of the former

Fig. 27. A view of the damage to the National Cemetery. Note the leaning headstones. Courtesy of Shiloh National Military Park.

lodge's location, replaced the one so devastated in the tornado. A new brick wall, also finished in 1911, went up on the western edge of the cemetery, completely enclosing the grounds. In the same year, a barn and toolshed replaced the structures devastated two years earlier, and a pump house with a gasoline engine was added for comfort. In 1912, two well houses and a "water closet" were built.[17]

Building a new park office proved to be a particularly difficult task. Reed reported that space in the old hotel had been unsatisfactory despite its being "quite commodious and in good condition." Fortunately, the War Department quickly approved a new office building, but the emergency appropriation did not cover its cost. As a result, the commission used what money it had to build a large foundation, begun on June 20, 1910, and later used future appropriations to finish the job. Workers completed the new office building, a two-story brick structure, in December 1910.[18]

Reed also began to rebuild the park's library. All the books had been lost in the storm, with those recovered so badly damaged as to be unfit for further use. Reed asked various states to provide regimental histories, but by mid-November, he had received only four books. John Obreiter, chairman of the Pennsylvania commission, sent several books and reminded Reed that "great oaks from small acorns grow." Reed himself placed another copy of his 12th Iowa history in the library, writing in the front, "Presented to 'Shiloh Library,' after New Office was completed in lieu of copy destroyed by Cyclone. By the author. D. W. Reed— January 2, 1911."[19]

The Iowa monument was also rebuilt at a total cost of $7,340, well under the appropriation. Iowa paid the bill, and the remainder of the delegated money was returned to the U.S. Treasury. Iowa officials, including the governor and "a large delegation of its citizens," held an elaborate rededication ceremony on April 6–7, 1912, exactly fifty years after the battle of Shiloh.[20]

Although the 1909 tornado had a devastating effect on government facilities at Pittsburg Landing, the rebuilding process created a newer and better-equipped park. Now, commissioners had a first-rate office building to carry on their work, as well as space for quarters, ending the need for tents. The park gained a new hotel and store, adding to visitor accommodations. The cemetery also received much-needed improvements. In his annual report for 1911, Reed summed up the good wrought in the terrible and tragic storm: "With the exception of the loss of valuable records, books, maps, relics, etc., [and, of course, lives] the restoration puts the park in much better order than before the storm." Even the loss of archives was less severe than it might have been because Cadle had kept a major portion of the files in Cincinnati, thereby preserving many letters and documents for future generations.[21]

The massive storm also produced the first major change in the commission's composition. It had previously endured deaths such as those of Buell, Looney, and Patterson, but these had made little real difference to the park's affairs. Even Thompson's departure had had little detrimental effect; in fact, it had forced Reed to move to Tennessee, consolidating the park's affairs even more firmly in the hands of Cadle and Reed.

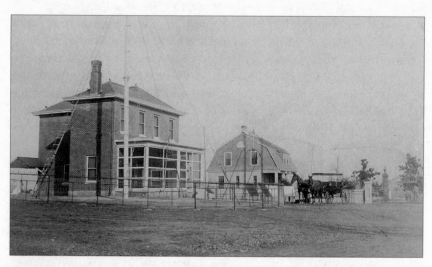

Fig. 28. The tornado resulted in a massive building program. The new headquarters building was the first permanent housing the commission had. Courtesy of Shiloh National Military Park.

Immediately after the storm, Reed asked the War Department to make F. A. Large the assistant superintendent, so that he could help Reed in the park cleanup. Cadle and Reed had encouraged this appointment before in recognition of Large's good work as Range Rider, but the War Department had refused, probably because of Large's August 1908 threat to resign over insufficient pay. As Range Rider and special deputy U.S. marshal, Large was also outside of civil service rules, having been originally appointed by a special order of the president. Large had been granted the pay raise in 1908, but then he resigned a few months later because of severe illness. Eldon R. Underhill replaced him as Range Rider. Because of the massive destruction, however, the department allowed Large's reemployment. Recovered completely from his illness, Large returned to work as assistant superintendent in November 1909.[22]

The major change occurred in January 1910. Cadle received notice from the secretary of war that "for some time past the Department has been thoroughly dissatisfied with your method of conducting business. . . . It is therefore requested that you immediately forward to me your resignation as a member of said commission." Without even giving notice to Reed, Cadle resigned as commission chairman, effective January 31, 1910.[23]

Very little is known about the causes of the War Department's action. Apparently, Cadle was no longer doing his job. But why? The only direct evidence, a biographical description of Cadle in the *Dictionary of Alabama Biography*, is that he suffered some type of health problems because of "exposure" resulting from the tornado "and became disabled." This makes little sense, however, because Cadle and the other commissioners stayed at Reed's residence at Review Field. Adding to the mystery is the secrecy with which he offered his resignation. Cadle did not even tell his trusted friend Reed, who had to read about it in the newspapers.[24]

Cadle had suffered from various ailments during his tenure as chairman. By 1909, he was seventy-three years old and, as recently as 1908, had suffered a severe case of lumbago, an arthritic condition. He missed the dedication of the Minnesota monument in April 1908 because of "my severe illness." The best possible guess is that Cadle's health deteriorated drastically with the increased activity of rebuilding the park, and he realized that such stress was something that his feeble health simply could not take. Supporting this supposition is the fact that Cadle died after an extended illness at his home in Cincinnati on January 13, 1913, only three years later. After a solemn funeral led by Union General Grenville Dodge and Rev. George A. Thayer, Cadle was cremated and buried in his hometown of Muscatine, Iowa.[25]

Apparently, there is more to the story than that. Reed and Cadle had always been close friends and confidants. Yet, Reed made no mention of Cadle's 1913 death. The only mention of Cadle after his resignation is found in minute records of the commission regarding an effort to retrieve from his possession the commission's "minute book." More importantly, there was apparently some correspondence between Reed and the War Department over Cadle's failure to respond to Reed's requests and inquiries. Although Cadle recommended that Reed replace him as commission chairman, Reed and Cadle's relationship apparently ended, indicating that some animosity had developed between the two men. No post-resignation correspondence between Reed and Cadle has been found.[26]

For whatever reason it occurred, Cadle's resignation caused a flurry of activity in the War Department to find his replacement. Of course, the logical choice was Reed, whom the secretary of war appointed. An added problem was the location of the official commission office and files at Cincinnati. Working through the War Department, Reed, as new chairman, began to deal with each problem systematically. While his appointment kept the park's affairs in the hands of the most knowledgeable individual, it also consolidated jurisdiction. The original leadership of three had dwindled to Cadle and Reed with Thompson's resignation and now consisted of Reed alone. He became the supreme park authority at Shiloh. Moreover, he now lived in the park, thus further consolidating his control. To replace Reed as secretary and historian, the War Department on February 4, 1910, appointed Colonel John T. Wilder, a veteran of the 17th Indiana.[27]

Reed's first major problem was moving the commission office from Cincinnati to Pittsburg Landing. The move took a great deal of effort, but the issue of where to store the records and house the office was the bigger concern. Reed had to do something quickly in light of the War Department's orders to clerk J. M. Riddell to pack up the office and move to Pittsburg Landing. Unwilling to leave Cincinnati and wishing to begin a full-time law practice, Riddell simply "refused to comply" and offered his resignation instead, effective February 21, 1910. Reed then obtained travel orders for J. H. Ashcraft, the healthiest of the remaining commissioners, to travel to Cincinnati and retrieve the commission's records and furniture. Then another problem arose. After the hotel's loss and before the new office's approval, Reed had no headquarters from which to operate the park and store the newly arrived documents. He reminded War Department officials of this deficiency every chance he had, stating that the records were stored at his home in boxes, with almost no shelter from the sun and the elements.[28]

When the new office building was completed, Reed had ample room for storage, as well as quarters for the visiting commission. Affairs of the park settled down once again but this time with Reed in charge. The tornado of 1909 had caused much damage and heartache, but it had nevertheless benefited the park in significant ways. For the first time, the park had an office of its own in which to do business and greet visitors. Most of all, a complete interpretation program, previously limited only to the battlefield itself, seemed a real possibility. Reed could now further advance the memory of the battle and, for that matter, of the Civil War itself.

Unfortunately, this new opportunity to advance Shiloh's interpretation and improve visitor accommodations did not come to fruition. Reed was an elderly man, and he soon had to bring in additional help to run the park. The national commission system soon underwent massive changes as well, again delaying desired alterations at Shiloh. As a result, it was years before all the possibilities the tornado had created could be fully realized.

Yet, Reed continually oversaw the building program of the park. A new flag-pole went up with great celebration in February 1911. In 1912, workers finished a new pavilion, 40 by 120 feet, just south of the park headquarters. The new facility was furnished with fifty new "settees," drinking fountains of the "bubbling kind," and a "rest room for women, toilet rooms and other conveniences." In 1914, Reed marked Grant's headquarters in the cemetery with a pyramid of cannon tubes. Other work went on, including re-fencing and concreting Bloody Pond, which had become "a filthy wallowing place for hogs." Reed was pleased with the progress he was making, writing in the "Daily Events" ledger book that "the Head-quarters Office and the new Park Pavilion proved to be [of] great convenience and comfort, this being the first time the Commission has had any suitable place for entertaining any visitors."[29]

Reed's solo administration of the park continued patterns already established in the past. He continued to defend his interpretation of the battle with vehe-mence, reissuing the second edition of his book in 1913. In fact, he became even more combative. He had a rocky relationship with owners of first the Stantonville Telephone Company and then the Sun Telephone and Telegraph Company, carrying on lengthy arguments over prices, locations of lines, and service.[30]

A new disagreement also emerged between him and cemetery officials. The secretary of war had given permission for these officials to take some seventy feet of land from the park and move the west wall that distance. This alteration was accomplished in 1904 and marked by a wire fence. When the park commission built the new office building in 1910, it rested only thirty feet from the new west boundary. Surveyors then found an error in the line, which forced the erection of the proposed cemetery iron gates within ten feet of the commission's office building. Reed complained and succeeded in getting the entrance gates moved farther south and the position of the west wall moved some five feet to the east.[31]

At times, Reed let his combative personality cause him unnecessary trouble. When he caught lawbreakers in the park, he sought not only to punish them but also to teach them a lesson, even if such action was not strictly within the law. He once fined several white boys for throwing rocks at their black neighbors and fined another child ten dollars for killing a squirrel in the park. He allowed the boys to work off their fines for a dollar a day, thus providing himself with help while teaching the boys a lesson they would not soon forget. Word of the kan-garoo court leaked out, however, and angry parents soon took the matter to the

Fig. 29. An aging D. W. Reed. Courtesy of Shiloh National Military Park.

judicial system. By the end of the incident, the United States attorney general had become involved, and Reed almost faced charges of extortion by threats of violence. On another occasion, Reed locked horns with U.S. marshals for not prosecuting park cases fast enough. He thought that quick judicial proceedings would curb lawlessness in the park, but busy marshals, swamped by other cases, did not act quickly enough for Reed.[32]

The most severe allegations came from park neighbors who complained of the way that Reed ran the battlefield. The often lawless locals were more disturbed about the sudden arrival of federal authority in their neighborhood than anything else. They complained about Range Rider Underhill, Assistant Superintendent Large, and Reed himself. The Justice Department sent the acting judge advocate general to the park to investigate, and Large and Underhill were suspended pending a ruling. Reed, however, faced no charges.[33]

Other problems also confronted the aging Reed. The hotel, rebuilt in 1910, burned on the night of December 23, 1913, causing "much inconvenience to visitors and some embarrassment to the authorities." Such a loss was not as devastating as the former hotel's loss because the commission now had ample room for offices and quarters. However, in a day of uncertain travel options to the park, accommodations in such a remote area were a necessity. Congress never appropriated the money to rebuild the hotel, however, thus continuing the emerging pattern of insufficient funding for the park.[34]

Perhaps the most pressing problem Reed faced was finding suitable help for the work at Shiloh. He discovered more and more that he could not handle the job alone and that he needed other, more able-bodied men present in the park to carry on day-to-day operations. Reed found that good workers were hard to locate, and as a result, he went through many individuals before he found competent workers he could trust with the future of the park.

Personnel changes took place on a regular basis. The job of Range Rider changed hands from E. R. Underhill to A. E. Emmons in October 1914. When Reed had taken the chairman's job, the War Department had appointed Colonel John T. Wilder as commission secretary and historian. The secretary of war quickly transferred Wilder on September 30, 1911, to a position as a full commissioner at Chickamauga. General Gates P. Thurston then became secretary at Shiloh on October 4, 1911, but remained only until his death on December 10, 1912. In his place, the War Department appointed DeLong Rice of Nashville, Tennessee, an appointment that was to prove significant in Shiloh's history.[35]

The task of finding a suitable clerk was even more demanding. The park, Reed complained, had "never been able to keep a clerk very long, and this has resulted in repeated embarrassment to the work here, in the necessity of installing a new clerk every few months." Indeed, Shiloh had gone through more than its quota of clerks. After Riddell refused to move south, Reed tried a number of other people, but he always ran into difficulties. First appointed was W. B. King in December 1910, but he soon transferred to the Surgeon General's Office. William M. Greene became clerk in the summer of 1912, but he soon found that his health would not permit residence at Pittsburg Landing. Solomon Pope also served as clerk between 1914 and 1916, but he, too, left. In between official clerks, Mrs. Lillie Hagy and Reed's daughter, Althea, served in temporary capacities. The quest for a permanent clerk ended, however, when the War Department hired a local resident, Robert A. Livingston.[36]

The arrival of Rice and Livingston marked a new phase in Shiloh's history. For the first time, the majority of the permanent members of the staff were not veterans of the battle or even of the Civil War. Yet, these two men had a love for Shiloh, just like Cadle, Reed, and the thousands of veterans who had built monuments and returned each year. Therefore, official attitudes toward the park remained favorable.

Born near Winchester, Tennessee, on July 5, 1872, DeLong Rice was the son of a Confederate veteran. After formal education and a year of law school, he worked several odd jobs, including one as a stenographer in Chattanooga, Tennessee. He also served on the staff of Robert L. Taylor, a former Tennessee governor. Later, he became secretary for the Tennessee Railroad Commission. In 1900, he established the Rice Lyceum Bureau in Nashville, which presented lecturers and theatrical performances. Interested in politics, Rice even ran unsuccessfully for state treasurer.[37]

Rice's appointment as Shiloh's secretary came on May 12, 1913, and he quickly made contact with his new boss, D. W. Reed. The elderly chairman immediately gave Rice a taste of what to expect. He said that he would like to meet with him as soon as possible in order to proceed with the work, "of which there is more than enough to do." He then proceeded to tell Rice the difficult circumstances at the park. "I have been for two weeks laid up with a broken thigh, and Major Ashcraft's wife is very sick and General Duke is in such poor health as to prevent his presence on the Park," Reed related. In short, Rice had a big job to do with little help.[38]

Robert A. Livingston, known as "Arby," was born on the western edge of the park on August 18, 1892. Hearing that clerk Solomon Pope was leaving, he wrote to Rice about the job. Rice interviewed him but found he "had no training or experience either as bookkeeper or typewriter." Additionally, when Livingston took the civil service exam, he did poorly. Nevertheless, Rice apparently liked Livingston and pushed for his consideration. He knew that Livingston lived near the park, and that "would settle the boarding house problem."[39]

Fortunately for Livingston, the only qualified applicant turned down the job. With the resignation of Mrs. Lillie Hagy, caused by her husband's wish that she stay at home "to keep house for him," the position remained open, and Livingston was able to gain temporary appointment. He began work on August 11, 1916. Rice found that Livingston could indeed do the job, stating that "his efficiency is in every way satisfactory." Rice nominated Livingston for permanent placement as clerk. After a probationary period, Livingston became the permanent clerk on September 13, 1916.[40]

Just as Shiloh gained a permanent clerk who would stay on-site, other events that created new problems were taking place. The great European war engulfed the United States, and the government drafted many young men, one of whom was R. A. Livingston. Rice tried to persuade the War Department to exempt Livingston, but it refused, pointing out that it did so only in cases where the draftee was "practically invaluable." Livingston thus had to resign as clerk, but he stated that "as my resignation is purely for the purpose of enabling me to perform my duty as a soldier, I trust that I may not lose my status in the Civil Service."[41]

Livingston did not serve in Europe; he was a corporal in Motor Transport Corps No. 787, stationed at Camp Sevier, near Greenville, South Carolina. Later, the unit served at Muscle Shoals, Alabama. During Livingston's absence, Rice succeeded in placing his son, Robert C. Rice, in the temporary position. Upon Livingston's discharge from the army, the younger Rice gave up the position. Rice lobbied for Livingston's early discharge, and Livingston was reinstated on June 17, 1919.[42]

The arrival of Rice and Livingston came at a critical point. By the 1910s, the veterans' ranks were thinning quickly, and so was the commission. Soon the remaining commissioners would die. Reed realized what was happening, and he worked with Rice to perpetuate the memory of Shiloh that he had literally created and overseen for much of his life.

The War Department also realized that the aging soldiers could no longer look after the battlefield parks, so they instituted a new policy. The old commission system, under attack as early as 1900, was scrapped, and superintendents acting under the secretary of war replaced it. Yet, the department did not fire the old soldiers; they established a system of phasing out the commissions. According to the Sundry Civil Bill passed in 1912, when a vacancy occurred because of resignation or death, it would simply not be filled. Thus, as the commissioners died, the care of the parks fell to civilian leadership operating under the secretary of war.[43]

This change in commission organization directly affected Shiloh. The aging Reed could no longer see to the day-to-day activities of the park. Likewise, Ashcraft and Duke, both older men, did not even live in the park. Thus, the need for a superintendent became acute by the mid-1910s. Fortunately, Rice was available on the scene and impressed Reed so much that the chairman supported his promotion to head the park. Rice officially took control of the park in February 1914, with the title "Secretary and Superintendent."[44]

As Rice assumed more and more responsibility, Reed and the other commissioners faded away. Duke died on September 16, 1916, leaving only Ashcraft and Reed. By this time, however, Reed was also very sick, having suffered for several years from deteriorating health. When called to Washington to testify about appropriations in 1912, he sent Duke because he was not "just now in very robust health." In May 1913, Reed was thrown from his carriage and "suffered a broken thigh." This event ended his mobility, and he was soon forced to hand over his on-site duties to Rice, although he remained the commission chairman. His health continued to deteriorate so much, however, that he had to leave his beloved Shiloh and return home to Waukon, Iowa. There he died on September 22, 1916. Shiloh's most knowledgeable historian was now gone.[45]

Veterans recognized Reed's dedication to and influence on the park and wanted to place a monument to him on the grounds, but the rules preventing glorification of individuals precluded such an act. Undaunted, the National Association of the Survivors of the Battle of Shiloh then planned to place a plaque to Reed on the office wall. The War Department also denied this request. But Reed's memory was preserved in the park itself and in the aging veterans' hearts.[46]

J. H. Ashcraft was now the only remaining commissioner, but he died on January 19, 1920. The War Department promoted Rice to director just two months later, although he would use the title "superintendent" for the remainder of his tenure. He moved his entire family to the park, building a new superintendent's house in 1918, partly out of materials taken from the razing of Reed's old residence at Review Field. This new residence was a large log structure with cannon as posts supporting the porches.[47]

As the number of proposed military parks grew in the 1910s and 1920s and as the War Department grew as a result of World War I, the parks became less and less a part of the secretary of war's duties. By the 1920s, the park's annual reports did not even appear in the War Department's published report. In 1923, the secretary of war transferred the five Civil War parks to the Office of the Quartermaster General, so Rice soon found his immediate bosses stationed in the Quartermaster Department in Atlanta. In 1930, the parks were transferred again, this time to the "commanding generals of the corps areas in which they are severally located." There was now no central governance for the parks. As the person in charge at Shiloh, Rice now had wide discretion, but he looked after the park with the same love and dedication that Reed had earlier demonstrated.[48]

Rice made the park more accessible and understandable to the public. He built a new superintendent's residence and oversaw the building of a magnificent hotel just south of the park boundary. The Pine Lodge Hotel, a huge structure built of pine and rock, was Rice's brainchild. This exquisite haven offered swimming pools, fountains, and lavishly decorated rooms. Rice sold stock in the venture, with stockholders owning lots adjacent to the hotel. Even Governor Gordon Browning of Tennessee purchased one such lot.[49]

The most notable piece of construction Rice oversaw was a highway linking the battlefield with Corinth, the nearest rail station. In 1924, the government bought from the Corinth, Shiloh, and Savannah Turnpike Company a toll road built in the 1910s. The idea of a road connecting Shiloh and Corinth was not new. As early as 1900, Cadle had requested such a thoroughfare, and Thompson had even surveyed the route. As late as 1912, Reed called for this road to be built in order to allow access to the park "so that more visitors may see, study, and get some good out of the large sums that have been expended here." Efforts to appropriate money failed in Congress, however, and the private company built the thoroughfare but charged for its use. Public sentiment ran heavily against the toll, prompting Congressman J. F. Rankin (Democrat) of Mississippi to offer legislation to buy the road. The government paid twenty-five thousand dollars for the thoroughfare in 1924 and spent more money in widening and modernizing it. The government also removed the toll. Where once veterans came to Shiloh by boat and carriage, now the general public drove their automobiles to the battlefield.[50]

Not only did Rice restart the construction program at Shiloh, but he also acted as the chief preservationist. He counted the number of trees, determining that there were some 280,000 on the battlefield, 220 of which were what he called "veterans" of the battle. He utilized the National Bureau of Forestry to help in saving these trees. In order to prevent forest fires, Rice cut a one-hundred-foot-wide fire strip around the heavily forested southeastern boundary of the park. Other instances of Rice's cultivation of natural resources were his building of a sod farm in one of the fields, planting grass, stopping erosion, and razing unsightly and unneeded buildings. To make life more pleasant, he initiated a program to eradicate mosquitoes and flies.[51]

Rice also modernized Shiloh in terms of the interpretation of the battle. Reed's interpretation had been aimed strictly at veterans who understood tactical deployments and maneuvers. With the continual passing of these former soldiers, however, Rice realized that the battlefield had a new audience, and these people required new interpretive methods. The recent war in Europe had also caused a surge in patriotism, which drove up visitation numbers at Shiloh. Rice even petitioned the War Department for a captured German gun to place in the park, but the military had none to spare. In all this activity, however, Rice firmly built on Reed's already-established Hornet's Nest interpretation.[52]

Rice also became involved in a number of other historical efforts. The only park publication until the 1920s was Reed's book. A new interpretive text, therefore, was needed. Rice utilized the battlefield itself to provide visitors with interpretive trails, such as the "Indian Mounds Trail," complete with its own written guide. More importantly, in 1927, Rice developed the first interpretive tour system at Shiloh,

Fig. 30. DeLong Rice would take the mantle of leadership from D. W. Reed and continue a passionate interpretation and preservation of the battlefield. Courtesy of DeLong Rice Collection, Pickwick, Tennessee.

creating a tour route consisting of some twenty-seven stops. He placed stakes at each stop with numbers corresponding to a printed guide. Rice had the Government Printing Office print thousands of these guides.[53]

Rice also continually sought the cooperation of river transit companies to advertise Shiloh in attractive pamphlets. He also became involved in scholarship. The War Department asked Rice to write a short article on the battlefield, which he did in 1925. The same year, he wrote an article dealing with transportation at Shiloh for the *Tennessee Highway and Public Works Magazine.* His most significant effort, however, was a small book entitled *The Story of Shiloh.*[54]

The Story of Shiloh showed just how much of an effect D. W. Reed and his Hornet's Nest interpretation had on Rice. The book began by noting the deeply cut road on the battlefield—what became known as the Sunken Road. It was this road, Rice claimed, that played such a pivotal role in the Battle of Shiloh. Throughout the book, Rice returned again and again to the Sunken Road and the Hornet's Nest that formed around it. He agreed wholeheartedly with D. W. Reed's interpretation of the battle.[55]

The work at Shiloh took the majority of Rice's time, but he also became involved in other War Department activities. Congress memorialized the death site of Meriwether Lewis, near Hohenwald, Tennessee, on July 1, 1926, and it fell to Rice to develop the National Historic Monument there, including construction and interpretation. He had to build not only the park but also the infrastructural support. Accordingly, he contracted for buildings, including tool and storage houses. He erected an eighty-two-foot flagpole, and decorated the area with cast-iron tablets similar to those at Shiloh. He also marked 107 graves at the site with government-bought headstones. Rice apparently sent many of his Shiloh laborers to the site to perform maintenance and finish the construction. For this extra work, Rice received a three-hundred-dollar-a-year pay increase, but there is no evidence that the Shiloh workforce received any extra pay.[56]

As Rice settled into his eighteenth year at Shiloh, however, tragedy struck. He and family members returned to the superintendent's residence from Memphis around half past six on the evening of September 20, 1929. Mrs. Rice and the two daughters went upstairs, while Rice and his sixteen-year-old son James remained on the first floor. Smelling a strong stench of the acetylene gas that lit the home, both men went to investigate. Rice was carrying a lantern, and it set off a massive explosion, burning both father and son severely and setting the house afire. James was knocked unconscious, and Rice, burned badly, could only try to roll out of the burning room. His wife and daughters rushed from upstairs, having realized that their first impression of an earthquake had been false. They wrapped themselves in bed sheets and braved the fire to remove the unconscious boy. Neighbors arrived shortly thereafter and put out the blaze, while an ambulance and physician arrived to care for the injured.[57]

Both Rice and his son were taken to the hospital in Corinth, where the son died shortly thereafter. In much pain, Rice himself lingered for four days, but on September 24, 1929, he also died. Buried originally in Henry Cemetery in Corinth, his body was later taken to Memphis and reburied in the Memorial Park Cemetery.[58]

This unfortunate tragedy took away yet another Shiloh expert. By the time of his death, Rice had served at Shiloh nearly as long as Reed had. Likewise, Rice had studied under Reed himself and had gained from him a thorough knowledge of the park. Whereas Reed was somewhat brash and hardheaded, Rice was a courtly gentleman who evidenced Southern hospitality in every word and deed and thus established much public good will for the park. An astute writer who often worked in a summer cottage atop the Indian mound on the bluff of the Tennessee River,

Rice filled his prose and poetry with the flowery Victorian language of that age. His book was written with a dramatic flair, as were his letters. In one series of letters written to various state governors asking that their respective legislatures erect monuments on the field, Rice wrote that such monuments would make the park "a badge of honor upon the lapel of the whole nation."[59]

Rice's legacy is clear. He took the park from an ailing Reed, and despite his old-fashioned ways, he made the park modern in the midst of the second American industrial revolution. He continually sought ways to bring the battlefield to a greater number of people and likewise to bring a greater number of people to the park. Most importantly, Rice was the first official to interpret the park to visitors not of the veteran generation. In so doing, he blazed a new trail. He never let go of his roots, however, and the interpretation of his mentor, D. W. Reed. Even amid the modernization of both physical management and up-to-date interpretation, Rice always advanced the traditional Reed thesis centering on the Hornet's Nest and Sunken Road.

With Rice gone, the reins of control over Shiloh National Military Park were transferred to another dedicated individual with his heart centered directly on Shiloh. R. A. Livingston, born and raised on the park, had served faithfully as clerk for nearly thirteen years. He knew the park and the duties of the superintendent. He was the logical choice to replace Rice, and he received the job.

Livingston's first four years were uneventful compared to what had earlier taken place in Shiloh's history. His major duty was to maintain the park and facilitate visitors who flocked to its grounds. Little unusual activity took place during Livingston's first four years as superintendent; he basically continued what he had learned from Rice—the Hornet's Nest thesis. Reed had trained Rice, and Rice trained Livingston. The Reed interpretation would continue.

Two major events in U.S. history took place in 1933, however, and these dramatically affected the future of Shiloh National Military Park. First, on March 4, 1933, Franklin Delano Roosevelt became president of the United States. Amid economic turmoil, Roosevelt instituted within a hundred days a major series of reform and recovery efforts commonly called the New Deal. Second, on August 10, 1933, Roosevelt reorganized the executive branch of the government. One of his many changes placed the military parks under the National Park Service.

These reforms had major implications for Shiloh. The change of stewardship placed the park in the hands of an agency with expertise in preservation and interpretation, activities with which the War Department had not been especially concerned. As a result, Shiloh experienced a developing interpretive program under the National Park Service. The ghost of D. W. Reed, however, still dominated these efforts. The interpretation that took place over the decades to come was firmly based on the Reed interpretation of the Hornet's Nest, and it built on Rice's early efforts at getting the visitor around the battlefield in a coherent manner.

Because of Roosevelt's New Deal, Shiloh ironically reaped benefits during a period in which most of America was drowning in economic crisis. Many government agencies sent workers to the park, such as two Civilian Conservation Corps camps, as well as Works Progress Administration workers writing histories of various aspects of the battlefield. In the end, the Great Depression drastically benefited the park, allowing construction on a scale not matched since the original days between 1900 and 1903. This New Deal building process even outmatched the flurry of construction after the 1909 tornado. Benefits received from the New Deal included a new visitor center, park employee housing, erosion control, and concrete roadways.

The crisis of the 1930s, however, spilled into a larger worldwide crisis in the 1940s. As the nation went to war, the large labor pools Shiloh had welcomed under the New Deal suddenly went to work in the war effort. Former road builders, erosion controllers, and writers were now soldiers, sailors, and shipyard and factory workers. The result was a lack of labor at the park, and several years of inadequate maintenance resulted. Historic wood lines began to creep into fields, historic buildings went without repairs, and general maintenance went lacking until the 1950s.

Shiloh was not the only national park suffering from a deficiency of labor and the general lack of maintenance. By the 1950s, the National Park Service recognized the critical state of its resources and implemented a renewal program named Mission 66. In the ten-year program from 1956 to 1966, millions of dollars would be funneled into efforts to renew and rejuvenate America's national parks.

Yet, Shiloh faced the same old problems it had endured for its entire existence. Historically, Shiloh had not received the attention that other, larger national military parks received. Each of the other four 1890s-era parks had better facilities, monuments, and resources than did Shiloh. The same occurred under Mission 66. Very little new construction and renewal took place. The New Deal–era visitor center remained, while other parks, such as Vicksburg, Gettysburg, and Antietam, received newer buildings. Although a fair amount of planning emerged, relatively few results materialized at Shiloh from Mission 66.

The pattern of little change continues through today. The park still shows its 1954 film, *Shiloh: Portrait of a Battle*. It still relies on its decades-old wayside exhibits that reflect none of the scholarship of the last thirty years. With the exceptions of modern cars, a visitor from earlier years would have trouble distinguishing whether he was living in 2004 or 1944. For that matter, with the exception of a few more changes, such as concrete roads and several buildings, veterans of the Civil War would have trouble distinguishing whether they were living in 2004 or 1904.

Perhaps it is fitting that the park has changed so little. Those veterans of the 1890s labored hard to create a park and a national memory of the Civil War for following generations to see. The battlefield is a testimony to the many brave soldiers of both North and South who fought the battle over issues larger than themselves and then fought just as hard to have their small place in history preserved in the memory of the American people. It is fitting that when visitors step onto Shiloh National Military Park, they are stepping back in time to the 1890s and 1900s. And if they listen closely, visitors can still hear what those veterans had to say to America.

CONCLUSION

History, Memory, and
Shiloh National Military Park

Between 1862 and 1933, the area around Pittsburg Landing, Tennessee, underwent a series of major changes at the hands of the United States government. In 1862, the area hosted as many as three major Union armies, totaling over one hundred thousand troops. As a result of the Union forces' presence, a pivotal battle took place near the landing. After the war, the government established a National Cemetery on the site. In 1894, the United States government went even further by building a national military park on the surrounding four thousand acres. Not content with merely remembering what had happened at Shiloh, the government sought to erect a tangible memorial to the brave soldiers of the Civil War.

If treated as a case study of American Civil War memory, Shiloh National Military Park demonstrates the existence of a late–nineteenth-century Civil War generational movement of national scope. This movement consisted of several essential agendas, all keying on the collective memory of the Civil War that sought to honor the veterans of the Civil War of both sides. This veterans' movement carried so much force that the federal government itself, relatively uninvolved to this point, became heavily engaged in memorializing the veterans and their battlefields. Beginning with the national cemetery movement and growing into battlefield preservation, the evolution of the national government's involvement is clearly seen. Indeed, the main function of Shiloh National Military Park, as outlined in the enabling legislation, was to preserve the scene of conflict and thus honor the veterans who fought there.

More importantly, this memorialization movement, of which Shiloh was a part, was an effort to limit controversy over the war. Big issues such as slavery and states' rights had separated the sections in the 1860s, and many of the same big issues, now in the form of Jim Crow segregation, still confronted the nation in the 1890s. Yet, there was a concerted effort to forget the controversies that had separated the nation in the 1860s and concentrate on the heroism and courage of the soldiers who had fought over those issues. As a result, few debated the central themes of the Civil War, such as slavery and race. Rather, American leaders emphasized the manliness and courage of the soldiers, both North and South.

Shiloh National Military Park, of course, illustrates this movement. The park commission did not try to interpret the causes or the results of the war, but rather concentrated on the battle itself and the courage and honor of the soldiers.

Most importantly, during the 1890s, a wave of reconciliation was sweeping the nation. For the first time in decades, Americans long torn by sectional disputes viewed themselves as a united people. The effort to reduce the post–Civil War sectionalism had a home in the battlefield parks such as Shiloh, where Americans of all ages, sections, and ideologies could come and witness the scene of destruction that had not only torn apart the nation but ultimately made it stronger. The dedication speeches and celebrations at Shiloh ignored racial and sectional differences and the many economic, social, and labor disputes of the decade while emphasizing nationalism and reconciliation.

Thus, the deliberate creation of memory by the Shiloh Park Commission on a local level and by national leaders on a broader level played a critical role in America's memory of the Civil War and the nation's self-identity. What the commission did for Shiloh and what policymakers did for the United States go hand in hand, the latter working through individual entities like the former. Thus, Shiloh National Military Park stands as a testament not only to the soldiers of 1862 but also to the veterans of 1894 who actively sought to honor their colleagues and, in the process, helped heal a nation of its sectional strife.

APPENDIX I

ENABLING LEGISLATION

Public—No. 9
AN ACT To establish a national military park at the battlefield of Shiloh.

Be it enacted by the Senate and House of Representatives of the United States of America in Congress assembled, That in order that the armies of the southwest which served in the civil war, like their comrades of the eastern armies at Gettysburg and those of the central west at Chickamauga, may have the history of one of their memorable battles preserved on the ground where they fought, the battlefield of Shiloh, in the State of Tennessee, is hereby declared to be a national military park, whenever title to the same shall have been acquired by the United States and the usual jurisdiction over the lands and roads of the same shall have been granted to the United States by the State of Tennessee; that is to say, the area inclosed by the following lines, or so much thereof as the commissioners of the park may deem necessary, to wit: Beginning at low-water mark on the north bank of Snake Creek where it empties into the Tennessee River; thence westwardly in a straight line to the point where the river road to Crumps Landing, Tennessee, crosses Snake Creek; thence along the channel of Snake Creek to Owl Creek; thence along the channel of Owl Creek to the crossing of the road to Purdy, Tennessee; thence southwardly in a straight line to the intersection of an east and west line drawn from the point where the road to Hamburg, Tennessee, crosses Lick Creek near the mouth of the latter; thence eastward along the said east and west line to the point where the Hamburg Road crosses Lick Creek; thence along the channel of Lick Creek to the Tennessee River; thence along low-water mark of the Tennessee River to the point of beginning, containing three thousand acres, more or less, and the area thus inclosed shall be known as the Shiloh National Military Park: Provided, That the boundaries of the land authorized to be acquired may be changed by the said commissioners.

SEC. 2. That the establishment of the Shiloh National Military Park shall be carried forward under the control and direction of the Secretary of War, who, upon the passage of this Act, shall proceed to acquire title to the same either under the Act approved August first, eighteen hundred and eighty-eight, entitled "An Act to authorize the condemnation of land for sites of public buildings, and for other purposes," or under the Act approved February twenty-seventh, eighteen hundred and sixty-seven, entitled "An Act to establish and protect national cemeteries," as he may select, and as title is procured to any portion of the lands and roads within the legal boundaries of the park he may proceed with the establishment of the park upon such portions as may thus be acquired.

SEC. 3. That the Secretary of War is hereby authorized to enter into agreements whereby he may lease, upon such terms as he may prescribe, with such present owners or tenants of the lands as may desire to remain upon it, to occupy and cultivate their present holdings upon condition that they will preserve the present buildings and roads and the present outlines of field and forest, and that they only will cut trees or underbrush under such regulations as the Secretary may prescribe, and that they will assist in caring for and protecting all tablets, monuments, or such other artificial works as may from time to time be erected by proper authority.

SEC. 4. That the affairs of the Shiloh National Military Park shall, subject to the supervision and direction of the Secretary of War, be in charge of three commissioners, to be appointed by the Secretary of War, each of whom shall have served at the time of the battle in one of the armies engaged therein, one of whom shall have served in the Army of the Tennessee, commanded by General U. S. Grant, who shall be chairman of the commission;

one in the Army of the Ohio, commanded by General D. C. Buell; and one in the Army of the Mississippi, commanded by General A. S. Johnston. The said commissioners shall have an office in the War Department building, and while on actual duty shall be paid such compensation out of the appropriations provided by this Act as the Secretary of War shall deem reasonable and just; and for the purpose of assisting them in their duties and in ascertaining the lines of battle of all troops engaged and the history of their movements in the battle, the Secretary of War shall have authority to employ, at such compensation as he may deem reasonable, to be paid out of the appropriations made by this Act, some person recognized as well informed concerning the history of the several armies engaged at Shiloh, and who shall also act as secretary of the commission.

SEC. 5. That it shall be the duty of the commission named in the preceding section, under the direction of the Secretary of War, to open or repair such roads as may be necessary to the purposes of the park, and to ascertain and mark with historical tablets or otherwise, as the Secretary of War may determine, all lines of battle of the troops engaged in the battle of Shiloh and other historical points of interest pertaining to the battle within the park or its vicinity, and the said commission in establishing this military park shall also have authority, under the direction of the Secretary of War, to employ such labor and services and to obtain such supplies and material as may be necessary to the establishment of the said park under such regulations as he may consider best for the interest of the Government, and the Secretary of War shall make and enforce all needed regulations for the care of the park.

SEC. 6. That it shall be lawful for any State that had troops engaged in the battle of Shiloh to enter upon the lands of the Shiloh National Military Park for the purpose of ascertaining and marking the lines of battle of its troops engaged therein: *Provided,* That before any such lines are permanently designated the position of the lines and the proposed methods of marking them by monuments, tablets, or otherwise shall be submitted to and approved by the Secretary of War, and all such lines, designs and inscriptions for the same shall first receive the written approval of the Secretary, which approval shall be based upon formal written reports, which must be made to him in each case by the commissioners of the park: *Provided,* That no discrimination shall be made against any State as to the manner of designating lines, but any grant made to any State by the Secretary of War may be used by any other State.

SEC. 7. That if any person shall, except by permission of the Secretary of War, destroy, mutilate, deface, injure, or remove any monument, column, statues, memorial structures, or work of art that shall be erected or placed upon the grounds of the park by lawful authority, or shall destroy or remove any fence, railing, inclosure, or other work for the protection or ornament of said park, or any portion thereof, or shall destroy, cut, hack, bark, break down, or otherwise injure any tree, bush, or shrubbery that may be growing upon said park, or shall cut down or fell or remove any timber, battle relic, tree or trees growing or being upon said park, or hunt within the limits of the park, or shall remove or destroy any breastworks, earthworks, walls, or other defenses or shelter on any part thereof constructed by the armies formerly engaged in the battles on the lands or approaches to the park, any person so offending and found guilty thereof, before any justice of the peace of the county in which the offense may be committed or any court of competent jurisdiction shall for each and every such offense forfeit and pay a fine, in the discretion of the justice, according to the aggravation of the offense, of not less than five nor more than fifty dollars, one-half for the use of the park and the other half to the informer, to be enforced and recovered before such justice in like manner as debts of like nature are now by law recoverable in the several counties where the offense may be committed.

SEC. 8. That to enable the Secretary of War to begin to carry out the purpose of this Act, including the condemnation or purchase of the necessary land, marking the boundaries of the park, opening or repairing necessary roads, restoring the field to its condition at the time of the battle, maps and surveys, and the pay and expenses of the commissioners and their assistant, the sum of seventy-five thousand dollars, or such portion thereof as may be necessary, is hereby appropriated, out of any moneys in the Treasury not otherwise appropriated, and disbursements under this Act shall require the approval of the Secretary of War, and he shall make annual report of the same to Congress.

Approved, December 27, 1894.

APPENDIX 2

LAND PURCHASES

	Name	Date	Acres	Price
1.	George W. L. Smith	Sept. 28, 1896	85.18	$851.80
2.	Samuel Chambers	Jan. 2, 1897	101	$1,010.00
3.	Thomas Walker	Jan. 2, 1897	206.05	$3,184.70
4.	W. G. Petty	Apr. 17, 1897	206.15	$2,061.50
5.	W. G. Petty	Apr. 17, 1897	204.97	$1,950.00
6.	P. N. Tilghman	Apr. 26, 1897	79.08	$790.60
7.	W. C. and O. C. Meeks (C)	Apr. 27, 1897	180.90	$6,000.00
8.	Samuel Chambers	Feb. 23, 1897	65.11	$651.10
9.	James J. Fraley	Aug. 26, 1897	160.45	$929.10
10.	James J. Fraley	Sept. 11, 1897	52.52	$525.20
11.	W. G. Petty	Nov. 29, 1897	151.31	$1,513.10
12.	Samuel Chambers	Dec. 1, 1897	385.77	$3,857.70
13.	W. A. Rowsey	Dec. 1, 1897	89.65	$1,200.00
14.	S. M. Rogers	Dec. 13, 1897	69.81	$723.10
15.	Samuel Chambers	Dec. 29, 1897	56.94	$569.40
16.	John R. Duncan	Jan. 8, 1898	168.84	$1,900.00
17.	D. H. Cantrell	Jan. 8, 1898	26.28	$362.50
18.	George H. Hurley	Jan. 8, 1898	43.50	$1,000.00
19.	J. W. Sowell	Jan. 8, 1898	37.54	$375.40
20.	Ervin P. Tillman	Jan. 8, 1898	35.55	$355.50
21.	F. M. Hagy	Dec. 28, 1898	211.54	$3,115.40
22.	W. G. Petty	Jan. 7, 1899	146.59	$1,965.90
23.	Samuel Chambers	Jan. 7, 1899	31.20	$3,300.00
24.	James W. Bell	Jan. 7, 1899	72.21	$1,000.00
25.	Hugh D. Harris	Jan. 7, 1899	1	$200.00
26.	A. W. Walker	Jan. 9, 1899	172.60	$1,726.00
27.	M. C. McDaniel	Aug. 10, 1899	7.26	$300.00
28.	Samuel Chambers	Mar. 16, 1903	2.4	$500.00
29.	O. H. P. Cantrell	July 14, 1903	75.08	$2,500.00
30.	D. C. McCullers	July 10, 1903	86.87	$2,100.00
31.	William J. Petty	Nov. 12, 1903	100.41	$1,800.00
32.	O. H. P. Cantrell	Sept. 1, 1908	88.74	$887.40
33.	D. C. McCullers (C)	June 8, 1911	52.43	$943.74
34.	W. E. Morris (C)	June 8, 1911	13.11	$235.98
35.	W. C. Meeks	June 8, 1911	32.08	$417.04
36.	H. Abernathy	Jan. 27, 1911	3.57	$35.70
37.	J. P. Cantrell	Feb. 1, 1911	15.67	$203.71
38.	E. R. Underhill	Feb. 2, 1911	10.95	$142.00
39.	Samuel Chambers	Feb. 20, 1911	1	$13.00
40.	G. H. Hurley	Feb. 28, 1911	4.83	$62.79
41.	I. W. Phillips	Aug. 1, 1911	2 tracts	$1.00
42.	Board of Education	July 6, 1918	1.01	$250.00
43.	Turnpike Co.	Mar. 24, 1925	road and 11.5	$28,000.00
44.	W. W. Harrison	June 6, 1928	4	$2,600.00
45.	Judy Ann Underhill	July 2, 1928	32.54	$4,500.00

(C) = Condemned

APPENDIX 3

SHILOH NATIONAL CEMETERY
SUPERINTENDENTS

The following is a list of cemetery superintendents, as complete as the scanty records will allow:

A. W. Wills	Quartermaster Department builder of cemetery, 1866–67
Peter Jecko	Nov. 26, 1867–Aug. 18, 1870
Thomas Jackson	*Acting* 1870
M. O'Connor	*Acting* 1871
Rufus C. Taylor	Letters dated May 1871 to July 1871
Enos P. Trussell	Letter dated Feb. 18, 1873
William A. Graham	Letter dated Aug. 1874
Thomas Frame	Letters dated Oct. 1874–Oct. 1875
Leonard S. Doolittle	Letters dated Apr. 1876–1888
Frederick Schmidt	Aug. 30, 1888–Mar. 31, 1894
Clayton Hart	Mar. 31, 1894–Oct. 17, 1896
John W. Shaw	Oct. 17, 1896–May 21, 1905
H. C. Lacy	May 21, 1905–Mar. 17, 1906
George P. Dean	Mar. 17, 1906–Sept. 30, 1926
Edna M. Harvey	*Acting* Sept. 30, 1926–Jan. 15, 1927
E. M. McDaniel	*Acting* Jan. 15–June 1927
Walter J. Pearce	June 1927–Jan. 1929
E. M. McDaniel	*Acting* Jan. 1929–Jan. 15, 1929
R. E. Gatewood	Jan. 15, 1929–Mar. 8, 1930
E. M. McDaniel	*Acting* Mar. 8, 1930–Mar. 20, 1930
John A. Myers	Mar. 20–Sept. 16, 1930
E. M. McDaniel	*Acting* Sept. 16–Nov. 23, 1930
R. H. Bailey	Nov. 23–July 31, 1943

Very little is known about the superintendents. A. W. Wills was the member of the Quartermaster Department who oversaw the building of the cemetery. Peter Jecko was the first official superintendent but died on August 18, 1870. Specific dates for superintendents Jackson through Doolittle are unknown. Scattered letters offer insights into when they served, however. No mention of Enos P. Trussell could be found besides the one letter mentioned. William C. Hershberger shows up on a list of Shiloh National Cemetery superintendents in the National Archives, but no reference to his actually taking the position was found. He received orders in 1881 to replace L. S. Doolittle, but those orders were soon revoked. Apparently, he never served at Shiloh. R. H. Bailey served as superintendent when the cemetery was transferred from the War Department to the National Park Service but remained as superintendent until Shiloh National Military Park superintendent Blair Ross took over on July 31, 1943. A few of the superintendents listed above were only acting superintendents for a very short period, and often superintendents would swap positions and hold the office on more than one occasion. Frederick Schmidt is an example of trading positions. He reported that Shiloh had such a terrible effect on his health that he requested a transfer. He swapped positions with Clayton Hart at the National Cemetery at Jefferson City, Missouri, in 1894.[1]

APPENDIX 4

COMMISSIONERS AND SUPERINTENDENTS

War Department (December 27, 1895–August 10, 1933)

Colonel Cornelius Cadle, Commission Chairman	Mar. 12, 1895–Jan. 31, 1910
General Don Carlos Buell, Commissioner	Mar. 12, 1895–Nov. 19, 1898
Colonel Robert F. Looney, Commissioner	Mar. 12, 1895–Nov. 19, 1899
Colonel Josiah Patterson, Commissioner	Jan. 1, 1900–Feb. 10, 1904
Major James H. Ashcraft, Commissioner	Jan. 12, 1899–Jan. 19, 1920
General Basil W. Duke, Commissioner	Feb. 20, 1904–Sept. 16, 1916
Major David W. Reed, Commission Chairman	Feb. 1, 1910–Sept. 22, 1916
DeLong Rice, Superintendent	Feb. 1, 1914–Sept. 24, 1929
Robert A. Livingston, Superintendent	1929–Aug. 10, 1933

National Park Service, Department of the Interior
(August 10, 1933–present)

Robert A. Livingston, Superintendent	Aug. 10, 1933–May 14, 1936
Charles S. Dunn, *Acting* Superintendent	Apr. 11, 1936–May 14, 1936
Charles S. Dunn, Superintendent	May 15, 1936–Dec. 31, 1937
William W. Luckett, *Acting* Superintendent	Jan. 1, 1938–Mar. 14, 1940
Blair A. Ross, Superintendent	Mar. 15, 1940–May 12, 1945
James W. Holland, Superintendent	June 4, 1945–Aug. 14, 1951
Ira B. Lykes, Superintendent	Aug. 15, 1951–Apr. 14, 1956
James W. Howell, *Acting* Superintendent	Apr. 15, 1956–July 9, 1956
Floyd B. Taylor, Superintendent	July 10, 1956–Apr. 11, 1959
Bernard T. Campbell, Superintendent	Apr. 12, 1959–Nov. 30, 1963
Ivan J. Ellsworth, Superintendent	Dec. 1, 1963–June 3, 1967
Herbert Olsen, Superintendent	June 18, 1967–Jan. 10, 1970
Alvoid L. Rector, Superintendent	Jan. 25, 1970–Mar. 27, 1976
Zeb V. McKinney, Superintendent	Mar. 28, 1976–June 1, 1990
George A. Reaves, *Acting* Superintendent	June 2, 1990–Aug. 25, 1990
Haywood S. Harrell, Superintendent	Aug. 26, 1990–present

APPENDIX 5

MONUMENTS AND DEDICATIONS

One by one, Northern states erected and dedicated monuments to their soldiers who fought at Shiloh. Ohio became the first state to do so, placing thirty-four regimental monuments all across the field. Built by the Hughes Granite and Marble Company of Clyde, Ohio, the monuments cost a total of $45,140. Ohio dedicated these memorials on June 6, 1902, in front of a crowd estimated at two thousand people. Judge David Pugh, an Ohio statesman and veteran of the 46th Ohio, turned the monuments over to the War Department, with Chairman Cornelius Cadle acting as accepting agent. Made of Barre granite, the monuments were of differing shapes and sizes, except those to the 15th, 46th, and 77th Ohio Infantry.[1]

Indiana dedicated its memorials next. The state commission called on John R. Lowe, a member of the 11th Indiana and a veteran of Shiloh, to design these monuments. He built a shapely obelisk of limestone, and the state placed twenty-two of these memorials across the battlefield. The total cost amounted to $22,250. At the dedication services, held on the forty-third anniversary of the battle—April 6–7, 1903—Governor Winfred Durbin turned over possession of the monuments to Assistant Secretary of War William Cary Sanger.[2]

The third Northern dedication took place on November 13, 1903, when the state of Pennsylvania dedicated one monument to the 77th Pennsylvania, the only eastern regiment that had fought at Shiloh. Designed by Julius C. Loester of New York, New York, the monument cost $3,000. It featured battle scenes of bronze and a statue of a soldier made from a portrait of the state commission's chairman, John Obrieter. Governor Samuel Pennypacker handed the monument over to the government, Cadle accepting on behalf of the War Department.[3]

Illinois next dedicated its forty monuments: twenty-eight infantry, ten artillery, one cavalry, and a large central monument. At a total cost of $42,025.05, Illinois contracted German designer R. W. Bock to build the memorials. Dedicated on May 17–18, 1904, the individual unit monuments were entirely uniform, while the cavalry monument resembled a thimble. The large, imposing central monument contains much symbolism, depicting a woman representing Illinois seated on a throne. The woman carries a sheathed sword, symbolizing a patient wait for a resumption of battle. The woman holds a historical book of Illinois, with her fingers marking the entry of April 6–7, 1862. The monument faces southeast, with the woman symbolically looking in the direction from which the attack came.[4]

Wisconsin dedicated her two monuments on April 7, 1906. The large central monument represents a mortally wounded color sergeant grasped in the arms of Lady Victory, who continually holds the flag upright. The other memorial marks the burial site of J. D. Putnam, a private of the 14th Wisconsin. He fell near the Hornet's Nest on April 7, 1862, and his friends buried him at the foot of a tree, upon which they carved his initials. The letters were still legible in 1901, although only the stump remained. Park employee F. A. Large dug up the stump and shipped it to Wisconsin. The state commission had an exact replica made of granite and placed it on the exact spot where the tree once stood. The total cost of the two monuments was $13,425. Governor James O. Davidson dedicated the monuments and turned them over to the government.[5]

After a long and heated controversy that delayed dedication ceremonies, Iowa turned over to the government its eleven regimental and one central monument on November 23, 1906. At a total cost of $43,051, the identical unit monuments were placed in the field while the imposing central monument was located atop the bluff at Pittsburg Landing. The tall shaft supporting a globe and eagle stands seventy-five feet high. At the base, a statue of Lady Fame writes a tribute to Iowa soldiers on the roll of honor. Governor Albert B. Cummins dedicated the monuments, designed by F. E. Triebel of New York City.[6]

On April 10, 1908, Minnesota dedicated one monument to the only unit from that state to fight at Shiloh, the 1st Minnesota Battery. Designed by John K. Daniels, the monument depicts an artilleryman standing ready to serve. Governor John A. Johnson dedicated the $4,000 monument, which the Minnesota commission placed in the Hornet's Nest.[7]

The last of the Northern states to dedicate a monument during the era of War Department administration was Michigan, which did so on May 30, 1919. Presented to the government by Governor Albert E. Sleeper, the central monument commemorates the state's units that served at Shiloh. Built by the Detroit Granite Company, the monument cost $3,900.[8]

Southerners erected seven different monuments on the field, but only two were state-supported. The first Southern dedication occurred on August 22, 1905, when Senator William Bate's monument to the 2nd Tennessee went up. War Department regulations would not allow monuments to honor individuals, so Bate's work was done on behalf of the regiment he commanded. Some three thousand people attended the ceremony as veterans dedicated the monument near Shiloh Church. Designed by the Foster and Herbert Cut Stone Company of Nashville, the monument cost $2,000 and depicts a soldier gazing through the smoke of battle. Unfortunately, Senator Bate died only several months before the dedication.[9]

United Daughters of the Confederacy (UDC) women in Alabama presented their monument next, dedicating it in a heavy rain on May 7, 1907. Morris Brothers of Memphis constructed the Alabama monument at a cost of $3,000. It features the Confederate flag, a gun, and a saber, all surmounted by a cluster of granite cannonballs. Decades later, Alabama partisans also erected a monument ostensibly to the 19th Alabama, but actually to its colonel, Joseph Wheeler. The Wheeler monument stands beside the Alabama memorial.[10]

Arkansas UDC women dedicated their monument on September 6, 1911. The women placed this monument, which resembled the courthouse monuments of the South, in the Hornet's Nest. Built by Morris Brothers, the monument cost $3,000. The keynote speaker at the dedication was R. G. Shaver, commander of an Arkansas brigade at Shiloh.[11]

On May 30, 1915, Louisiana veterans dedicated a monument to the New Orleans Crescent Regiment. The originator and financier of the monument, Dr. Y. R. Lemonnier, unfortunately could not attend because of ill health. Crossed rifles and a wreath cover the face of the memorial, while a new moon represents the Crescent Regiment. Albert Weiblen of New Orleans designed the monument.[12]

The most famous Confederate memorial on the field is the massive UDC monument. Dedicated on May 17, 1917, in front of a crowd of fifteen thousand people, the UDC monument cost $50,000. Designed by Frederick C. Hibbard of Chicago, the memorial is heavily endowed with symbolism. The center cluster of figures represents death and night stealing victory from the Confederates, while each branch of the Confederate army is represented on each flank. The upward-looking carved heads on the right denote victory on the first day of Shiloh while the downtrodden heads on the left denote defeat on the second day and the loss of life. The UDC women placed in the cornerstone of the monument an impressive collection of memorabilia, including a lock of Albert Sidney Johnston's hair. With money left over from the project, the UDC members erected a small memorial at the largest Confederate burial trench. In 1935, the Tennessee chapter of the UDC placed similar monuments at the other four trenches.[13]

APPENDIX 6

SHILOH CHURCH

The Battle of Shiloh received its name from Shiloh Church; ironically, one meaning of *Shiloh* is "Place of Peace." The original church in the area sat near the present-day Michigan monument, a mile southwest from the landing. Built in 1835 and named the Union Church, its congregation split around 1845 over the slavery issue. In 1851, J. J. Ellis gave some four acres of land to the local school district, on which a new church was built. The result was the Shiloh Church, built in the 1850s and located on the tall ridge just north of Shiloh Branch, some three miles southwest of the landing.

At the time of the battle, Shiloh Church was a small log structure measuring twenty-five by thirty feet. Confederate general P. G. T. Beauregard used the church as his headquarters during the battle, and others no doubt used it as a hospital or shelter. The church survived the battle but not the war. Accounts differ concerning the destruction of the church: some say soldiers took it apart for use in campfires and bridges, while others say it collapsed because of damage sustained during the battle.

In the original church's place, members later built a brush arbor and worshiped there until enough money could be raised to build a large board building of simple style. This church, built in 1881, remained in service during the 1890s, when the park was established. This church likewise did not last, with the congregation tearing it down in 1929.

Church members began building the present structure in 1929, but a lack of funding during the Great Depression forced the congregation to stop construction. Work began again in 1949, and by 1952 the members had finished the uncompleted shell, made of native stone, with brick, giving the present church a two-toned look.

The relationship between the park and the church, which holds the only private land within the boundaries of the park, has been somewhat rocky. Efforts to buy the land and the church have failed, and the church retains its sovereignty over its landlocked area. It maintained a school on the premises for years and in 2001 allowed erection of a replica of the original Shiloh Church.

Other churches existed on the battlefield throughout the years. The Union Church has vanished from existence, and no traces can be found either on the park or on battle maps. Apparently, it was gone by the time of the battle. After the war, the Northern branch of the Methodist Episcopal Church built a structure just north of the Shiloh Church, which was a member of the Southern branch of the Methodist Episcopal Church. This church stood less than a quarter of a mile north of the more famous Shiloh Church. Shake-a-Rag Church stood near Confederate artillery positions south of Locust Grove Branch. Yet another church stood near the headwaters of Locust Grove branch. The isolated area around Pittsburg Landing was not lacking in churches.[1]

APPENDIX 7

SHILOH HISTORIOGRAPHY

Historical writing on Shiloh falls into four distinct schools of thought. The first school, written from the time of the battle to the late 1880s, is simply a recounting of the battle by its participants. The second school of thought, the dominant school even today, began with the establishment of the park in 1894. With access to published reports, veterans' accounts, and, most importantly, the battlefield itself, this school insisted that the Hornet's Nest and Sunken Road were the keys to the Battle of Shiloh. A more recent third school argues that Albert Sidney Johnston's death, not the Hornet's Nest, determined the fate of the battle. The fourth and final school, just emerging and very revisionist in nature, has taken an almost radical approach to the battle. This school argues that neither the Hornet's Nest nor Johnston's death was the key to the battle. Rather, it was the Confederates' misunderstanding of enemy positions, deployment, and geography that led to their defeat.

The first school includes postwar memoirs and articles by participants, which often caused heated controversies. These accounts can be found in hundreds of memoirs and reminiscences. In almost all of these, veterans promoted their own agendas, whether to defend their actions or lay blame at someone else's feet. The best collection of material is in *Battles and Leaders of the Civil War* (1884–87). The Shiloh articles offer insight into historiographical arguments that emerged on both sides after the war.

These controversies generally raged between partisans on each side, not between Confederates and Federals. Ulysses S. Grant, in "The Battle of Shiloh" in *Battles and Leaders of the Civil War*, and Don Carlos Buell, in "Shiloh Reviewed" in the same volume, vehemently argued over the battle and the role played by the respective Union armies. Grant maintained that he had the battle won by the time Buell's troops arrived, while Buell argued that his army's arrival turned the tide.

The Confederates likewise argued over details of the battle but without one key player. Johnston was, of course, dead and could not defend himself, but his son took up the standard and blamed Beauregard for the Confederate defeat. The younger Johnston, in "Albert Sidney Johnston at Shiloh" in *Battles and Leaders of the Civil War*, argued that his father had the battle won, only to have Beauregard throw it away. Beauregard's article in the same volume, "The Campaign of Shiloh," denied Johnston's allegations.

While the first school of partisan bickering had little to do with the formulation of the park, the second school directly affected park formation and continues to do so in the early years of the twenty-first century. Within this school exists the work of the park commission historian D. W. Reed: the still-valuable *The Battle of Shiloh and the Organizations Engaged* (1902). Reed is the father of this school, which emphasized the importance of the Hornet's Nest to the battle. Other historians and park officials, such as DeLong Rice and Albert Dillahunty, continued the thesis. The first major academic monograph on the battle, James Lee McDonough's *Shiloh: In Hell Before Night* (1977) carried this thesis to the academic community, and most scholarly studies even today perpetuate Reed's theory.

The more recent, if less acknowledged, third school of thought concentrates not on the Hornet's Nest but rather upon Albert Sidney Johnston's death as the key to the battle. In his biography, *Albert Sidney Johnston: Soldier of Three Republics* (1964), Charles Roland argued that the Confederate general's death caused the Southern defeat. He stated that Beauregard inherited an army on the verge of victory and that just because Beauregard lost the battle did not mean that Johnston would have. Roland stressed his subject's leadership abilities in an effort to argue that Johnston could have spurred the army on to victory when Beauregard could not. Wiley Sword, in *Shiloh: Bloody April* (1974), continued the thesis that Johnston's death was the critical point in the battle, causing a lull on the Confederate right flank. Sword went to great lengths to establish the circumstances of Johnston's death, including in an appendix a detailed medical explanation. He even attempted to relocate the place of Johnston's wounding, arguing that Isham G. Harris identified the wrong location.

The fourth school is revisionist in nature, questioning Reed's contention about the Hornet's Nest's importance, as well as other arguments, such as the magnitude of Ruggles' Battery. Stacy D. Allen, chief ranger at the park, has written two full-length articles in *Blue and Gray* magazine: "Shiloh! The Campaign and First Day's Battle" and "Shiloh! The Second Day's Battle and Aftermath," both published in 1997. After years of intense study, Allen offered a completely different analysis, taken from a study of the effects of geography on the time and space factors of unit maneuvers. He argued that the Confederate command authority, most notably Johnston, misread the Union deployment at Pittsburg Landing in the context of the geography of the site. Johnston believed the Union camps lay in a line from north to south, facing west, but in actuality, the front line of camps ran east and west, facing south. With this faulty information, Johnston came to believe that he had actually turned Grant's left flank early in the day, thereby mistakenly placing emphasis on the Confederate left in order to drive the enemy into the swamps of Owl Creek north of Pittsburg Landing.

The most recent monograph is a political analysis: Larry J. Daniel's *Shiloh: The Battle That Changed the Civil War* (1997). He placed the battle in the context of political concerns and incorporated some of the revisionist arguments of the Allen thesis, such as questioning the importance of Ruggles' Battery. He stated that Johnston's death made little difference and even argued that the Confederates never really had a chance for victory in the campaign anyway. Even if Johnston had won an impressive victory at Shiloh, the gains would have been strategically negligible.

The revisionist school is nowhere near finished in its examination of Shiloh. To be sure, it has questioned many longstanding myths that have stood for decades, but there has yet to be written a comprehensive study of the battle from the revisionists' standpoint. As a result, in 2004, no one work fully incorporates all the research and interpretation done by the revisionist historians.

Amid all the historiographical chaos, however, one school remains the most influential. The Reed school that emphasized the Hornet's Nest still dominates Shiloh history. Visitors to Shiloh want to see the Hornet's Nest more than any other part of the battlefield. The wayside exhibits that interpret the action there take the Reed approach. Even the most recent studies of the battle still present the Reed interpretation. D. W. Reed, the father of Shiloh National Military Park, continues to dominate the battle's history. His one-hundred-year-old book and the interpretation it produced, though challenged, has not yet been replaced.

NOTES

ABBREVIATIONS

CCNMP   Chickamauga and Chattanooga National
Military Park

FHS   Filson Historical Society

LC   Library of Congress

MSCPL   Memphis Shelby County Public Library

NARA   National Archives and Records Administration

OR   *War of the Rebellion: A Compilation of the Official Records of
the Union and Confederate Armies.* 128 vols. Washington, D.C.:
Government Printing Office, 1880–1901.

SNMP   Shiloh National Military Park

INTRODUCTION

1. The 1890s were turbulent years in American history. This was the decade of the Panic of 1893, Coxey's Army, the Populist Party, free silver, William Jennings Bryan and the "Cross of Gold," the Pullman Strike, *Plessy* v. *Ferguson* and Jim Crowism, urban reform, and hard-fought presidential campaigns. It was a time when the nation faced a variety of problems and challenges. This book does not concentrate on these issues, important as they were. Instead, it views the creation of Shiloh National Military Park from the perspective of the movement to reunite North and South, still split by Civil War animosities. Emphasis on the sectional reconciliation resided in the joint acceptance of the bravery of soldiers on both sides in the 1860s conflict. These other major issues were passed over in the movement to heal the sectional split.

2. See David L. Schalk, *War and the Ivory Tower: Algeria and Vietnam* (New York: Oxford Univ. Press, 1991), for a discussion of the agreement between the interest groups necessary to memorialize a war successfully.

3. *House Reports,* 53rd Cong., 2nd sess., Rept. 1139, 1; George Mason, *Illinois at Shiloh* (Chicago: M. A. Donohue and Company, n.d.), 175, 181–82; T. J. Lindsey, *Ohio at Shiloh: Report of the Commission* (Cincinnati: C. J. Krehbiel and Company, 1903), 195.

4. Mason, *Illinois at Shiloh,* 181; Lindsey, *Ohio at Shiloh,* 200, 205; F. H. Magdeburg, *Wisconsin at Shiloh: Report of the Commission* (Milwaukee: Riverside Printing Company, 1909), 82, 112, 115, 117.

5. David Blight, *Race and Reunion: The Civil War in American Memory* (Cambridge: Harvard Univ. Press, 2001); Edward T. Linenthal, *Sacred Ground: Americans and Their Battlefields* (Urbana: Univ. of Illinois Press, 1991); Gaines M. Foster, *Ghosts of the Confederacy: Defeat, The Lost Cause, and the Emergence of the New South* (New York: Oxford Univ. Press, 1987); G. Kurt Piehler, *Remembering War the American Way* (Washington, D.C.: Smithsonian Institution Press, 1995).

6. Charles E. Shedd, *A History of Shiloh National Military Park, Tennessee* (Washington, D.C.: Government Printing Office, 1954); Herman Hattaway and A. J. Meek, *Gettysburg to Vicksburg: The Five Original Civil War Battlefield Parks* (Columbia: Univ. of Missouri Press,

2001); Richard L. Kiper, *Major General John Alexander McClernand: Politician in Uniform* (Kent, Ohio: Kent State Univ. Press, 1999); Stephen D. Engle, *Don Carlos Buell: Most Promising of All* (Chapel Hill: Univ. of North Carolina Press, 1999).

7. See Stacy D. Allen, "Shiloh! The Campaign and First Day's Battle," *Blue and Gray* 14, no. 3 (Winter 1997): entire issue; Stacy D. Allen, "Shiloh! The Second Day's Battle and Aftermath," *Blue and Gray* 14, no. 4 (Spring 1997): entire issue; Larry J. Daniel, *Shiloh: The Battle That Changed the Civil War* (New York: Simon and Shuster, 1997); James Lee McDonough, *Shiloh: In Hell Before Night* (Knoxville: Univ. of Tennessee Press, 1977); Wiley Sword, *Shiloh: Bloody April* (New York: William Morrow and Company, 1974).

CHAPTER 1

1. Haywood S. Harrell to Herb Harper, July 21, 1998, Vertical File, Indian Mounds, Shiloh National Military Park, hereafter cited as SNMP. The Shiloh Indian Mounds were made a National Historic Landmark in 1989.

2. W. H. Holmes to Superintendent Shiloh NMP, Apr. 17, 1914; Secretary and Superintendent Shiloh NMP to W. H. Holmes, Apr. 21, 1914; W. H. Holmes to DeLong Rice, Apr. 28, 1914, all in Series 1, Box 15, Folder 203, SNMP; Shedd, *A History of Shiloh National Military Park*, 2.

3. Ronald F. Lee, "Report of Historical Work at Shiloh National Military Park," Vertical File, Indian Mounds, SNMP; Lindsay Christine M. Beditz, "Excavations at Mound A, Shiloh National Military Park, Tennessee," (Tallahassee: Southeast Archaeological Center, 1890), 4; Clarence B. Moore, "Aboriginal Sites on Tennessee River," Vertical File, Indian Mounds, 224, SNMP.

4. P. M. Harbert, *Early History of Hardin County, Tennessee* (Memphis: Tri-State Printing and Binding Company, 1968), 42–43; Shedd, *A History of Shiloh National Military Park*, 6, 8–9.

5. "Chain of Title," W. C. Meeks land, Series 1, Box 22, Folder 312, SNMP; "Pittsburg Landing Name Explained," *Memphis Commercial Appeal*, May 3, 1952; B. G. Brazelton, *A History of Hardin County* (Nashville: Cumberland Presbyterian Publishing House, 1885), 35; Shedd, *A History of Shiloh National Military Park*, 6. For a history of Shiloh Church, see Appendix 6.

6. Shedd, *A History of Shiloh National Military Park*, 8.

7. Brazelton, *A History of Hardin County*, 67.

8. Ibid, 58–66.

9. Ibid.

10. David W. Reed, *The Battle of Shiloh and the Organizations Engaged*, 2nd ed. (Washington, D.C.: Government Printing Office, 1909), 8. Subsequent references to Reed's book will be to either this edition or the original 1902 edition; citations of the second edition will be indicated as "2nd ed.," as here.

11. *War of the Rebellion: A Compilation of the Official Records of the Union and Confederate Armies* (Washington, D.C.: Government Printing Office, 1880–1901), series 1, vol. 10, pt. 1:27. Subsequent references to this source will be abbreviated *OR* and followed by series, volume, part number, and page reference.

12. This short account of the battle is taken from the published literature on the engagement. See Appendix 7 for a discussion of Shiloh historiography.

13. George B. Davis to Secretary of War, Mar. 18, 1895, Series 1, Box 19, Folder 267, SNMP; Brazelton, *A History of Hardin County*, 35; George W. McBride, "Shiloh, After Thirty-Two Years," in *Under Both Flags: A Panorama of the Great Civil War As Represented in Story, Anecdote, Adventure, and the Romance of Reality* (Philadelphia: People's Publishing Company, 1896), 221.

14. "Shocking Conditions of the Confederate Dead at Shiloh," Jan. 2, 1878, *Talladega* (Ala.) *Reporter and Watchtower;* Brazelton, *A History of Hardin County*, 82. The Park Commission claimed to have located nine Confederate burial trenches. However, only five of these burial trenches are now marked at Shiloh National Military Park. There are, no doubt, other Union and Confederate dead still interred on the battlefield itself.

15. For the continual discovery of soldiers on the field, see Jesse H. Curtis Statement, Feb. 19, 1898, and John W. Shaw to J. W. Scully, Feb. 21, 1898, both in Series 4, Box 1, Folder 2, SNMP; R. H. Bailey to Quartermaster General, Feb. 7, 1934, Series 4, Box 15, Folder 191, SNMP; "Resting Place," *Raleigh News and Observer*, May 27, 1979, in "Request For Permission For Interment Of Two Confederate Soldiers On The Shiloh National Military Park," SNMP; Otis H. Jones, "Building Shiloh Park," Vertical File, 10, 13–14, SNMP; *Report of the Proceedings of the Society of the Army of the Tennessee at the Twenty-Fifth Meeting held at Chicago, Ills. September 12th and 13th, 1893* (Cincinnati: F. W. Freeman, 1893), vol. 25:8, 60–61. The two Confederate soldiers found in 1977 were later buried in front of one of the Confederate burial trenches in the park.

16. David Charles Sloane, *The Last Great Necessity: Cemeteries in American History* (Baltimore: Johns Hopkins Univ. Press, 1991); James J. Farrell, *Inventing the American Way of Death, 1830–1920* (Philadelphia: Temple Univ. Press, 1980); Piehler, *Remembering War the American Way*, 6, 50; Dept. Quartermaster to F. E. Kirk, July 30, 1888, RG 92, E 576, Box 61, National Archives and Records Administration, hereafter cited as NARA; Regional Chief of Operations to Superintendent Shiloh National Military Park, June 1, 1960, Series 4, Box 15, Folder 200, SNMP; Dean W. Holt, *American Military Cemeteries: A Comprehensive Illustrated Guide to the Hallowed Grounds of the United States, Including Cemeteries Overseas* (Jefferson, N.C.: McFarland and Company, 1992), 2–3; Brian Keith McCutchen, "Of Monuments and Remembrance: A History and Structural Analysis of the Monuments of Shiloh," M.A. thesis, Southeast Missouri State Univ., 1995, 14; *Annual Report of the Secretary of War—1866* (Washington, D.C.: Government Printing Office, 1866), 50, 116. The government created an initial series of cemeteries, mostly in the North, but waited until after the war ended and tempers cooled before creating cemeteries on southern battlefields. Wartime building of cemeteries in the South would not only take manpower away from the war effort but also expose laborers to still-active Confederate forces that might be lurking in the areas.

17. War Dept. Memo, Jan. 6, 1869, RG 92, Office of the Quartermaster General, General Correspondence File, Box 2116, Folder 601.1, NARA; Chain of Title and Final Decree, Mar. 4, 1869, Series 4, Box 1, Folder 9, SNMP; Shedd, *A History of Shiloh National Military Park*, 67.

18. Regional Chief of Operations to Superintendent Shiloh National Military Park, June 1, 1960, Series 4, Box 15, Folder 200, SNMP; E. B. Whitman to J. L. Donelson, Apr. 29, 1866, RG 92, E 576, Box 53, NARA.

19. Regional Chief of Operations to Superintendent Shiloh National Military Park, June 1, 1960, Series 4, Box 15, Folder 200, SNMP; D. W. Reed, "Full of Interest: Magnificent Paper on National Cemeteries and Parks—Major David W. Reed Makes a Plea for the Establishment and Maintenance of National Military Parks on Famous Battlefields," Series 3, Box 4, Folder 219, SNMP; Charles E. Burr letter, Aug. 1866, RG 92, E 225, Box 1028, NARA; U. S. Quartermaster Dept., *Roll of Honor: Names of Soldiers Who Died in Defense of the American Union Interred in the National Cemeteries*, 27 vols. (Washington, D.C.: Government Printing Office, 1869), 20: 119.

20. Ephraim P. Abbott to Mother, July 11, 1867, Vertical File, Shiloh National Cemetery, SNMP; Regional Chief of Operations to Superintendent Shiloh National Military Park, June 1, 1960, Series 4, Box 15, Folder 200, SNMP; Quartermaster Dept., *Roll of Honor*, 20: 119; Michael A. Capps, "Shiloh National Military Park: An Administrative History," unpublished draft, 1993, 100.

21. "Monthly Report of Utilization of Gravesites," Dec. 1982, Series 4, Box 14, Folder 188, SNMP; Quartermaster Dept., *Roll of Honor*, 20: 119.

22. A. W. Wills to C.H. Folsom, Mar. 24, 1868, RG 92, E 576, Box 53, NARA; Lera Durbin, "Historical Reports: Shiloh National Cemetery," Vertical File, Shiloh National Cemetery, 2, SNMP.

23. Report of Inspection, Pittsburg Landing National Cemetery, Aug. 8, 1867, RG 92, E 576, Box 53, NARA; Quartermaster Dept., *Roll of Honor,* 20: 119; James Gall to A. F. Rockwell, Feb. 13, 1876, Series 4, Box 10, Folder 109, SNMP; *Annual Report of the Secretary of War—1873*, 119; *Annual Report of the Secretary of War—1877*, 195; *Annual Report of the Secretary of War—1865*, 177. Many soldiers from the Spanish-American War, both World Wars, the Korean War, and the Vietnam conflict have joined the Civil War servicemen. Even one veteran of the Persian Gulf War is memorialized in the cemetery.

24. Hiliary A. Tolson et al, *Historic Listing of National Park Service Officials* (Washington, D.C.: United States Dept. of the Interior, 1991), 173. For a full list of the cemetery superintendents, see Appendix 3.

25. Thomas Frame to H. B. Larson, Nov. 8, 1875, RG 92, E 576, Box 53, NARA; Report of Inspection, Pittsburg Landing National Cemetery, Aug. 8, 1867, RG 92, E 576, Box 53, NARA; Cemetery Superintendent Monthly Report, Feb. 1894 and Mar. 1894, Series 4, Box 8, Folder 98, SNMP; H. B. Sansau to Superintendent Shiloh National Cemetery, Jan. 3 and June 12, 1876, both in Series 4, Box 11, Folder 142, SNMP; *Annual Report of the Secretary of War—1876*, 288–89; *Annual Report of the Secretary of War—1870*, 229.

26. *Annual Report of the Secretary of War—1872*, 152; *Annual Report of the Secretary of War—1891*, 485; *Annual Report of the Secretary of War—1892*, 360; Cemetery Superintendent Monthly Report, Feb. 1894 and Mar. 1894, Series 4, Box 8, Folder 98, SNMP; D. H. Rhodes to R. N. Batchelder, Nov. 25, 1893, Series 4, Box 10, Folder 108, SNMP; for the steps, see Frederick Schmidt to J. W. Scully, June 20, 1891, Series 4, Letters Sent, vol. 1:34, SNMP; for the gates, see Superintendent Shiloh National Cemetery to Chief Quartermaster, Feb. 15, 1911, and Superintendent Shiloh National Cemetery to Chief Quartermaster, May 18, 1911, both in Series 4, Box 12, Folder 146, SNMP.

27. Report of Inspection, Pittsburg Landing National Cemetery, Nov. 8, 1867, RG 92, E 576, Box 53, NARA; Report of Inspection, Shiloh National Cemetery, Jan. 8, 1889, RG 92, E 576, Box 61, NARA; *Annual Report of the Secretary of War—1871*, 176, 186; D. H. Rhodes to R. N. Batchelder, Nov. 25, 1893, Series 4, Box 10, Folder 108, SNMP.

28. Cemetery Superintendent Monthly Report, Apr. 1894, Series 4, Box 8, Folder 98, SNMP; Frederick Schmidt to John L. Clem, June 18, 1893, Letters Sent, Vol. 1: 98, SNMP; Durbin, "Historical Reports: Shiloh National Cemetery," 3.

29. Clayton Hart to J. L. Clem, Apr. 29, 1896, Series 4, Letters Sent, Vol. 1:186, SNMP; Atwell Thompson to Cornelius Cadle, June 9, 1896, Series 1, Box 37, Folder 621, SNMP; *OR*, series 1, vol. 10, pt. 1:101.

30. J. W. Scully to Superintendent Shiloh National Cemetery, July 12, 1889, Series 4, Box 1, Folder 11, SNMP; *Annual Report of the Secretary of War—1891*, 485.

31. Unknown to Henry W. Halleck, Apr. 11, 1871, RG 92, E 576, Box 52, NARA; James Gall to M. C. Meigs, Apr. 30, 1874, Series 4, Box 11, Folder 140, and J. E. Bloom to Superintendent Shiloh National Cemetery, July 13, 1903, Series 4, Box 11, Folder 140, both in SNMP.

32. L. S. Doolittle to C. A. Reynolds, June 22, 1884, RG 92, E 576, Box 53, NARA; John W. Shaw to Samuel R. Jones, June 4, 1904, Shiloh National Cemetery, Letters Sent, Vol. 2:6, SNMP; Shiloh National Military Park Commission Daily Events, June 8, 1904, 194, SNMP.

33. James Williams to John W. Shaw, Feb. 19, 1897, Series 4, Box 11, Folder 128, SNMP; Reed, "Full of Interest"; Commanding Officer to Superintendent Shiloh National Cemetery, June 29, 1908; Apr. 8, 1923; and Mar. 11, 1930, all in Series 4, Box 11, Folder 129, SNMP; H. W. Weeks to John W. Shaw, May 29, 1897, Series 4, Box 1, Folder 5, SNMP; S. S. Frowe to Superintendent Shiloh National Cemetery, Apr. 11, 1906, Series 4, Box 7, Folder 90, SNMP.

CHAPTER 2

1. For background, see James M. McPherson, *Battle Cry of Freedom: The Civil War Era* (New York: Oxford Univ. Press, 1988); William W. Freehling, *The Road to Disunion: Secessionists at Bay, 1776–1854* (New York: Oxford Univ. Press, 1990); Eric Foner, *Reconstruction: America's Unfinished Revolution, 1863–1877* (New York: Harper Collins, 1989).

2. For background, see Nell Irvin Painter, *Standing at Armageddon: The United States, 1877–1919* (New York: W. W. Norton, 1987); Vincent P. DeSantis, *The Shaping of Modern America, 1877–1920* (Wheeling, Ill.: Forum Press, 1973); C. Vann Woodward, *The Strange Career of Jim Crow,* 3rd ed. (New York: Oxford Univ. Press, 1989); Ronald F. Lee, *The Origin and Evolution of the National Military Park Idea* (Washington, D.C.: National Park Service, 1973), 6–7, 12; Piehler, *Remembering War the American Way,* 64–66.

3. Lee, *The Origin and Evolution,* 6; Piehler, *Remembering War the American Way,* 65, 71; Brent K. Ashabranner, *No Better Hope: What the Lincoln Memorial Means to America* (Brookfield, Conn.: Twenty First Century Books, 2001).

4. Lee, *The Origin and Evolution,* 13, 16.

5. *Report of the Proceedings of the Society of the Army of the Tennessee,* 25:58, 60–61.

6. Ibid.

7. Ibid., 59–61.

8. Ibid., 59, 62.

9. Ibid., 60–61. At least some of the vice presidents were named without their prior knowledge or consent.

10. Ibid., 59; *Report of the Proceedings of the Society of the Army of the Tennessee at the Twenty-Sixth Meeting held at Council Bluffs, Iowa. October 3rd and 4th, 1894* (Cincinnati: F. W. Freeman, 1895), vol. 26:126; Memphis *Commercial Appeal,* Dec. 5, 1894, 1.

11. *Report of the Proceedings of the Society of the Army of the Tennessee,* 25:59.

12. Lee, *The Origin and Evolution,* 38.

13. Piehler, *Remembering War the American Way,* 51.

14. Ibid., 3.

15. "List of Lands Optioned to John A. McClernand, President, E. T. Lee, Secretary, and J. W. Coleman, Treasurer, of the Shiloh Battlefield Association," undated, Series 1, Box 19, Folder 268, SNMP; "Copy of Option Form," blank and undated, Series 1, Box 19, Folder 268, SNMP; "Memorandum of Agreement," Mar. 26, 1895, Series 1, Box 21, Folder 295, SNMP; *Report of the Proceedings of the Society of the Army of the Tennessee,* 26:125.

16. *Report of the Proceedings of the Society of the Army of the Tennessee*, 25:59.

17. David B. Henderson Compiled Service Record, NARA; *Biographical Directory of the United States Congress* (Washington, D.C.: Government Printing Office, 1989), 1170; David W. Reed, *Campaigns and Battles of the Twelfth Regiment Iowa Veteran Volunteer Infantry: From Organization, September , 1861, to Muster-Out, January 20, 1866* (n.p., n.d.), 64.

18. *Report of the Proceedings of the Society of the Army of the Tennessee*, 26:127.

19. For a complete copy of H.R. 6499, see Appendix 1.

20. *Congressional Record*, 53rd Cong., 3rd sess., 27, pt. 1:19.

21. Ibid.

22. Ibid.

23. Ibid., 19–20.

24. Ibid., 20.

25. Ibid.

26. Ibid.

27. Ibid.

28. Ibid., 19; *Congressional Record*, 53rd Cong., 2nd sess., 26, pt. 4:3368.

29. *Congressional Record*, 53rd Cong., 2nd sess., 26, pt. 7:6722; *House Reports*, 53rd Cong., 2nd sess., Rept. 1139, 1–5.

30. *House Reports*, 53rd Cong., 2nd sess., Rept. 1139, 1–5.

31. Ibid.

32. *Report of the Proceedings of the Society of the Army of the Tennessee*, 26:127–28.

33. *Congressional Record*, 53rd Cong., 3rd sess., 27, pt. 1:20.

34. Ibid.

35. Ibid.

36. Ibid., 21.

37. Ibid.

38. Ibid.

39. Ibid., 73, 270; *Senate Reports*, 53rd Cong., 3rd sess., Rept. 722, 1–4.

40. *Congressional Record*, 53rd Cong., 3rd sess., 27, pt. 1:393. Of course, Bate and Harris, both Shiloh veterans, were interested in the project because the proposed park was in their state.

41. Ibid., 430.

42. Ibid., 651. Grover Cleveland was no stranger to Civil War memory controversy. In his first term, he had returned Confederate battle flags to southern states, earning the ire of many northern Republicans.

43. Shedd, *A History of Shiloh National Military Park*, 19; Lee, *The Origin and Evolution*, 35–36.

44. *Report of the Proceedings of the Society of the Army of the Tennessee*, 26:128.

45. George W. Davis to George B. Davis, Oct. 9, 1895, "Letter Book of Shiloh National Military Park Commission," RG 92, E713, NARA; Shedd, *A History of Shiloh National Military Park*, 19–21; Lee, *The Origin and Evolution*, 40–42. The Antietam Plan was an effort to save

money and government intervention at key battlefield sites. This policy of buying as little land as possible was implemented first at Antietam and later at parks such as Fort Donelson, Appomattox, and Kennesaw Mountain.

46. Lee, *The Origin and Evolution*, 14.

CHAPTER 3

1. Lee, *The Origin and Evolution*, 14.

2. Daniel S. Lamont to Cornelius Cadle, Mar. 14, 1895, Box 91, Book 7, Daniel S. Lamont Papers, 336, Library of Congress, hereafter cited as LC; Henry J. Baker to John C. Black, May 28, 1895; Augustus Laubscher to Cornelius Cadle, Mar. 14, 1895; Charles P. Westerfield to Cornelius Cadle, D. C. Buell, and R. F. Looney, Mar. 18, 1895; G. W. Wooldridge to W. B. Allison, Mar. 26, 1895; W. B. Allison to G. M. Dodge, Mar. 27, 1895; Samuel Lyon to Cornelius Cadle, Apr. 6, 1895, all in Series 1, Box 36, Folder 583, SNMP; A. T. Andreas to George B. Davis, Jan. 31, 1895, and A. W. Wills to George B. Davis, Feb. 14, 1895, both in RG 92, E 712, Box 1, NARA. For a complete list of park commissioners and superintendents, see Appendix 4.

3. E. C. Dawes to George B. Davis, Dec. 29, 1894, RG 92, E 712, Box 1, NARA.

4. For Cadle, see Cornelius Cadle, Jr., in Vertical File, SNMP; Cornelius Cadle Compiled Service Record, NARA; *OR*, series I, vol. 10, pt. 1:121, 125; *Roster and Record of Iowa Soldiers in the War of the Rebellion Together with Historical Sketches of Volunteer Organizations, 1861–1866* (Des Moines: Emory H. English, 1908), vol. 2:284, 306; Frank W. Mahin, *Genealogy of the Cadle Family Including English Decent* (n.p., 1915), 95.

5. Francis B. Heitman, *Historical Register and Dictionary of the United States Army, From Its Organization, September 29, 1789, to March 2, 1903* (Washington, D.C.: Government Printing Office, 1903), vol. 1: 272; *Roster and Record of Iowa Soldiers*, 2: 284, 306.

6. Heitman, *Historical Register*, 1: 272; Mahin, *Genealogy of the Cadle Family*, 95–100.

7. Daniel S. Lamont to Cornelius Cadle, Mar. 12, 1895, RG 92, E 713, NARA; E. C. Dawes to George B. Davis, Jan. 24, 1895, RG 92, E 712, Box 1, NARA; W. S. Yeatman to Cornelius Cadle, July 6, 1895, Series 1, Box 9, Folder 67, SNMP; Biographical Sketch of Ephraim C. Dawes, Apr. 1895, Series 1, Box 13, Folder 127, SNMP; D. B. Henderson to D. W. Reed, Mar. 28, 1895, Series 3, Box 1, Folder 91, SNMP.

8. George B. Davis to Secretary of War, Mar. 12, 1895, RG 92, E 713, NARA.

9. For Buell, see Ezra J. Warner, *Generals in Blue: Lives of the Union Commanders* (Baton Rouge: Louisiana State Univ. Press, 1964), 51–52; Engle, *Don Carlos Buell*.

10. George B. Davis to Secretary of War, Mar. 12, 1895, RG 92, E 713, NARA; "Col. R. F. Looney," *Confederate Veteran* 8, no. 1 (Jan. 1900): 36–37; Robert F. Looney Compiled Service Record, NARA.

11. J. W. Irwin Compiled Service Record, NARA; "Capt. James William Irwin," *Confederate Veteran* 22, no. 5 (May 1914): 220.

12. James W. Irwin Appointment, Feb. 11, 1895, RG 92, E 713, NARA; J. W. Irwin to William B. Bate, Jan. 4, 1895, RG 92, E 712, Box 1, NARA.

13. James W. Irwin Appointment, Feb. 11, 1895, RG 92, E 712, Box 1, NARA; Allen R. Adams to Cornelius Cadle, July 18, 1895, RG 92, E 713, NARA; F. A. Large Appointment, Sept. 24, 1897, RG 92, E 712, Box 1, NARA; J. M. Riddell Appointment, June 1, 1895, Series 1, Box 37,

Folder 618, SNMP; F. A. Large Compiled Service Record, NARA; Cornelius Cadle to D. W. Reed, Mar. 22, 1899, Series 1, Box 13, Folder 114, SNMP.

14. Atwell Thompson Appointment, May 1, 1895, Series 1, Box 37, Folder 618, SNMP.

15. Atwell Thompson to Chickamauga and Chattanooga National Military Park, Feb. 13, 1895, Series 1, Box 37, Folder 618, SNMP; Atwell Thompson appointment, May 1, 1895, Series 1, Box 37, Folder 618, SNMP; H. V. Boynton to Cornelius Cadle, Mar. 21, 1895, Series 1, Box 35, Folder 570, SNMP; Cornelius Cadle to Willard Warner, June 8, 1896, Series 1, Box 37, Folder 621, SNMP; Ray H. Mattison to Regional Director, Apr. 13, 1948, Series 1, Box 56, Folder 866, SNMP.

16. Alexander P. Stewart to Chickamauga and Chattanooga National Military Park Commission, Feb. 14, 1895, Series 1, Box 37, Folder 618, SNMP; J. S. Fullerton, Frank Smith, and H. V. Boynton to War Dept., Feb. 18, 1895, Series 1, Box 37, Folder 618, SNMP; Atwell Thompson to Chickamauga and Chattanooga National Military Park, Feb. 13, 1895, Series 1, Box 37, Folder 618, SNMP.

17. A. J. Gahagan et al to Congress, Apr. 14, 1896; Atwell Thompson to Cornelius Cadle, May 21, 1896; Cornelius Cadle to Willard Warner, June 8, 1896, all in Series 1, Box 37, Folder 621, SNMP.

18. D. W. Reed Appointment, Mar. 26, 1895, RG 92, E 713, NARA.

19. D. W. Reed to Cornelius Cadle, Aug. 5, 1895, Series 1, Box 37, Folder 619, SNMP; Charles B. Clark and Roger B. Bowen, *University Recruits—Company C: 12th Iowa Infantry Regiment, U.S.A, 1861–1865* (Elverson, Pa.: Mennonite Family History, 1991), 34.

20. D. W. Reed photograph, Series 3, Box 5, Folder 241, SNMP.

21. D. W. Reed Compiled Service Record, NARA; Clark and Bowen, *University Recruits,* 34.

22. Various D. W. Reed documents and commissions, all in Series 3, Artifact Cabinet 7, Drawer 1, Folders 282–87, SNMP; Reed, *Campaigns and Battles of the Twelfth Regiment Iowa Veteran Volunteer Infantry,* 250–51.

23. D. W. Reed to Cornelius Cadle, Aug. 5, 1895, Series 1, Box 37, Folder 619, SNMP; D. B. Henderson to D. W. Reed, Jan. 13, 1895, Series 3, Box 1, Folder 90; SNMP; D. W. Reed appointment, Mar. 26, 1895, RG 92, E 713, NARA.

24. George B. Davis to R. F. Looney, Apr. 16, 1895, Series 1, Box 37, Folder 618, SNMP; Jim Ogden, Historian, Chickamauga and Chattanooga National Military Park, interview by author, May 21, 2001; Terry Winschel, historian, Vicksburg National Military Park, interview by author, May 21, 2001; D. Scott Hartwig, historian, Gettysburg National Military Park, interview by author, May 22, 2001; Ted Alexander, historian, Antietam National Battlefield, interview by author, May 25, 2001. Actually, Looney's experience on the Shiloh Commission may reflect a general pattern of northern domination in the national military parks and certainly highlights a lack of central control over the various battlefields. The southern representatives at Chickamauga and Antietam apparently wielded no real power, while those at Vicksburg and Gettysburg held much authority.

25. George B. Davis to D. B. Henderson, Feb. 20, 1895, RG 92, E 713, NARA; D. B. Henderson to Cornelius Cadle, Mar. 29, 1895, Series 1, Box 35, Folder 531, SNMP; D. B. Henderson to Cornelius Cadle, July 7, 1895, Series 1, Box 13, Folder 153, SNMP; D. B. Henderson to D. W. Reed, Jan. 13, 1895, Series 1, Box 35, Folder 555, SNMP; D. B. Henderson to D. W. Reed, Mar. 28, 1895, Series 3, Box 1, Folder 91, SNMP.

26. See each individual's Compiled Service Record, NARA.

27. Daniel S. Lamont to Cornelius Cadle, Mar. 12, 1895, RG 92, E 713, NARA; George B. Davis to Secretary of War, Mar. 18, 1895, Series 1, Box 19, Folder 267, SNMP.

28. George B. Davis to Cornelius Cadle, Mar. 28, 1895, Series 1, Box 37, Folder 618, SNMP.

29. "Boundary Description: By Metes and Bounds," undated, Series 1, Box 40, Folder 644, SNMP; "Preliminary Map: Battlefield of Shiloh," Dec. 1, 1895, Series 7, Drawer 1, Folder 7, SNMP.

30. George B. Davis to Cornelius Cadle, May 6, 1895, Series 1, Box 37, Folder 618, SNMP.

31. Daniel S. Lamont Order, Feb. 11, 1895; George B. Davis to Cornelius Cadle, Mar. 26, 1895; Daniel S. Lamont to Cornelius Cadle, Mar. 26, 1895; Daniel S. Lamont to Cornelius Cadle, Apr. 20, 1895; Daniel S. Lamont to Cornelius Cadle, May 10, 1895, all in RG 92, E 713, NARA; George B. Davis to Cornelius Cadle, Apr. 8, 1895, Series 1, Box 37, Folder 618, SNMP.

32. George B. Davis to War Dept., Oct. 2, 1895, RG 92, E 713, NARA; George B. Davis to Cornelius Cadle, Mar. 28, 1895, Series 1, Box 37, Folder 618, SNMP.

33. George B. Davis to Cornelius Cadle, Apr. 27, 1895 and May 13, 1895, Series 1, Box 37, Folder 618, SNMP; Clayton Hart to John L. Clem, Apr. 17, 1895, Series 4, Letters Sent, Vol. 1: 157, SNMP; Jones, "Building Shiloh Park," 6.

34. Joseph B. Doe to George W. Davis, Aug. 23, 1895, Series 1, Box 37, Folder 619, SNMP.

CHAPTER 4

1. Isabell Borgeson, "Character Sketch of Colonel E. T. Lee," Series 1, Box 13, Folder 153, SNMP; "Feel Indignant," newspaper clipping, no date, no heading, Series 1, Box 39, Folder 635, SNMP.

2. *Report of the Proceedings of the Society of the Army of the Tennessee*, 26:124–26.

3. John A. McClernand to E. T. Lee, Aug. 6, 1895, Series 1, Box 39, Folder 635, SNMP; John A. McClernand to Cornelius Cadle, Aug. 12, 1895 and Oct. 11, 1895, Series 1, Box 39, Folder 635, SNMP.

4. D. C. Buell to Robert F. Looney, June 9, 1895, Robert F. Looney Collection, Folder 64, Memphis Shelby County Public Library, hereafter cited as MSCPL; R. F. Looney to Cornelius Cadle, Aug. 21, 1895, Series 1, Box 39, Folder 635, SNMP; John A. McClernand to Cornelius Cadle, Sept. 26, and Oct. 11, 1895, Series 1, Box 39, Folder 635, SNMP.

5. E. T. Lee to Robert F. Looney, May 9, 1895, Robert F. Looney Collection, Folder 63, MSCPL; John A. McClernand to Cornelius Cadle, Nov. 12, 1895, Series 1, Box 39, Folder 635, SNMP; William H. Busby to D. W. Reed, Feb. 6, 1896, Series 1, Box 14, Folder 173, SNMP; Unknown to Editor, *Commercial-Gazette*, Dec. 24, 1895, Series 1, Box 13, Folder 153, SNMP; E. T. Lee to J. W. Petty, June 24, 1895, Series 1, Box 13, Folder 153, SNMP. Boynton was active in Chickamauga's affairs, and had caused major controversy over William T. Sherman's memoirs by publishing *Sherman's Historic Raid: The Memoirs in the Light of the Record* (Cincinnati: Wilstach, Baldwin, and Company, 1875).

6. "Circular," 1896, Robert F. Looney Collection, Folder 71, MSCPL; John A. McClernand to Cornelius Cadle, Mar. 25, 1896, Series 1, Box 39, Folder 635, SNMP; D. W. Reed to Cornelius Cadle, Feb. 3, 1896, Series 1, Box 37, Folder 620, SNMP; Atwell Thompson to Cornelius Cadle, June 9, 1896, Series 1, Box 37, Folder 621, SNMP; John A. McClernand to Cornelius Cadle, Jan. 21, 1896, Series 1, Box 13, Folder 153, SNMP; for Lee's expulsion from the GAR, see D. W. Reed to Cornelius Cadle, May 8, 1896, Series 1, Box 14, Folder 173, SNMP.

7. George B. Davis to Cornelius Cadle, Apr. 17 and June 25, 1895, "Letter Book of the Shiloh National Military Park Commission," RG 92, E713, NARA. As the majority of the association's officers, Lee and Coleman held the fate of the land in their hands.

8. George B. Davis to Cornelius Cadle, Sept. 24, 1895, RG 92, E 713, NARA.

9. Daniel S. Lamont to Cornelius Cadle, Apr. 20, 1895 and Daniel S. Lamont to George B. Davis, Mar. 19, 1895, both in RG 92, E 713, NARA; George B. Davis to Cornelius Cadle, Mar. 23, 1895, Series 1, Box 35, Folder 570, SNMP.

10. Shiloh National Military Park Commission engineering appointments, May 1, 1895, Series 1, Box 37, Folder 618, SNMP.

11. Atwell Thompson to Cornelius Cadle, July 9, 1895, Series 1, Box 17, Folder 249, SNMP; Atwell Thompson to Shiloh National Military Park Commission, July 10, 1896, Series 1, Box 40, Folder 640, SNMP.

12. S. M. Rogers to Atwell Thompson, July 31, 1895, Series 1, Box 37, Folder 619, SNMP; Jones, "Building Shiloh Park," 7–9.

13. Jones, "Building Shiloh Park," 8–9. The lack of cash also displayed why the soft-money advocates of the time had a valid point.

14. Atwell Thompson to Cornelius Cadle, July 9, 1895, Series 1, Box 17, Folder 249, SNMP; Atwell Thompson to Shiloh National Military Park Commission, July 10, 1896, Series 1, Box 40, Folder 640, SNMP; Atwell Thompson to Cornelius Cadle, July 20 and Aug. 6, 1895, both in Series 1, Box 37, Folder 619, SNMP.

15. Atwell Thompson to Cornelius Cadle, July 9, 1895, Series 1, Box 17, Folder 249, SNMP; Atwell Thompson to Shiloh National Military Park Commission, July 10, 1896, Series 1, Box 40, Folder 640, SNMP.

16. "Preliminary Map, Battlefield of Shiloh," Dec. 1, 1895, Series 7, Drawer 1, Folder 7, SNMP.

17. Atwell Thompson to Shiloh National Military Park Commission, July 10, 1896, Series 1, Box 40, Folder 640, SNMP.

18. George B. Davis to J. W. Irwin, Feb. 23, Mar. 1, and Mar. 7, 1895, all in RG 92, E 713, NARA; J. W. Irwin to Shiloh Commission, Mar. 5, 1895, RG 92, E 714, NARA; Cornelius Cadle to J. G. Cannon, Jan. 22, 1897, Series 1, Box 40, Folder 641, SNMP.

19. Elihu Root to Cornelius Cadle, Mar. 26, 1902, Series 1, Box 37, Folder 601, SNMP; J. W. Irwin to Cornelius Cadle, Sept. 3, 1896, Series 1, Box 18, Folder 265, SNMP; Atwell Thompson to Cornelius Cadle, Dec. 8, 1898, Series 1, Box 40, Folder 641, SNMP.

20. "Boundary Description: By Metes and Bounds," undated, Series 1, Box 40, Folder 644, SNMP; G. W. L. Smith Land Acquisition Folder, Series 1, Box 22, Folder 325, SNMP.

21. "Boundary Description: By Metes and Bounds," undated, Series 1, Box 40, Folder 644, SNMP; Thomas Walker Land Acquisition Folder, Series 1, Box 23, Folder 333, SNMP.

22. "Boundary Description: By Metes and Bounds," undated, Series 1, Box 40, Folder 644, SNMP; W. C. Meeks Land Acquisition Folder, Series 1, Box 22, Folder 312, SNMP.

23. Cornelius Cadle to J. G. Cannon, Jan. 22, 1897, Series 1, Box 40, Folder 641, SNMP.

24. Cornelius Cadle to J.G. Cannon, Jan. 22, 1897, Series 1, Box 40, Folder 641, SNMP; "Boundary Description: By Metes and Bounds," undated, Series 1, Box 40, Folder 644, SNMP.

25. "Boundary Description: By Metes and Bounds," undated, Series 1, Box 40, Folder 644, SNMP; list of land owned by SNMP, May 28, 1903, Series 1, Box 18, Folder 265, SNMP; "List

of Lands Optioned to . . . Shiloh Battlefield Association," undated, Series 1, Box 19, Folder 268, SNMP. For a complete list of land acquisition, see Appendix 2.

26. *Annual Report of the Secretary of War–1907,* 332; *Annual Report of the Secretary of War–1908,* 178; Jones, "Building Shiloh Park," 7.

27. J. W. Irwin Discharge, July 16, 1906; Cornelius Cadle to J. W. Irwin, July 19, 1906; Cornelius Cadle to Assistant Secretary of War, Apr. 6, 1908, all in Series 1, Box 35, Folder 523, SNMP; Cornelius Cadle to J. W. Irwin, July 19, 1902, Series 1, Box 38, Folder 628, SNMP.

CHAPTER 5

1. *Congressional Record,* 53rd Cong., 3rd sess., 27, pt. 1:19.

2. For these historical controversies, see Ulysses S. Grant, "The Battle of Shiloh" and Don Carlos Buell, "Shiloh Reviewed," both in *Battles and Leaders of the Civil War,* 4 vols. (New York: Century Company, 1884–87). See also Grant's *Memoirs,* as well as secondary biographies such as Engle, *Don Carlos Buell,* and Brooks D. Simpson, *Ulysses S. Grant: Triumph Over Adversity, 1822–1865* (New York: Houghton Mifflin Company, 2000). For a history of the Army of the Ohio, see Gerald J. Prokopowicz, *All for the Regiment: The Army of the Ohio, 1861–1862* (Chapel Hill: Univ. of North Carolina Press, 2001).

3. See William Preston Johnston, "Albert Sidney Johnston at Shiloh," and P. G. T. Beauregard, "The Campaign of Shiloh," both in *Battle and Leaders.*

4. Ulysses S. Grant, "The Battle of Shiloh," 1:465.

5. D. C. Buell to George W. Davis, Oct. 18, 1897, RG 92, E 713, NARA; D. C. Buell to George W. Davis, June 24, 1896, Series 1, Box 37, Folder 621, SNMP; Cornelius Cadle to D. W. Reed, Mar. 6, 1896, Series 1, Box 37, Folder 621, SNMP; Cornelius Cadle to D. W. Reed, Nov. 9, 1897, Series 1, Box 38, Folder 624, SNMP; George W. Davis to Cornelius Cadle, June 30, 1896, Series 1, Box 37, Folder 621, SNMP.

6. Rules of action for the Shiloh Battlefield Commission, July 20, 1896, Series 1, Box 38, Folder 624, SNMP; Cornelius Cadle to D. W. Reed, Aug. 6, 1896, Series 1, Box 38, Folder 622, SNMP.

7. "Regulations Governing the Erection of Monuments, Tablets, and Markers in the Chickamauga and Chattanooga National Park," Dec. 14, 1895, Series 1, Box 37, Folder 620, SNMP; "Rules to be Observed in Preparing the Battle Map," Apr. 8, 1896, Vertical File, Shiloh Battlefield Commission, SNMP.

8. "Rules to be Observed in Preparing the Battle Map," Apr. 8, 1896, Vertical File, Shiloh Battlefield Commission, SNMP.

9. "Regulations," undated, Series 1, Box 38, Folder 624, SNMP.

10. Jones, "Building Shiloh Park," 13.

11. D. W. Reed to Cornelius Cadle, Jan. 30, 1897, Series 1, Box 38, Folder 623, SNMP; D. W. Reed to Cornelius Cadle, June 1, 1897, Series 1, Box 38, Folder 624, SNMP; Shiloh National Military Park Commission Daily Events, May 20 and June 4, 1901, 29, 31, SNMP; "Federal Veterans at Shiloh," *Confederate Veteran* 3, no. 4 (Apr. 1895): 104. Similar visits of fellow park commissioners from Gettysburg and Chickamauga also helped Reed plan construction and interpretation.

12. Shiloh National Military Park Commission Daily Events, Nov. 21, 1901, 49, SNMP. For Monocacy, see Benjamin F. Cooling, *Monocacy: The Battle That Saved Washington* (Shippensburg, Pa.: White Mane, 1997).

13. Shiloh National Military Park Commission Daily Events, Nov. 19–21, 1901, 48–50, SNMP.

14. Ibid., 50–52.

15. Ibid., 52–56.

16. Ibid.

17. D. W. Reed to Basil W. Duke, July 20, 1906, Series 1, Box 13, Folder 140, SNMP.

18. Preliminary Map, Battlefield of Shiloh, Dec. 1, 1895, Series 7, Drawer 1, Folder 7, SNMP; D. W. Reed to Basil W. Duke, July 20, 1906, Series 1, Box 13, Folder 140, SNMP.

19. D. W. Reed to Basil W. Duke, July 20, 1906, Series 1, Box 13, Folder 140, SNMP.

20. Ibid.

21. Ibid.

22. Ibid. Harris's testimony, of course, did not end speculation. Reed reported in his 1912 Annual Report that as many as six men disputed Harris's claim, and even today, historians speculate that Johnston may have fallen elsewhere. See *Annual Report of the Secretary of War–1912*, 196, and Sword, *Shiloh*, 443–46.

23. D. W. Reed to Basil W. Duke, July 20, 1906, Series 1, Box 13, Folder 140, SNMP.

24. Cornelius Cadle to George W. Davis, Sept. 30, 1896, RG 92, E 712, Box 1, NARA.

25. Cornelius Cadle to Secretary of War, Feb. 23, 1901, Shiloh National Military Park Commission Daily Events, Feb. 20, 1901, 23, SNMP; Cornelius Cadle to Robert F. Looney, Aug. 10, 1895, Robert F. Looney Collection, MSCPL.

26. Atwell Thompson to Cornelius Cadle, Jan. 27, 1896, Series 1, Box 37, Folder 620, SNMP; D. W. Reed to Cornelius Cadle, Mar. 4, 1896, Series 1, Box 37, Folder 621, SNMP; Atwell Thompson to Shiloh National Military Park Commission, July 10, 1896, Series 1, Box 40, Folder 640, SNMP.

27. D. C. Buell to George W. Davis, Nov. 13, 1897, RG 92, E 712, Box 1, NARA; D. C. Buell to George W. Davis, Nov. 10, 1897, RG 92, E 713, NARA; Atwell Thompson to D. W. Reed, Nov. 14, 1900, Series 1, Box 25, Folder 369, SNMP; *Annual Report of the Secretary of War–1901*, 384.

28. Atwell Thompson to D. W. Reed, Mar. 8, 1901, Series 1, Box 25, Folder 369, SNMP; Atwell Thompson to D. W. Reed, June 23, 1899; Cornelius Cadle to John C. Scofield, Nov. 11, 1899; and D. W. Reed to Cornelius Cadle, July 12, 1899, all in Series 1, Box 25, Folder 368, SNMP.

29. Atwell Thompson to D. W. Reed, June 11, 1901, Series 1, Box 25, Folder 369; SNMP; *Annual Report of the Secretary of War–1900*, 213; *Annual Report of the Secretary of War–1901*, 384; *Annual Report of the Secretary of War–1902*, 23; *Annual Report of the Secretary of War–1903*, 236; *Annual Report of the Secretary of War–1904*, 267; *Annual Report of the Secretary of War–1905*, 150; *Annual Report of the Secretary of War–1906*, 318; *Annual Report of the Secretary of War–1908*, 178; Shiloh National Military Park Commission Daily Events, Feb. 10, 1902, 85, 113.

30. J. E. Evans to Cornelius Cadle, Sept. 9, 1902, Series 1, Box 25, Folder 370, SNMP; Shiloh National Military Park Commission Daily Events, Nov. 23, 1900, Jan. 9, 1901, and Oct. 23, 1901, 9, 16, 39, SNMP; Shiloh National Military Park Commission Annual Report, Oct. 31, 1899, Series 1, Box 40, Folder 641, SNMP. Reed even made the foundry correct the misspelling of Prentiss's name as "Prentice" on the 61st Illinois monument.

31. J. W. Irwin to J. M. Riddell, Mar. 5, 1897, Series 1, Box 25, Folder 361, SNMP; Cornelius Cadle to Secretary of War, Nov. 14, 1896, RG 92, E 713, NARA; "List of Cannon to be turned over to the Shiloh Battlefield Commission," undated, Series 1, Box 24, Folder 359, SNMP.

32. George W. Davis to Cornelius Cadle, Mar. 13, 1897, Series 1, Box 25, Folder 361, SNMP; Atwell Thompson to Cornelius Cadle, Dec. 8, 1898, Series 1, Box 40, Folder 641, SNMP.

33. John P. Nicholson to Cornelius Cadle, Apr. 23, 1897, Series 1, Box 38, Folder 623, SNMP; J. E. Evans to Cornelius Cadle, Apr. 10, 1897 and Calvin Gilbert to Cornelius Cadle, Apr. 27, 1897, both in Series 1, Box 24, Folder 360, SNMP.

34. "Request to Publish Advertisement," various newspapers, Dec. 29, 1900, Series 1, Box 25, Folder 361, SNMP; Cornelius Cadle to Atwell Thompson, Jan. 29, 1901, Series 1, Box 25, Folder 361, SNMP; Cornelius Cadle to J. W. Foley and Company, Feb. 18, 1901, Series 1, Box 25, Folder 361, SNMP.

35. Cornelius Cadle to Chief of Ordinance, May 13, 1901, Series 1, Box 25, Folder 361, SNMP; Cornelius Cadle to John C. Scofield, June 7, 1901, Series 1, Box 25, Folder 361, SNMP.

36. Cornelius Cadle to Ross-Meehan Foundry Company, Dec. 12, 1901, Series 1, Box 25, Folder 361, SNMP; Shiloh National Military Park Commission Daily Events, July 13 and Aug. 10, 1901, Jan. 2, 5, 17, 18, 28, Feb. 10, Mar. 22, Nov. 17, and Dec. 27, 1902, and Jan. 13 and 31, May 1, Aug. 1, and Sept. 18, 1903, 34–35, 59–60, 150, 161, 163, 164, 172, 176, 178, SNMP.

37. D. W. Reed to Atwell Thompson, July 19, 1901, Series 1, Box 25, Folder 361, SNMP.

38. Cornelius Cadle to Ross-Meehan Foundry Company, Dec. 12, 1901, Series 1, Box 25, Folder 361, SNMP; Shiloh National Military Park Commission Daily Events, July 13 and Aug. 10, 1901, Jan. 2, 5, 17, 18, 28, Feb. 10, Mar. 22, Nov. 17, and Dec. 27, 1902, and Jan. 13 and 31, May 1, Aug. 1, and Sept. 18, 1903, 34–35, 59–60, 150, 161, 163, 164, 172, 176, 178, SNMP.

39. Cornelius Cadle to John C. Scofield, Nov. 13, 1902, RG 92, E 712, Box 1, NARA; H. V. Boynton to Secretary of War, May 21, 1900, Series 1, Box 25, Folder 361, SNMP; Shiloh National Military Park Commission Daily Events, Mar. 9, 1906, 225, SNMP. The park also sent trees from the battlefield to the residents of Sacramento, California, to commemorate the battle in a local park.

40. Reed Map, First and Second Days, 1900, Series 6, Boxes 1 and 2, SNMP.

41. David W. Reed, *The Battle of Shiloh and the Organizations Engaged* (Washington, D.C.: Government Printing Office, 1902); "First Reunion of Iowa Hornet's Nest Brigade," Oct. 12–13, 1887, Series 3, Box 4, Folder 216, SNMP; "12th Iowa Veteran Volunteer Infantry," Series 3, Box 4, Folder 218, SNMP.

42. Reed, *The Battle of Shiloh and the Organizations Engaged*.

43. Reed, *The Battle of Shiloh and the Organizations Engaged*, 2nd ed., 5.

44. Atwell Thompson to Cornelius Cadle, Jan. 27, 1896, Series 1, Box 37, Folder 620, SNMP; D. W. Reed to Cornelius Cadle, Mar. 4, 1896, Series 1, Box 37, Folder 621, SNMP.

45. "The Bloody Pond," two-page history by WPA writers, Vertical File, Shiloh–Bloody Pond, SNMP; Allen, "Shiloh! The Campaign and First Day's Battle," 53.

46. Reed, *The Battle of Shiloh and the Organizations Engaged*, 7–23, 48–49; "First Reunion of Iowa Hornet's Nest Brigade," Oct. 12–13, 1887, Series 3, Box 4, Folder 216, SNMP; *OR*, series 1, vol. 10, pt. 1:277–80.

47. Regional Chief of Operations to Superintendent Shiloh National Military Park, June 1, 1960, Series 4, Box 15, Folder 200, SNMP; *OR*, series 1, vol. 10, pt. 1:101.

48. Reed, *The Battle of Shiloh and the Organizations Engaged*, 50.

49. Ibid., 19, 23, 62–63.

50. See Allen, "Shiloh! The Campaign and First Day's Battle," and "Shiloh! The Second Day's Battle and Aftermath." For a full historiographical analysis of Shiloh and how Reed's interpretation dominates it, see Appendix 7. Ironically, in his 1912 Annual Report, Reed argued against veterans creating myths. "It seems hard for them to realize that oft-repeated camp-fire stories, added to and enlarged, become impressed on the memory as real facts," he stated. Such is exactly what he had done with the Hornet's Nest, however. See *Annual Report of the Secretary of War–1912*, 196.

CHAPTER 6

1. *Congressional Record*, 53rd Cong., 3rd sess., 27, pt. 1:19–20.

2. "Division Headquarters Monuments," and "Brigade Headquarters Monuments," both in Series 1, Box 26, Folder 373, SNMP; *Annual Report of the Secretary of War–1903*, 236; *Annual Report of the Secretary of War–1902*, 23.

3. Cornelius Cadle to D. W. Reed, June 21, 1901, Series 1, Box 27, Folder 389, SNMP; *Annual Report of the Secretary of War–1902*, 23; *Annual Report of the Secretary of War–1903*, 236.

4. D. W. Hagler to Cornelius Cadle, July 15, 1897, Series 1, Box 24, Folder 359, SNMP; Atwell Thompson to Cornelius Cadle, Aug. 2, 1897, Series 1, Box 38, Folder 624, SNMP.

5. This number of brigade headquarters includes Everett Peabody's, which was combined with his mortuary monument. Lew Wallace's division or brigades received no monuments, despite some talk about it.

6. "Mortuary Monuments," Series 1, Box 26, Folder 373, SNMP; *Annual Report of the Secretary of War–1902*, 23.

7. "Mortuary Monuments," Series 1, Box 26, Folder 373, SNMP.

8. *Annual Report of the Secretary of War–1903*, 237.

9. Regional Chief of Operations to Superintendent Shiloh National Military Park, June 1, 1960, Series 4, Box 15, Folder 200, SNMP.

10. Cornelius Cadle to Robert Shaw Oliver, Aug. 5, 1907; Cornelius Cadle to Francis Gunther et al. Mar. 20, 1909; Robert Shaw Oliver to Cornelius Cadle, Apr. 30, 1909; Cornelius Cadle to D.W. Reed, May 5, 1909, all in Series 1, Box 33, Folder 450, SNMP.

11. Cornelius Cadle to John C. Scofield, Oct. 12, 1909, and Robert Shaw Oliver to Cornelius Cadle, Oct. 18, 1909, both in Series 1, Box 33, Folder 450, SNMP.

12. "U.S. Regular Monuments," Series 1, Box 26, Folder 373, SNMP.

13. "U.S. Regular Monuments," Series 1, Box 26, Folder 373, SNMP; D. W. Reed to W. R. Hodges, Dec. 9, 1910, Series 1, Box 33, Folder 451, SNMP.

14. Cornelius Cadle to D. W. Reed, Nov. 9, 1899, Series 1, Box 25, Folder 368, SNMP.

15. For a discussion of the monuments, see Appendix 5.

16. Jones, "Building Shiloh Park," 15–17.

17. Cornelius Cadle to Atwell Thompson, June 19, 1901, Series 1, Box 32, Folder 440, SNMP.

18. Cornelius Cadle to Atwell Thompson, June 19, 1901, Series 1, Box 32, Folder 440, SNMP; Jones, "Building Shiloh Park," 15–16.

19. Cornelius Cadle to D. W. Reed, Mar. 23, 1903, Series 1, Box 28, Folder 403, SNMP.

20. Jones, "Building Shiloh Park," 1.

21. T. J. Lindsey to Cornelius Cadle, Sept. 6, 1901, Series 1, Box 32, Folder 442, SNMP; Cornelius Cadle to D. W. Reed, Nov. 9, 1899, Series 1, Box 25, Folder 368, SNMP.

22. T. M. Page to Cornelius Cadle, June 2, 1899, and D. W. Reed to Cornelius Cadle, June 15, 1899, both in Series 1, Box 27, Folder 376, SNMP; Cornelius Cadle to T. M. Page, Apr. 4, 1899, and D. W. Reed, "Appeal to the Commissioners," undated, both in Series 1, Box 14, Folder 166, SNMP.

23. D. W. Reed to H. G. Keplinger, July 31, 1906; H. G. Keplinger to D. W. Reed, July 2, 1906; H. G. Keplinger to William Howard Taft, Dec. 5, 1906, all in Series 1, Box 28, Folder 399, SNMP; D. W. Reed to John R. Palmer, Jan. 7, 1910, Series 1, Box 28, Folder 401, SNMP.

24. "Memorandum," undated, and John C. Scofield to Cornelius Cadle, Apr. 26, 1902, both in Series 1, Box 32, Folder 444, SNMP.

25. T. J. Lindsey to D. W. Reed, Jan. 21, 1902, Series 1, Box 32, Folder 444, SNMP.

26. W. H. Chamberlain et al to Elihu Root, Apr. 9, 1902, and Cornelius Cadle to John C. Scofield, Apr. 26, 1902, both in Series 1, Box 32, Folder 444, SNMP.

27. Private Secretary to Assistant Secretary of War, Feb. 7, 1906, Series 8, Vol. 61, Reel 393, William Howard Taft Papers, LC; W. H. Chamberlain to Shiloh National Military Park Commission, undated, Series 1, Box 32, Folder 444, SNMP.

28. William Howard Taft to Cornelius Cadle, Oct. 12, 1905, Series 8, Vol. 47, Reel 486, William Howard Taft Papers, LC; D. W. Reed to Cornelius Cadle, May 17, 1902, and T. J. Lindsey to Cornelius Cadle, June 23, 1902, both in Series 1, Box 32, Folder 444, SNMP; W. H. Taft to Cornelius Cadle, Oct. 12, 1905, Series 1, Box 32, Folder 445, SNMP; T. J. Lindsey, *Ohio at Shiloh: Report of the Commission* (Cincinnati: C.J. Krehbiel and Company, 1903), 48.

29. L. S. Tyler to Cornelius Cadle, June 24, 1901, Series 1, Box 29, Folder 409, SNMP.

30. Cornelius Cadle to H. C. McArthur, July 25, 1901, Series 1, Box 29, Folder 409, SNMP; Albert B. Cummins to Elihu Root, Sept. 15, 1902, Series 1, Box 29, Folder 410, SNMP; Elihu Root to Cornelius Cadle, May 11, 1903, and F. C. Ainsworth to Elihu Root, Mar. 28, 1903, both in Series 1, Box 29, Folder 411, SNMP.

31. The veterans' affidavits are in RG 92, E 712, Box 3, NARA; Cornelius Cadle to J. H. Ashcraft and Josiah Patterson, Feb. 3, 1904, and Albert B. Cummins to Cornelius Cadle, Feb. 6, 1904, both in Series 1, Box 31, Folder 427, SNMP; minutes of various commission meetings, undated; "Conclusions of the Commission," undated; Albert B. Cummins, "In the Matter of the Controversy Between the Shiloh National Military Park Commission and the Iowa Shiloh Commission relating to Inscriptions Upon the Regimental Monuments of the 15th and 16th Iowa Volunteer Infantry," undated, all in Series 1, Box 31, Folder 428, SNMP.

32. Robert Shaw Oliver to Albert B. Cummins, Sept. 16, 1904; Albert B. Cummins to Robert Shaw Oliver, Sept. 19, 1904; Albert B. Cummins to Robert Shaw Oliver, Nov. 30, 1904; D. W. Reed to Cornelius Cadle, Dec. 8, 1904, all in Series 1, Box 31, Folder 430, SNMP.

33. Robert Shaw Oliver to Cornelius Cadle, Feb. 2, 1905, Series 1, Box 31, Folder 431, SNMP.

34. John Hayes to Walter I. Smith, Jan. 6, 1906, RG 92, E 712, Box 3, NARA; J. B. Randolph to Cornelius Cadle, June 5, 1905, Series 1, Box 31, Folder 431, SNMP; Robert Shaw Oliver to Cornelius Cadle, Feb. 2, 1906, Series 1, Box 32, Folder 432, SNMP.

35. Lew Wallace to Cornelius Cadle, May 12, 1903, Series 1, Box 18, Folder 253, SNMP; Memo, undated, Series 1, Box 17, Folder 249, SNMP; Lew Wallace to Cornelius Cadle, Feb. 22, 1896, and Lew Wallace to D. W. Reed, Mar. 8, 1902, both in Series 1, Box 15, Folder 194, SNMP.

36. Lew Wallace to Cornelius Cadle, May 12, 1903; D. W. Reed to Cornelius Cadle, Apr. 14, 1903; Cornelius Cadle to D. W. Reed, June 3, 1903, all in Series 1, Box 18, Folder 253, SNMP.

37. D. C. Buell to Cornelius Cadle, Feb. 9, 1896, Robert F. Looney Collection, Folder 66, MSCPL; D. C. Buell to H.V. Boynton, Jan. 9, 1895, Series 9, Chickamauga and Chattanooga National Military Park, hereafter cited as CCNMP; Robert F. Looney to D. C. Buell, Mar. 11, 1896, Don Carlos Buell Papers, Filson Historical Society, hereafter cited as FHS.

38. F. C. Ainsworth to War Dept., Oct. 14, 1904, Series 1, Box 11, Folder 89, SNMP; Daniel, *Shiloh*, 304–5.

39. Whitelaw Reid to Secretary of War, Oct. 11, 1904 and Cornelius Cadle to D. W. Reed, Oct. 27, 1904, both in Series 1, Box 11, Folder 88, SNMP.

40. John C. Paige and Jerome A. Greene, *Administrative History of Chickamauga and Chattanooga National Military Park* (Denver: Denver Service Center, 1983), 10.

41. D. W. Reed to Cornelius Cadle, Feb. 20, 1905, Series 1, Box 11, Folder 91, SNMP.

42. H. V. Boynton to Secretary of War, Mar. 7, 1905, Series 1, Box 12, Folder 92, SNMP.

43. H. V. Boynton to Secretary of War, Mar. 25, 1905, Series 1, Box 12, Folder 92, SNMP.

44. D. W. Reed to Cornelius Cadle, Mar. 27, 1905, and Robert Shaw Oliver to Cornelius Cadle, Mar. 30, 1905, both in Series 1, Box 12, Folder 93, SNMP; D. W. Reed to Cornelius Cadle, Apr. 13, 1905, Series 1, Box 12, Folder 94, SNMP.

45. D. W. Reed to Cornelius Cadle, Apr. 1, 1905, Series 1, Box 12, Folder 94, SNMP; H. V. Boynton to Assistant Secretary of War, Apr. 27, 1905, Series 1, Box 12, Folder 95, SNMP.

46. Robert Shaw Oliver to Cornelius Cadle, May 5, 1905, Series 1, Box 12, Folder 95, SNMP; W. W. Wotherspoone Memo, Sept. 2, 1909, Series 1, Box 39, Folder 630, SNMP.

47. Atwell Thompson to D. W. Reed, Aug. 25, 1903, Series 1, Box 28, Folder 405, SNMP; D. W. Reed to Harrison Granite Company, Oct. 29, 1910, Series 1, Box 28, Folder 407, SNMP.

48. *House Reports,* 53rd Cong., 2nd sess., Rept. 1139, 5.

49. *Annual Report of the Secretary of War—1904,* 269.

50. For the Lost Cause, see Foster, *Ghosts of the Confederacy.*

51. Lindsey, *Ohio at Shiloh,* 195, 200, 210.

52. John W. Coons, *Indiana at Shiloh: Report of the Commission* (Indianapolis: William B. Burford, 1904), 296; *The Seventy-seventh Pennsylvania at Shiloh: History of the Regiment* (Harrisburg: Harrisburg Publishing Company, 1905), 50.

53. Alonzo Abernathy, *Dedication of Monuments Erected by the State of Iowa* (Des Moines: Emory H. English, 1908), 256; Mason, *Illinois at Shiloh,* 177; Magdeburg, *Wisconsin at Shiloh,* 236–37.

54. "Alabama's Shiloh Monument," *Confederate Veteran* 15, no. 6 (June 1907): 249; "The Confederate Monument at Shiloh," *Confederate Veteran* 13, no. 10 (Oct. 1905): 441.

55. "Dedication of the Monument at Shiloh," *Confederate Veteran* 25, no. 6 (June 1917): 251–52; Joe Gillis, *The Confederate Monument: Shiloh National Military Park* (n.p., 1994), 16.

CHAPTER 7

1. Atwell Thompson to Cornelius Cadle, Mar. 9, 1899, Series 1, Box 38, Folder 626, SNMP.

2. Cornelius Cadle to Atwell Thompson, Jan. 18, 1897, Series 1, Box 38, Folder 623, SNMP; Atwell Thompson to Cornelius Cadle, Mar. 9 and 10, 1897, Series 1, Box 38, Folder

623, SNMP; Robert Shaw Oliver to Cornelius Cadle, Oct. 7, 1903, Series 1, Box 13, Folder 116, SNMP; Cornelius Cadle to D. W. Reed, June 4, 1898, Series 1, Box 13, Folder 114, SNMP; Cornelius Cadle to D. W. Reed, Mar. 1, 1901, Series 1, Box 38, Folder 627, SNMP; Cornelius Cadle to D. W. Reed, Jan. 23, 1899, Series 1, Box 38, Folder 626, SNMP; DeB. Randolph Keim, *Sherman: A Memorial in Art, Oratory, and Literature by the Society of the Army of the Tennessee with the aid of the Congress of the United States of America* (Washington, D.C.: Government Printing Office, 1904), 9.

3. Cornelius Cadle to D. W. Reed, Mar. 22, 1899, Series 1, Box 13, Folder 114, SNMP; D. W. Reed to J. M. Riddell, Mar. 30, 1899, Series 1, Box 38, Folder 627, SNMP; Cornelius Cadle to D. W. Reed, Aug. 28, 1903, Series 1, Box 38, Folder 628, SNMP.

4. Cornelius Cadle to Allen R. Adams, Oct. 24, 1898, RG 92, E 712, Box 1, NARA; Atwell Thompson to J. M. Riddell, Nov. 27, 1898, Series 1, Box 38, Folder 626, SNMP. Buell's replacement, James H. Ashcraft, attended Robert F. Looney's funeral in 1899, and Cadle himself attended the funeral of Looney's replacement, Josiah Patterson, in 1904. See Shiloh National Military Park Commission Daily Events, Feb. 10, 1904, 185, SNMP,; *Annual Report of the Secretary of War—1900*, 216.

5. J. H. Ashcraft Compiled Service Record, NARA; Cornelius Cadle to J. H. Ashcraft, Mar. 1, 1901, and J. H. Ashcraft Appointment, Jan. 12, 1899, both in Series 1, Box 34, Folder 470, SNMP.

6. "Col. R. F. Looney," 36.

7. Cornelius Cadle to Secretary of War, Nov. 27, 1899, RG 79, Box 11, Press Copies of Letters Sent, NARA–Southeast Region, Atlanta; *Biographical Directory of the United States Congress*, 1619; James D. Porter, *Confederate Military History: Tennessee* 10 (Wilmington, N.C.: Broadfoot Publishing Company, 1987), 662–67.

8. Cornelius Cadle to D. W. Reed, Jan. 23, 1899, Series 1, Box 38, Folder 626, SNMP; *Biographical Directory of the United States Congress*, 1619.

9. Basil W. Duke Compiled Service Record, NARA; Ezra J. Warner, *Generals in Gray: The Lives of the Confederate Commanders* (Baton Rouge: Louisiana State Univ. Press, 1959), 76–77; *Annual Report of the Secretary of War—1904*, 268.

10. Lee, *The Origin and Evolution*, 38–46.

11. H.R. 12092, Mar. 4, 1902, Series 1, Box 38, Folder 628, SNMP; H. V. Boynton to John P. Nicholson, Apr. 22, 1902, Series 1, Box 38, Folder 628, SNMP; Lee, *The Origin and Evolution*, 38–46.

12. Lee, *The Origin and Evolution*, 38–46.

13. Atwell Thompson to Cornelius Cadle, Sept. 5, 1895, Series 1, Box 37, Folder 620, SNMP; Jones, "Building Shiloh Park," 5–6; Atwell Thompson to Cornelius Cadle, Dec. 8, 1898, Series 1, Box 40, Folder 641, SNMP; *Annual Report of the Secretary of War—1900*, 215.

14. Atwell Thompson to D. C. Buell, Oct. 20, 1898, Don Carlos Buell Papers, FHS; Cornelius Cadle to S. D. Lee, Aug. 19, 1899, RG 79, Box 1, NARA–Southeast Region; Cornelius Cadle to Secretary of War, Mar. 3, 1899, RG 92, E 712, Box 1, NARA; George B. Davis to Cornelius Cadle, May 10, 1895, RG 92, E 713, NARA; Atwell Thompson to Cornelius Cadle, Dec. 8, 1898, Series 1, Box 40, Folder 641, SNMP; Cornelius Cadle to D. W. Reed, Apr. 23, 1901, Series 1, Box 25, Folder 371, SNMP; Cornelius Cadle to D. W. Reed, Sept. 2, 1899, Series 1, Box 13, Folder 115, SNMP; Atwell Thompson to Cornelius Cadle, Mar. 9, 1899, Series 1, Box 38, Folder 626, SNMP; Atwell Thompson to D. W. Reed, July 20, 1903, Series 1, Box 18, Folder 253, SNMP; Cornelius Cadle to Secretary of War, Oct. 31, 1899, Series 1, Box 40, Folder 641, SNMP;

Annual Report of the Secretary of War–1900, 215; *Annual Report of the Secretary of War–1901,* 383; *Annual Report of the Secretary of War–1906,* 317; Atwell Thompson to D. W. Reed, May 7, 1901, Series 1, Box 14, Folder 188, SNMP.

15. Atwell Thompson to Cornelius Cadle, Sept. 4, 1896, Series 1, Box 38, Folder 622, SNMP; *Annual Report of the Secretary of War–1901,* 385; *Annual Report of the Secretary of War–1903,* 237; *Annual Report of the Secretary of War–1904,* 265; *Annual Report of the Secretary of War–1905,* 149; *Annual Report of the Secretary of War–1906,* 319; *Annual Report of the Secretary of War–1907,* 333; *Annual Report of the Secretary of War–1908,* 177–79; Shiloh National Military Park Commission Daily Events, Aug. 11, 1906, 234. Engineers began surveying and placing stakes for the railroad, without permission, but park officials stopped the action.

16. Cornelius Cadle to S. D. Lee, Aug. 2, 1899, RG 79, Box 1, NARA–Southeast Region; Cornelius Cadle to R. F. Looney, Aug. 10, 1895, Robert F. Looney Collection, MSCPL; Secretary and Superintendent to employees, June 19, 1914, Series 1, Box 36, Folder 595, SNMP; John W. Shaw to Sam R. Jones, Sept. 12, 1904, Series 4, Letters Sent, Vol. 4:21, SNMP; Shiloh National Military Park Commission Daily Events, Nov. 29, 1901, Dec. 21, 1901, and Oct. 31, 1905, 11, 58, 221, SNMP. While the work force at Shiloh was primarily white, there were African Americans on the labor rolls at various times.

17. Atwell Thompson to Cornelius Cadle, Apr. 5 and Aug. 3, 1899, both in Series 1, Box 38, Folder 627, SNMP; Cornelius Cadle to D. W. Reed, Sept. 26, 1901, Series 1, Box 13, Folder 115, SNMP; Shiloh National Military Park Commission Daily Events, Sept. 17, 1901, 37, SNMP; A. E. Demaray to Superintendent, Shiloh National Military Park, Jan. 11, 1934, Series 2, Box 19, Folder 309, SNMP; Cornelius Cadle to Atwell Thompson, Mar. 22, 1905, Series 1, Box 35, Folder 564, SNMP.

18. Cornelius Cadle to D. W. Reed, Nov. 13, 1905, and Cornelius Cadle to John C. Scofield, Oct. 15, 1906, both in Series 1, Box 35, Folder 570, SNMP; D. W. Reed to Cornelius Cadle, June 23, 1905, Series 1, Box 38, Folder 629, SNMP.

19. Cornelius Cadle to D. W. Reed, Jan. 29, 1907, Series 1, Box 35, Folder 570, SNMP; Cornelius Cadle to Basil W. Duke, May 17, 1907, Series 1, Box 32, Folder 437, SNMP.

20. Cornelius Cadle to D. W. Reed, Nov. 6, 1905, Series 1, Box 38, Folder 629, SNMP; D. W. Reed to DeLong Rice, Nov. 10, 1914, Series 1, Box 39, Folder 632, SNMP; Shiloh National Military Park Commission Daily Events, Oct. 31, 1905, 221, SNMP.

21. D. W. Reed to Cornelius Cadle, June 23, 1905, Series 1, Box 38, Folder 629, SNMP; Cornelius Cadle to F. C. Ainsworth, Jan. 29, 1906, Series 1, Box 31, Folder 431, SNMP.

22. Atwell Thompson to Cornelius Cadle, Feb. 12, 1896, Series 1, Box 37, Folder 621, SNMP; J. Fairbanks to William Howard Taft, Oct. 10, 1904, and "Resolutions Adopted by the 72nd Regt. Ohio Vet. Vol. Association," Sept. 21, 1904, both in Series 1, Box 11, Folder 88, SNMP; Cornelius Cadle to D. W. Reed, Oct. 5, 1904, Series 1, Box 32, Folder 443, SNMP; Cornelius Cadle to Atwell Thompson, Aug. 19, 1904, Series 1, Box 33, Folder 448, SNMP; William B. Bate to Atwell Thompson, Oct. 5, 1904, Series 1, Box 33, Folder 449, SNMP; Reed, *The Battle of Shiloh and the Organizations Engaged,* 2nd ed.

23. Cornelius Cadle to John C. Scofield, Jan. 11, 1904, Series 1, Box 25, Folder 363, SNMP; Shiloh National Military Park Commission Daily Events, Apr. 1, 1904, and Aug. 1, 1904, 189, 197, SNMP; *Annual Report of the Secretary of War–1904,* 268–69; *Annual Report of the Secretary of War–1905,* 150.

24. Shiloh National Military Park Commission Daily Events, Aug. 11, 1906, 234, SNMP; Shedd, *A History of Shiloh National Military Park,* 61–62.

25. Shiloh National Military Park Commission Daily Events, Aug. 11, 1906, 234, SNMP; Shedd, *A History of Shiloh National Military Park,* 61–62.

26. Atwell Thompson to D. W. Reed, Sept. 2, 1903, Series 1, Box 28, Folder 405, SNMP; Cornelius Cadle to F. C. Ainsworth, Jan. 29, 1906, Series 1, Box 31, Folder 431, SNMP; Atwell Thompson to D. W. Reed, May 25, 1898, Series 1, Box 38, Folder 625, SNMP; Atwell Thompson to D. W. Reed, Jan. 5, 1903, Series 1, Box 23, Folder 344, SNMP; Jones, "Building Shiloh Park," 11, 17.

27. Shiloh National Military Park Commission Daily Events, May 30, 1904, and May 30, 1907, 194, 249, SNMP; Atwell Thompson to D. W. Reed, Jan. 5, 1903, Series 1, Box 23, Folder 344, SNMP; Shedd, *A History of Shiloh National Military Park*, 33, 38.

28. Cornelius Cadle to Secretary of War, May 7, 1898, RG 94, E 25, Box 599, NARA; George W. Davis to Cornelius Cadle, Feb. 23, 1897, RG 92, E 713, NARA; Atwell Thompson to Cornelius Cadle, Apr. 29, 1898; Atwell Thompson to Cornelius Cadle, May 16, 1898; Atwell Thompson to D. W. Reed, July 9, 1898, all in Series 1, Box 38, Folder 625, SNMP.

29. Atwell Thompson to Cornelius Cadle, Sept. 6, 1898, Series 1, Box 38, Folder 626, SNMP; Shiloh National Military Park Commission Daily Events, Feb. 13 and Sept. 11 and 28, 1901, 21, 37–38, SNMP.

30. George B. Davis to Cornelius Cadle, Apr. 27, 1895, Series 1, Box 37, Folder 618, SNMP; Clayton Hart to John L. Clem, Apr. 17, 1895, Series 4, Letters Sent, Vol. 1:157, SNMP.

31. R.A. Livingston Statement, July 24, 1929, Series 1, Box 7, Folder 52, SNMP; W. H. Noble to R. A. Livingston, Mar. 8, 1933, Series 1, Box 13, Folder 154, SNMP; for use of grave stones, see John W. Shaw to J. W. Scully, Feb. 1, 1900, Series 4, Letters Sent, Vol. 1:293, SNMP; for transfer of relics, see John A. Myers to Superintendent Shiloh National Cemetery, Apr. 15, 1930, Series 4, Box 1, Folder 1, SNMP; John L. Clem to Chairman Shiloh National Military Park, Dec. 22, 1913, Series 1, Box 27, Folder 388, SNMP.

32. Cornelius Cadle to Secretary of War, Feb. 8, 1898, RG 92, E 712, Box 1, NARA; Cornelius Cadle to Atwell Thompson, Feb. 16, 1905, Series 1, Box 38, Folder 628, SNMP; J. B. Bellinger to Cornelius Cadle, Jan. 28, 1905, Series 1, Box 38, Folder 629, SNMP; Shiloh National Military Park Commission Daily Events, Oct. 14, 1909, 276, SNMP.

33. J. B. Bellinger to Cornelius Cadle, Jan. 28, 1905, Series 1, Box 38, Folder 629, SNMP; Cornelius Cadle to Atwell Thompson, Mar. 22, 1905, Series 1, Box 35, Folder 564, SNMP; Atwell Thompson to D. W. Reed, Mar. 18, 1905, Series 1, Box 38, Folder 628, SNMP.

34. D. W. Reed to Robert F. Looney, July 14, 1899, Robert F. Looney Collection, Folder 76, MSCPL; F. A. Large to Atwell Thompson, Jan. 20, 1899, Series 1, Box 38, Folder 626, SNMP; Atwell Thompson to D. W. Reed, May 25, 1898, Series 1, Box 38, Folder 625, SNMP; Shiloh National Military Park Commission Daily Events, Nov. 21, 1900, and June 1, 1901, 8, 31, SNMP.

35. Cornelius Cadle to Secretary of War, June 26, 1899, RG 92, E 712, Box 2, NARA; Cornelius Cadle to D. W. Reed, Jan. 3, 1901, Series 1, Box 38, Folder 627, SNMP; Atwell Thompson to Cornelius Cadle, Feb. 23, 1897, Series 1, Box 38, Folder 623, SNMP; Cornelius Cadle to D. W. Reed, Jan. 23, 1899, Series 1, Box 38, Folder 626, SNMP; Atwell Thompson to D. W. Reed, June 23, 1899, Series 1, Box 25, Folder 368, SNMP.

CHAPTER 8

1. Shiloh National Military Park Commission Daily Events, Oct. 14, 1909, 274–77, SNMP. Shedd, *A History of Shiloh National Military Park*, 32. Shedd was historian in the 1950s.

2. "Mt. Vinson–Shiloh Illustrated Account of the Cyclone, October 14, 1909," Vertical File, Cyclone–1909, 2, SNMP.

3. Shiloh National Military Park Daily Events, Oct. 14, 1909, 274–77, SNMP; *Annual Report of the Secretary of War—1910*, 307.

4. "Mt. Vinson–Shiloh Illustrated Account of the Cyclone, October 14, 1909," Vertical File, Cyclone—1909, 15–17, SNMP.

5. Ibid., 4, 17, 22.

6. Shiloh National Military Park Daily Events, Oct. 14, 1909, 274–77, SNMP; "Mt. Vinson–Shiloh Illustrated Account of the Cyclone, October 14, 1909," Vertical File, Cyclone—1909, 17, 22, SNMP.

7. "Mt. Vinson–Shiloh Illustrated Account of the Cyclone, October 14, 1909," Vertical File, Cyclone—1909, 20, 22, SNMP.

8. Ibid., 3–4, 16.

9. Ibid., 3–4, 16; *Annual Report of the Secretary of War—1910*, 307.

10. Shiloh National Military Park Daily Events, Oct. 14, 1909, 274–77, SNMP; *Annual Report of the Secretary of War—1910*, 307; "Mt. Vinson–Shiloh Illustrated Account of the Cyclone, October 14, 1909," Vertical File, Cyclone—1909, 20, SNMP; D. W. Reed to B. F. Carroll, Dec. 3, 1909, Series 1, Box 28, Folder 406, SNMP; Cemetery Superintendent's Quarterly Report, Dec. 31, 1909, Series 4, Box 9, Folder 106, SNMP; Shiloh National Military Park Commission Daily Events, Oct. 14, 1909, 274–77, SNMP; George Dean to Quartermaster General, Oct. 16, 1909, Series 4, Letters Sent, Vol. 4:31, SNMP.

11. Shiloh National Military Park Daily Events, Oct. 14, 1909, 274–77, SNMP; *Annual Report of the Secretary of War—1910*, 308.

12. DeLong Rice to R. Rathbun, Aug. 5, 1914, Series 1, Box 15, Folder 203, SNMP; Shiloh National Military Park Daily Events, Oct. 14, 1909, 274–77, SNMP; *Annual Report of the Secretary of War—1910*, 307; "Mt. Vinson–Shiloh Illustrated Account of the Cyclone, October 14, 1909," Vertical File, Cyclone—1909, 24, SNMP; A. L. Lindsey to Cornelius Cadle, Oct. 24, 1909; Cornelius Cadle to N. L. Wilson, Nov. 8, 1909; Cornelius Cadle to William Riley, Dec. 14, 1909, all in Series 1, Box 13, Folder 116, SNMP.

13. Cornelius Cadle to Sydney E. Smith, Nov. 25, 1909, Series 1, Box 4, Folder 28, SNMP; Shiloh National Military Park Daily Events, Oct. 14, 1909, 274–77, SNMP.

14. "Mt. Vinson–Shiloh Illustrated Account of the Cyclone, October 14, 1909," Vertical File, Cyclone—1909, 22, SNMP.

15. Robert Shaw Oliver to Cornelius Cadle, Dec. 22, 1909, RG 107, E 82, Vol. 44, NARA; Cornelius Cadle to Sydney E. Smith, Nov. 25, 1909, Series 1, Box 4, Folder 28, SNMP; "An Act Making Appropriations to Supply Deficiencies in Appropriations for the Fiscal Year Nineteen Hundred and Ten, for other purposes," undated, Series 1, Box 5, Folder 32, SNMP; John C. Scofield to D. W. Reed, Feb. 28, 1910, Series 1, Box 4, Folder 28, SNMP; *Annual Report of the Secretary of War—1910*, 308.

16. D. W. Reed to John C. Scofield, Aug. 16, 1910, Series 1, Box 3, Folder 21, SNMP; *Annual Report of the Secretary of War—1910*, 307–8.

17. E. M. McDaniel to Commanding Officer Quartermaster Dept., Nov. 20, 1928, Series 4, Box 12, Folder 152, SNMP; H. W. Jones to Superintendent Shiloh National Cemetery, Feb. 14, 1925, Sheet Nos. 3–5, Series 4, Box 10, Folder 109, SNMP.

18. "To Accompany Deficiency Estimate of the Commission, dated Nov. 10, 1909," and D. W. Reed to Robert Shaw Oliver, May 23, 1910, both in Series 1, Box 4, Folder 28, SNMP; *Annual Report of the Secretary of War—1910*, 307; Shedd, *A History of Shiloh National Military Park*, 35.

19. John Obreiter to D. W. Reed, Nov. 17, 1909, Series 1, Box 14, Folder 164, SNMP.

20. *Annual Report of the Secretary of War–1912*, 191.

21. *Annual Report of the Secretary of War–1911*, 331.

22. John C. Scofield to D. W. Reed, Nov. 26, 1909; Cornelius Cadle to John C. Scofield, Aug. 8, 1908; John C. Scofield to Cornelius Cadle, Aug. 31, 1908; Cornelius Cadle to D. W. Reed, Sept. 11, 1908; Cornelius Cadle to John C. Scofield, Oct. 24, 1908; D. W. Reed to Secretary of War, May 27, 1909, all in Series 1, Box 35, Folder 531, SNMP; Shiloh National Military Park Commission Daily Events, Aug. 9, 1907, 253, SNMP.

23. Jacob Dickinson to Cornelius Cadle, Jan. 15, 1910, RG 107, E 82, Vol. 44, NARA.

24. D. W. Reed et al to John B. Randolph, July 5, 1911, Series 1, Box 36, Folder 589, SNMP; Cornelius Cadle to D. W. Reed, Jan. 31, 1910, Series 1, Box 39, Folder 630, SNMP; Thomas McAdory Owen, *History of Alabama and Dictionary of Alabama Biography*, 4 vols. (Spartanburg, S.C.: Reprint Company, Publishers, 1978), 3: 279.

25. J. M. Riddell to J. H. Ashcraft, May 5, 1908, Series 1, Box 13, Folder 116, SNMP; Stacy D. Allen to Charles E. Adams, Dec. 14, 1998, Vertical File, Cornelius Cadle, Jr., SNMP; Mahin, *Genealogy of the Cadle Family*, 95–100; *Cincinnati Commercial Tribune*, Jan. 16, 1913.

26. Assistant and Chief Clerk to D. W. Reed, Dec. 6, 1909, RG 107, E 82, Vol. 44, NARA; Minutes of Commission Meeting, Oct. 26, 1911, hard copy in Shiloh National Military Park Commission Daily Events, SNMP.

27. D. W. Reed et al to John B. Randolph, July 5, 1911, Series 1, Box 36, Folder 589, SNMP; Cornelius Cadle to D. W. Reed, Jan. 31, 1910, Series 1, Box 39, Folder 630, SNMP; John T. Wilder Compiled Service Record, NARA.

28. War Dept. Order, Feb. 12, 1910, Series 1, Box 5, Folder 33, SNMP; Minutes of Commission Meeting, Feb. 21, 1910, Series 1, Box 39, Folder 630, SNMP; War Dept. Memo, Mar. 7, 1910, and J. M. Riddell to D. W. Reed, Feb. 8, 1910, both in Series 1, Box 35, Folder 561, SNMP.

29. D. W. Reed to Robert Shaw Oliver, Jan. 22, 1912, and D. W. Reed to Chicago House Wrecking Company, Jan. 8, 1912, both in RG 79, Box 8, NARA–Southeast Region; Shiloh National Military Park Daily Events, Feb. 22, 1911, and Apr. 1912, 3, 20, SNMP; *Annual Report of the Secretary of War–1912*, 192; Chief Quartermaster to Chairman Shiloh National Military Park, Dec. 22, 1913, Series 1, Box 27, Folder 388, SNMP.

30. Terry W. Allen to D. W. Reed, Aug. 20, 1910, Series 1, Box 40, Folder 650, SNMP; Reed, *The Battle of Shiloh and the Organizations Engaged*, 2nd ed.

31. D. W. Reed to John C. Scofield, Mar. 7, 1911, Series 1, Box 14, Folder 174, SNMP.

32. George B. Randolph to Attorney General, May 10, 1909, and D. W. Reed to Cornelius Cadle, May 24, 1909, both in RG 92, E 712, Box 2, NARA. The details of the cases are hard to construct because of scarce sources. Only brief mentions of the affairs are made in letters.

33. Shiloh National Military Park Daily Events, Sept. 1913, 32, SNMP. Again, the details are not fully discernable.

34. *Annual Report of the Secretary of War–1914*, 656.

35. "Invoices" Ledger Book, RG 75, Box 5, NARA–Southeast Region; Shiloh National Military Park Daily Events, Oct. 1911, Dec. 1912, and May 1913, 14, 26, 29, SNMP; *Annual Report of the Secretary of War–1912*, 196; *Annual Report of the Secretary of War–1913*, 200.

36. DeLong Rice to A. J. Earl, Apr. 20, 1916, Series 1, Box 35, Folder 533, SNMP; "Invoices" Ledger Book, RG 75, NARA–Southeast Region; Shiloh National Military Park Daily Events, Feb., Apr., and Aug. 1912, 18, 20, 24, SNMP; William M. Green Diary, Vertical File, SNMP.

37. "DeLong Rice—Candidate for State Treasurer," undated, in private collection of DeLong Rice, Pickwick, Tennessee; Otto Eisenschiml, *The Story of Shiloh* (Chicago: Civil War Roundtable, 1946), 70.

38. DeLong Rice Appointment, May 12, 1913, and Secretary of War to DeLong Rice, May 14, 1913, both in private collection of DeLong Rice, Pickwick, Tennessee; D. W. Reed to DeLong Rice, May 20, 1913, and Record of Civil Employee, July 1, 1916, both in Series 1, Box 35, Folder 558, SNMP.

39. DeLong Rice to A. J. Earl, Apr. 20, 1916; R. A. Livingston to DeLong Rice, Dec. 20, 1915; Record of Civil Employee, July 1, 1916, all in Series 1, Box 35, Folder 533, SNMP.

40. R. A. Livingston to DeLong Rice, July 3, 1916; DeLong Rice to R. A. Livingston, Aug. 8, 1916; A. J. Earl to Secretary and Superintendent, July 19, 1916; DeLong Rice to Secretary Fifth Civil Service District, Aug. 25, 1916; R. A. Livingston Appointment, Sept. 13, 1916, all in Series 1, Box 35, Folder 533, SNMP.

41. John C. Scofield to DeLong Rice, Dec. 15, 1917, RG 79, Box 8, NARA—Southeast Region; R. A. Livingston to Secretary of War, Apr. 18, 1918, Series 1, Box 35, Folder 534, SNMP.

42. DeLong Rice to Secretary of War, June 11, 1919, RG 79, Box 8, NARA—Southeast Region; DeLong Rice to Secretary of War, Jan. 30, 1919; R. A. Livingston Appointment; DeLong Rice to Charles J. Hamlin, Mar. 5, 1919, and June 17, 1919, all in Series 1, Box 35, Folder 534, SNMP.

43. Lee, *the Origin and Evolution*, 45.

44. *Annual Report of the Secretary of War—1914*, 659.

45. Commission Minutes, Apr. 6, 1912, found in Shiloh National Military Park Commission Daily Events, Apr. 1912, 20, SNMP; Shiloh National Military Park Commission Daily Events, May 1913, 29, SNMP; *Annual Report of the Secretary of War—1917*, 1008; "David Wilson Reed," in *Memorials of Deceased Companions of the Commandery of the State of Illinois, Military Order of the Loyal Legion of the United States* (Wilmington: Broadfoot, 1993), 353.

46. DeLong Rice to Secretary of War, Apr. 27, 1917, and DeLong Rice to Assistant Secretary of War, June 18, 1917, both in RG 92, E 588, Box 5, NARA.

47. Labor Roll, Aug. 1916, in Time Books, RG 79, Box 5, NARA—Southeast Region; *Annual Report of the Secretary of War—1920*, 1963; *Annual Report of the Secretary of War—1918*, 1480.

48. *Annual Report of the Secretary of War—1923*, 161; *Annual Report of the Secretary of War—1931*, 21.

49. "Historic Pine Lodge Destroyed," unidentified newspaper clipping in private collection of DeLong Rice, Pickwick, Tennessee. Unfortunately, the hotel was never a success. It faced long periods of dormancy, only to burn in the 1980s. The massive rock foundation is still viewable, however.

50. *Annual Report of the Secretary of War—1900*, 215; *Annual Report of the Secretary of War—1912*, 195; "Boundary Description: By Metes and Bounds," undated, Series 1, Box 40, Folder 644, SNMP; Shedd, *A History of Shiloh National Military Park*, 37–38; DeLong Rice to Quartermaster General, Feb. 23, 1926, RG 79, Box 10, NARA—Southeast Region.

51. *Annual Report of the Secretary of War—1914*, 654–56; *Annual Report of the Secretary of War—1915*, 882–83.

52. DeLong Rice to Assistant Secretary of War, Jan. 24, 1919, and Benedict Crowell to DeLong Rice, Jan. 28, 1919, both in RG 92, E 588, Box 5, NARA; *Annual Report of the Secretary of War—1919*, 5255.

53. "Indian Mounds Trail Guide," undated, Series 1, Box 15, Folder 203, SNMP; "Shiloh Battlefield Guide," undated, Series 1, Box 17, Folder 248, SNMP.

54. DeLong Rice to C. A. DeSaussure, June 20, 1917, Series 1, Box 15, Folder 208, SNMP; R. P. Harbold to DeLong Rice, Feb. 9, 1925, and John F. Conklin to DeLong Rice, Mar. 27, 1928, both in Series 1, Box 17, Folder 248, SNMP; "St. Louis & Tennessee River Packet Co.," brochure, in private collection of DeLong Rice, Pickwick, Tennessee.

55. DeLong Rice, *The Story of Shiloh* (Jackson, Tenn.: McCowat-Mercer, 1924).

56. DeLong Rice to Corinth Machinery Company, June 18, 1927; DeLong Rice to Florence Marble Works, June 21, 1927; DeLong Rice to International Steel and Iron Company, Aug. 26, 1926; DeLong Rice to W. L. Jones, Sept. 6, 1926, all in RG 75, Box 11, NARA–Southeast Region; "Payroll for Personal Services," Oct. 1927, RG 75, Box 12, NARA–Southeast Region; DeLong Rice to Quartermaster General, July 26, 1926, Series 1, Box 35, Folder 558, SNMP.

57. "Rice and Son Burned in Explosion," Sept. 21, 1929, Corinth newspaper clipping, in private collection of DeLong Rice, Pickwick, Tennessee; DeLong Rice, grandson of DeLong Rice, interview by author, Mar. 30, 2001.

58. "Application for Payment of Accumulated Deductions," Oct. 25, 1929, and R. A. Livingston to Quartermaster General, Oct. 26, 1929, both in Series 1, Box 35, Folder 558, SNMP; Eisenschiml, *The Story of Shiloh*, 69.

59. DeLong Rice to Theodore G. Bilbo, Feb. 19, 1916, Series 1, Box 32, Folder 438, SNMP; DeLong Rice, grandson of DeLong Rice, interview by author, Mar. 30, 2001.

APPENDIX 3

1. For records on the superintendents, see the voluminous cemetery correspondence at SNMP. Most helpful in compiling this list were monthly and quarterly reports of the superintendents and letter books of letters sent and received. See also "List of Superintendents at National Cemeteries, 1867–83," RG 92, E 607, NARA; "Register of Superintendents at National Cemeteries, 1867–75," RG 92, E 606, NARA; and Cemetery Records in RG 75, NARA–Southeast Region.

APPENDIX 5

1. "Ohio Regimental Monuments," Series 1, Box 26, Folder 373, SNMP; Shedd, *A History of Shiloh National Military Park*, 40–42; Memphis *Commercial Appeal*, June 9, 1902.

2. "Indiana Regimental Monuments," Series 1, Box 26, Folder 373, SNMP; Shedd, *A History of Shiloh National Military Park*, 40–42; Memphis *Commercial Appeal*, Apr. 8, 1903.

3. "77th Pennsylvania Monument," Series 1, Box 26, Folder 373, SNMP; Shedd, *A History of Shiloh National Military Park*, 40–42.

4. "Illinois State Monument," "Illinois Regimental Monuments," and "Illinois Cavalry Monument," all in Series 1, Box 26, Folder 373, SNMP; Shedd, *A History of Shiloh National Military Park*, 40–42; *Chicago Evening Post*, May 23, 1904.

5. "Wisconsin State Monument" and "Putnam Stump Monument," both in Series 1, Box 26, Folder 373, SNMP; Shiloh National Military Park Commission Daily Events, Dec. 5, 1901, 57, SNMP; Shedd, *A History of Shiloh National Military Park*, 40–42.

6. "Iowa State Monument" and "Iowa Regimental Monuments," both in Series 1, Box 26, Folder 373, SNMP; Shedd, *A History of Shiloh National Military Park*, 40–42.

7. "First Minnesota Battery Monument," Series 1, Box 26, Folder 373, SNMP; Shedd, *A History of Shiloh National Military Park,* 40–42.

8. "Michigan State Monument," Series 1, Box 26, Folder 373, SNMP; Shedd, *A History of Shiloh National Military Park,* 40–42.

9. "Second Tennessee Regiment Monument," Series 1, Box 26, Folder 373, SNMP; Shedd, *A History of Shiloh National Military Park,* 40–42; *Memphis Commercial Appeal,* Aug. 23, 1905.

10. "Alabama Monument" and "Joe Wheeler Monument," both in Series 1, Box 26, Folder 373, SNMP; Shedd, *A History of Shiloh National Military Park,* 40–42; *Birmingham News,* May 8, 1907.

11. "Arkansas Monument," Series 1, Box 26, Folder 373, SNMP; Shedd, *A History of Shiloh National Military Park,* 40–42.

12. "Louisiana Crescent Regiment Monument," Series 1, Box 26, Folder 373, SNMP; Shedd, *A History of Shiloh National Military Park,* 40–42.

13. "The Confederate Monument" and "Confederate Burial Trench Monument," both in Series 1, Box 26, Folder 373, SNMP; Shedd, *A History of Shiloh National Military Park,* 40–42.

APPENDIX 6

1. For information concerning details of Shiloh Church and its relationship with the park, see Vertical File, Shiloh–Shiloh Church, SNMP; Series 1, Box 61, Folder 924, SNMP; Series 1, Box 33, Folders 323 and 324, SNMP; and "Shiloh Log Church: The Story of a Famous Church in American History" (n.p., n.d.).

BIBLIOGRAPHY

Manuscripts

Chickamauga and Chattanooga National Military Park, Fort Oglethorpe, Ga.
  Series 9–Shiloh Battlefield Commission, 1881–1906.

Filson Historical Society, Louisville, Ky.
  Don Carlos Buell Papers.

Library of Congress, Washington, D.C.
  Daniel S. Lamont Papers.
  William Howard Taft Papers.

Memphis Shelby County Public Library.
  Robert F. Looney Collection.

National Archives and Records Administration–Southeast Region, Atlanta, Ga.
  RG 79–Records of the National Park Service.
    Shiloh National Military Park, Tennessee, 1869–1950.
    Vicksburg National Military Park, Mississippi, 1865–1949.

National Archives and Records Administration, Washington, D.C.
  RG 92–Records of the Office of the Quartermaster General.
    E 225–Consolidated Correspondence File, 1794–1890.
    E 576–General Correspondence and Reports Relating to National and Post Ceme-
      teries, 1865–90.
    E 588–Correspondence, Maps, and Other Papers of the Mail and Record Division,
      Office of the Secretary of War, Relating to National Battlefield Parks at Chicka-
      mauga-Chattanooga, Vicksburg, and Other Battlefield Parks, 1913–23.
    E 606–Register of Superintendents at National Cemeteries, 1867–75.
    E 607–List of Superintendents at National Cemeteries, 1867–83.
    E 712–General Correspondence, Chiefly Letters Received, 1895–1911.
    E 713–Press Copies of Letters Sent, Feb. 1895–Apr. 1899.
    E 714–Register of Letters Received, Feb. 1895–July 1899.
  RG 94–Records of the Adjutant General's Office, 1780s–1917.
    E 25–Document File, 1890–1917.
  RG 107–Records of the Office of the Secretary of War.
    E 82–Press Copies of Letters Sent, Jan. 1896–July 1913.
  Compiled Service Records.
    J. H. Ashcraft.
    Cornelius Cadle.
    Basil W. Duke.
    David B. Henderson.
    J. W. Irwin.
    F. A. Large.
    Robert F. Looney.
    D. W. Reed.
    John T. Wilder.

DeLong Rice Collection, Pickwick, Tenn.

Shiloh National Military Park, Shiloh, Tenn.
  Series 1–Administration #1.
  Series 2–Administration #2.
  Series 3–D. W. Reed Papers.

Series 4–National Cemetery.

Series 5–Civil War Items.

Series 6–Maps #1.

Series 7–Maps #2.

Series 8–Blueprints/Plans.

Series 9–Photographs.

"Request For Permission For Interment Of Two Confederate Soldiers On The Shiloh National Military Park."

Vertical File.

Jones, Otis H. "Building Shiloh Park."

Cornelius Cadle, Jr.

Cyclone–1909.

"Mt. Vinson–Shiloh Illustrated Account of the Cyclone, October 14, 1909."

William M. Green Diary.

Indian Mounds.

Lee, Ronald F. "Report of Historical Work at Shiloh National Military Park."

Moore, Clarence B. "Aboriginal Sites on Tennessee River."

Shiloh National Cemetery.

Durbin, Lera. "Historical Reports: Shiloh National Cemetery."

Shiloh–Bloody Pond.

"The Bloody Pond."

Shiloh–Shiloh Church.

Shiloh Battlefield Commission.

"Rules to be Observed in Preparing the Battle Map," Apr. 8, 1896.

Newspapers

Birmingham Age Herald, Jan. and Feb. 1901.

Birmingham News, May 8, 1907.

Chattanooga Times, Jan. and Feb. 1901.

Chicago Evening Post, May 23, 1904.

Cincinnati Commercial-Gazette, Dec. 24, 1895.

Cincinnati Commercial-Tribune, Jan. and Feb. 1901; Jan. 16, 1913.

Memphis Commercial Appeal, Dec. 5, 1894; June 9, 1902; Apr. 8, 1903; Aug. 23, 1905; May 3, 1952.

Talladega (Ala.) *Reporter and Watchtower,* Jan. 2, 1878.

Raleigh News and Observer, May 27, 1979.

Published Primary Sources

Abernathy, Alonzo. *Dedication of Monuments Erected by the State of Iowa.* Des Moines: Emory H. English, 1908.

"Alabama's Shiloh Monument." *Confederate Veteran* 15, no. 6 (June 1907): 247–50.

Annual Report of the Secretary of War–1866–1933. Washington, D.C.: Government Printing Office, 1866–1933.

Beauregard, P. G. T. "The Campaign of Shiloh." In *Battles and Leaders of the Civil War,* vol. 1:569–93. New York: Century Company, 1884–87.

Beditz, Lindsay Christine M. "Excavations at Mound A, Shiloh National Military Park, Tennessee." Tallahassee: Southeast Archaeological Center, 1980.

Boynton, Henry Van Ness. *Sherman's Historical Raid: The Memoirs in the Light of the Record.* Cincinnati: Wilstach, Baldwin, and Company, 1875.

Buell, Don Carlos. "Shiloh Reviewed." In *Battles and Leaders of the Civil War,* vol. 1:487–536. New York: Century Company, 1884–87.

"Capt. James William Irwin." *Confederate Veteran* 22, no. 5 (May 1914): 220–21.

"Col. R. F. Looney." *Confederate Veteran* 8, no. 1 (Jan. 1900): 36–37.

"The Confederate Monument at Shiloh." *Confederate Veteran* 13, no. 10 (Oct. 1905): 437–43.

Congressional Record. 53rd Cong. Washington, D.C.

Coons, John W. *Indiana at Shiloh: Report of the Commission.* Indianapolis: William B. Burford, 1904.

"David Wilson Reed." *Memorials of Deceased Companions of the Commandery of the State of Illinois, Military Order of the Loyal Legion of the United States.* Wilmington, N.C.: Broadfoot Publishing Company, 1993.

"Dedication of the Monument at Shiloh." *Confederate Veteran* 25, no. 6 (June 1917): 250–52.

Eisenschiml, Otto. *The Story of Shiloh.* Chicago: Civil War Roundtable, 1946.

"Federal Veterans at Shiloh." *Confederate Veteran* 3, no. 4 (Apr. 1895): 104–5.

Grant, Ulysses S. "The Battle of Shiloh." In *Battles and Leaders of the Civil War,* vol. 1:465–86. New York: Century Company, 1884–87.

———. *Personal Memoirs of U. S. Grant.* 2 vols. New York: Charles L. Webster and Company, 1885–86.

Heitman, Francis B. *Historical Register and Dictionary of the United States Army, From Its Organization, September 29, 1789, to March 2, 1903.* 2 vols. Washington D.C.: Government Printing Office, 1903.

House Reports, 53rd Cong., 2nd sess., Rept. 1139. Washington, D.C.

Johnston, William Preston. "Albert Sidney Johnston at Shiloh." In *Battles and Leaders of the Civil War,* vol. 1:540–68. New York: Century Company, 1884–87.

Keim, DeB. Randolph. *Sherman: A Memorial in Art, Oratory, and Literature by the Society of the Army of the Tennessee with the Aid of the Congress of the United States of America.* Washington, D.C.: Government Printing Office, 1904.

Lindsey, T. J. *Ohio at Shiloh: Report of the Commission.* Cincinnati: C. J. Krehbiel and Company, 1903.

Magdeburg, F. H. *Wisconsin at Shiloh: Report of the Commission.* Milwaukee: Riverside Printing Company, 1909.

Mahin, Frank W. *Genealogy of the Cadle Family Including English Decent.* N.p., 1915.

Mason, George. *Illinois at Shiloh.* Chicago: M. A. Donohue and Company, n.d.

McBride, George W. "Shiloh, After Thirty-Two Years." In *Under Both Flags: A Panorama of the Great Civil War As Represented in Story, Anecdote, Adventure, and the Romance of Reality.* Philadelphia: People's Publishing Company, 1896. 220–27.

Michigan at Shiloh: Report of the Michigan Shiloh Soldiers' Monument Commission. Lansing: Michigan Historical Commission, 1920.

Porter, James D. *Confederate Military History: Tennessee.* Wilmington, N.C.: Broadfoot Publishing Company, 1987.

Reed, David W. *Campaigns and Battles of the Twelfth Regiment Iowa Veteran Volunteer Infantry: From Organization, September , 1861, to Muster-Out, January 20, 1866.* N.p., n.d.

———. *The Battle of Shiloh and the Organizations Engaged.* Washington, D.C.: Government Printing Office, 1902.

——. *The Battle of Shiloh and the Organizations Engaged,* 2nd ed. Washington, D.C.: Government Printing Office, 1909.

Report of the Proceedings of the Society of the Army of the Tennessee at the Twenty-Fifth Meeting held at Chicago, Ills. September 12th and 13th, 1893. Vol. 25. Cincinnati: F. W. Freeman, 1893.

Report of the Proceedings of the Society of the Army of the Tennessee at the Twenty-Sixth Meeting held at Council Bluffs, Iowa. October 3rd and 4th, 1894. Vol. 26. Cincinnati: F. W. Freeman, 1895.

Rice, DeLong. *The Story of Shiloh.* Jackson, Tenn.: McCowat-Mercer, 1924.

Roll of Honor: Names of Soldiers Who Died in Defense of the American Union Interred in the National Cemeteries. 27 vols. Washington D.C.: Government Printing Office, 1869.

Roster and Record of Iowa Soldiers in the War of the Rebellion Together with Historical Sketches of Volunteer Organizations, 1861–1866. 6 vols. Des Moines: Emory H. English, 1908.

Senate Reports, 53rd. Cong., 3rd sess., Rept. 722. Washington, D.C.

The Seventy-seventh Pennsylvania at Shiloh: History of the Regiment. Harrisburg, Pa.: Harrisburg Publishing Company, 1905.

War of the Rebellion: A Compilation of the Official Records of the Union and Confederate Armies, 128 vols. Washington, D.C.: Government Printing Office, 1880–1901.

SECONDARY SOURCES

Allen, Stacy D. "Shiloh! The Campaign and First Day's Battle." *Blue and Gray* 14, no. 3 (Winter 1997): entire issue.

——. "Shiloh! The Second Day's Battle and Aftermath." *Blue and Gray* 14, no. 4 (Spring 1997): entire issue.

Ashabranner, Brent K. *No Better Hope: What the Lincoln Memorial Means to America.* Brookfield, Conn.: Twenty First Century Books, 2001.

Biographical Directory of the United States Congress. Washington D.C.: Government Printing Office, 1989.

Blight, David. *Race and Reunion: The Civil War in American Memory.* Cambridge: Harvard Univ. Press, 2001.

Brazelton, B. G. *A History of Hardin County.* Nashville: Cumberland Presbyterian Publishing House, 1885.

Capps, Michael A. "Shiloh National Military Park: An Administrative History." Unpublished draft, 1993.

Clark, Charles B., and Roger B. Bowen. *University Recruits—Company C: 12th Iowa Infantry Regiment, U.S.A, 1861–1865.* Elverson, Pa.: Mennonite Family History, 1991.

Cooling, Benjamin F. *Monocacy: The Battle That Saved Washington.* Shippensburg, Pa.: White Mane, 1997.

Daniel, Larry J. *Shiloh: The Battle That Changed the Civil War.* New York: Simon and Shuster, 1997.

DeSantis, Vincent P. *The Shaping of Modern America, 1877–1920.* Wheeling, Ill.: Forum Press, 1973.

Engle, Stephen D. *Don Carlos Buell: Most Promising of All.* Chapel Hill: Univ. of North Carolina Press, 1999.

Farrell, James J. *Inventing the American Way of Death, 1830–1920.* Philadelphia: Temple Univ. Press, 1980.

Foner, Eric. *Reconstruction: America's Unfinished Revolution, 1863–1877.* New York: Harper Collins, 1989.

Foster, Gaines M. *Ghosts of the Confederacy: Defeat, The Lost Cause, and the Emergence of the New South.* New York: Oxford Univ. Press, 1987.

Freehling, William W. *The Road to Disunion: Secessionists at Bay, 1776–1854*. New York: Oxford Univ. Press, 1990.

Gillis, Joe. *The Confederate Monument: Shiloh National Military Park*. N.p., 1994.

Harbert, P. M. *Early History of Hardin County, Tennessee*. Memphis: Tri-State Printing and Binding Company, 1968.

Hattaway, Herman, and A. J. Meek. *Gettysburg to Vicksburg: The Five Original Civil War Battlefield Parks*. Columbia: Univ. of Missouri Press, 2001.

Holt, Dean W. *American Military Cemeteries: A Comprehensive Illustrated Guide to the Hallowed Grounds of the United States, Including Cemeteries Overseas*. Jefferson, N.C.: McFarland and Company, 1992.

Kiper, Richard L. *Major General John Alexander McClernand: Politician In Uniform*. Kent, Ohio: Kent State Univ. Press, 1999.

Lee, Ronald F. *The Origin and Evolution of the National Military Park Idea*. Washington, D.C.: National Park Service, 1973.

Linenthal, Edward T. *Sacred Ground: Americans and Their Battlefields*. Urbana: Univ. of Illinois Press, 1991.

McCutchen, Brian Keith. "Of Monuments and Remembrance: A History and Structural Analysis of the Monuments of Shiloh." M.A. thesis, Southeast Missouri State Univ., 1995.

McDonough, James Lee. *Shiloh: In Hell Before Night*. Knoxville: Univ. of Tennessee Press, 1977.

McPherson, James M. *Battle Cry of Freedom: The Civil War Era*. New York: Oxford Univ. Press, 1988.

Owen, Thomas McAdory. *History of Alabama and Dictionary of Alabama Biography*, 4 vols. Spartanburg, S.C.: Reprint Company, Publishers, 1978.

Paige, John C., and Jerome A. Greene. *Administrative History of Chickamauga and Chattanooga National Military Park*. Denver: Denver Service Center, 1983.

Painter, Nell Irvin. *Standing at Armageddon: The United States, 1877–1919*. New York: W. W. Norton, 1987.

Piehler, G. Kurt. *Remembering War the American Way*. Washington, D.C.: Smithsonian Institution Press, 1995.

Prokopowicz, Gerald J. *All for the Regiment: The Army of the Ohio, 1861–1862*. Chapel Hill: Univ. of North Carolina Press, 2001.

Roland, Charles. *Albert Sidney Johnston: Soldier of Three Republics*. Austin: Univ. of Texas Press, 1964.

Schalk, David L. *War and the Ivory Tower: Algeria and Vietnam*. New York: Oxford Univ. Press, 1991.

Shedd, Charles E. *A History of Shiloh National Military Park, Tennessee*. Washington D.C.: Government Printing Office, 1954.

"Shiloh Log Church: The Story of a Famous Church in American History." N.p., n.d.

Simpson, Brooks D. *Ulysses S. Grant: Triumph Over Adversity, 1822–1865*. New York: Houghton Mifflin Company, 2000.

Sloane, David Charles. *The Last Great Necessity: Cemeteries in American History*. Baltimore: Johns Hopkins Univ. Press, 1991.

Sword, Wiley. *Shiloh: Bloody April*. New York: William Morrow and Company, 1974.

Tolson, Hiliary A., et al. *Historic Listing of National Park Service Officials*. Washington, D.C.: United States Dept. of the Interior, 1991.

Warner, Ezra J. *Generals in Gray: Lives of the Confederate Commanders*. Baton Rouge: Louisiana State Univ. Press, 1959.

———. *Generals in Blue: Lives of the Union Commanders*. Baton Rouge: Louisiana State Univ. Press, 1964.

Woodward, C. Vann. *The Strange Career of Jim Crow*, 3rd ed. New York: Oxford Univ. Press, 1989.

PERSONAL INTERVIEWS

Alexander, Ted, historian, Antietam National Battlefield. Interview by author, May 25, 2001.

Allen, Stacy, chief ranger, Shiloh National Military Park. Interview by author, numerous dates.

Hartwig, D. Scott, historian, Gettysburg National Military Park. Interview by author, May 22, 2001.

Ogden, Jim, historian, Chickamauga and Chattanooga National Military Park. Interview by author, May 21, 2001.

Rice, DeLong, grandson of Delong Rice. Interview by author, Mar. 30, 2001.

Winschel, Terry, historian, Vicksburg National Military Park. Interview by author, May 21, 2001.

INDEX